The

Millennial

Money Tree

Published By

The Millennial Money Tree

How to (literally) Insure

Financial Security

in Your Golden Years

By John Logan

This book is for educational purposes only. While it is written to provide competent and reliable information on the subject matter, no part of this book should be construed as investment, legal or accounting advice. The views expressed are those of the author alone. The reader is responsible for his or her own actions. Adherence to all applicable laws and regulations, including international, federal, state, and local governing professional licensing, business practices, advertising, and all other aspects of doing business in the United States, or any other jurisdiction is the sole responsibility of the purchaser or reader. Neither the author nor the publisher assumes any responsibility or liability whatsoever on the behalf of the purchaser or reader of these materials.

First edition published in 2020.

Second edition published in 2023

ISBN: 978-1-7340027-7-5 paperback

ISBN: 978-1-7340027-6-8 ebook

Library of Congress Cataloging-in-Publication Data has been applied for

THIRD EDITION

For more information about this book or to book John Logan for a speaking engagement, visit millennialmoneytree.com

Table of Contents

Forward

There's an old proverb that says "The best time to plant a tree was twenty years ago. The second best time is now". That axiom can be applied to a number of things in our lives but in the realm of saving for the future, it is spot on with regard to the time value of money.

If you want to easily accumulate real wealth and keep it, there are three simple rules:

First, start saving early. Like the proverb says, now is a good time, years ago was smarter.

Next, take advantage of the magic of compound interest whenever you can.

And lastly, don't lose money.

The latter may sound obvious, but surprisingly most Americans invest in a way that puts their hard-earned dollars at risk every single day. We'll get into that in detail but first I want to tell you what you'll learn in this book.

This book will teach you a battle-tested, decades old, but too often overlooked method of saving for the future that you've probably never heard of. And if you *have* heard of it, you probably don't know how it works or how to implement it for your benefit. This book will educate you about the herd mentality of the common savings/investing practices taught by most financial gurus and exactly why you should have no part of most of them. It will also teach you that you don't have to be a genius to have a million dollars saved up by the time you're in your golden years, even if you haven't saved a dime yet.

The methods taught in this book do require help from a licensed expert for set up, but ones that are not hard to find, don't require any upfront fees or "load" charges or take some percentage of your profit as it grows.

What the methods in this book *don't* require is that you have a degree in finance to understand them. They don't require tens of thousands of dollars to buy into or hoarding some commodity like gold or silver or to learn some strict daily regimen of following the rollercoaster actions of the market to time your investment or divestiture. Nor does it require you to live like a Spartan either now or later. No so-called "rice and beans" diet is needed, financial or otherwise.

What it does explain is a guaranteed (yes, I said guaranteed) method of significantly growing capital for the future without the risk of loss of a single dime in the stock market. EVER.

The rapid growth of this kind of savings vehicle is a good indicator of the public's interest. In fact, in the now quarter century plus history of this kind of savings method, the market has grown from a single provider in 1997 with sales of less than $500,000 that year to 52 providers as of 2024 with over $3 billion invested annually.

Obviously, some people know something you don't.

All that said, here's how to gain the most from this book.

1st – Read the whole thing. That may sound obvious, but you'd be surprised how many people skip around in it because they think they already know about something, but they really don't have all the facts. Not that you're under-educated – on the contrary, chances are, since you bought this book, you're already one smart cookie – but because in my over 20+ years in financial services, I've encountered a whole lot of people who don't know what they don't know about stuff they think they're experienced in. I'll wager there will be something in this book that you're already pretty familiar with. If it's redundant anywhere, pat yourself on the back for what you already know, but it never hurts to look twice.

2nd – Sign up for my mailing list here: www.millennialmoneytree.blog/transform-your-future-opt-in/

I'm always finding new ways to earn without trading time for money that may be of interest to you. I promise I won't be flooding your inbox with daily emails. The only time you'll hear from me is when I've proven a 'new' (to me anyway) method of passive income works and how you can take advantage of it, or when there are substantial changes to laws or limitations noted in this book.

3rd – Act on what it tells you. Knowledge without execution is worthless. If you have questions on how best to do that, email me: john.logan@moneytree.ventures. I will be happy to help you in any way I can.

4th – Spread the word. The easiest way to do that is to write a review and post it on the Millennial Money Tree Amazon page here: https://www.amazon.com/Millennial-Money-Tree-literally-Financial/dp/1734002700

Lastly - Make notes! Scribble in the margins. Highlight stuff you want to quickly 're-find'. Especially if you plan to pass it on to others in your family. Your notes will give them your opinion on certain things without them having to ask. Not to mention it's kinda fun.

Chapter One

Why you're so hopelessly lost.

Face it. Most people are financially illiterate. You might be one of them.

Research from behavioral economist Dan Goldstein found that 70% of Americans say they have postponed decisions about money matters because they weren't sure what they should do. Over half said they hadn't made large purchases, actively managed investments, or reallocated retirement account assets within three plus years.

According to that study, people who feel they lack sufficient financial knowledge are 64% more likely to delay making these types of decisions — no matter what their income level. Procrastination becomes a huge obstacle when you consider that only three in ten respondents in that study said they are comfortable with their level of financial know-how.

The latter may include you, but if it does, consider yourself one of the learned minority.

In a study done by LIMRA (the Life Insurance Market Research Association) in 2013, they found that many don't have even a rudimentary understanding of their own finances. Chances are pretty good that despite the plethora of information available, that hasn't changed much…if at all…in the last decade.

LIMRA asked 2,000 Americans a series of basic financial and retirement questions — 10 multiple choice and true/false questions — and found that about one-third are financially illiterate. What the LIMRA quiz found was that about half of those polled had a mid-level understanding of financial topics, 36% answered five or fewer questions correctly, and only one in eight correctly answered nine or more of the questions.

Older respondents (age 55 and older) are nearly twice as likely as those younger than 55 to have a high level of financial literacy — almost 40% versus more than 20% of consumers which is not really a surprise since most of those who are 55 and older still remember lessons from their "home economics" class in high school; and also unsurprisingly, Americans who worked within a financial profession, had a college education and more than $100,000 in household assets were more likely to have a higher financial literacy.

Add to that, however, when then President Barack Obama signed the Dodd-Frank Wall Street Reform and Consumer Protection Act in July of 2010 (better known as simply the Dodd-Frank Act), Section 917 of Title IX of the Act required the Securities and Exchange Commission (the "SEC") to immediately conduct a study to identify the existing level of financial literacy of "retail investors" (meaning consumers that buy and sell securities of any type) as well as what could and should be done to increase the financial literacy of investors.

Note that the definition of "retail investor" is the average American who buys and sells stocks and bonds and other securities on a regular basis. Not someone who simply invests in their 401(k) or IRA through work, but individuals who actively monitor their investment holdings and trade those securities at least once per year. In other words, people who should know what they're doing, right? The operative word there is "should".

What the two-year SEC study found was "U.S. retail investors lack basic financial literacy". Individual investors, who own about a quarter of all equities in the market, have "a weak grasp of elementary financial concepts…" (like mortgage interest and inflation) "…and lack critical knowledge of ways to avoid investment fraud". The takeaway: we're mostly poster children for the Dunning-Kruger effect (a cognitive bias in which people think they're way smarter than they actually are), and easy marks.

The 4,800-person sample showed that women, African Americans, Hispanics, the poorly educated, and the very elderly are the least informed, and most vulnerable.

I know. You're thinking "Yeah, sure, but that was years ago. People have wised up since then. Right?"

You'd think so, considering a 2017 survey by financial services company Financial Engines (now Edelman Financial Engines) which found that over 47% of Americans felt more secure about their finances that year than they did five years prior.

However, feelings aren't the same as facts. When Financial Engines gave those same survey respondents an 11-question financial literacy quiz, 94% failed...miserably.

In truth, many Americans might feel that they're making responsible financial decisions when they could be inadvertently setting themselves up for ruin.

How hard was the test? Try it yourself. Below are the exact questions and answers used in the survey.

1. How many months of living expenses should you aim to have in an emergency fund?

   a. 1-2 months
   b. 3-6 months
   c. 1 year or more

2. How much Life Insurance should you have if your income is $75,000?

   a. $75,000
   b. $150,000
   c. $750,000
   d. $1,500,000

3. What is the average inflation rate for college tuitions around the country?

   a. 2%
   b. 5%
   c. 8%
   d. 11%

4. True or False: Only individuals with a net worth of $5.45 million or couples with a net worth of at least $10 million, need to worry about having estate plans.

   a. True

   b. False

5. If you take out a loan of $20,000 with an annual interest rate of 20%, but don't make any payments, how much will you owe at the end of four years?

   a. Less than $20,000

   b. $20,000

   c. $30,000

   d. $40,000

   e. Over $40,000

6. Is it better to take your pension as a lump sum or as a lifetime monthly paycheck?

   a. Lump sum

   b. Lifetime pension payments

   c. It depends

7. How much should the typical healthy married couple, retiring this year at age 65, covered by Medicare, expect to spend for out-of-pocket costs for healthcare throughout retirement (in today's dollars)?

   a. $50,000

   b. $100,000

   c. $157,000

   d. $200,000

   e. $266,000

f. $330,000

8. Which of the following is NOT covered by Medicare parts A or B?

a. Hospital Care
b. Dental Care
c. Ambulance Services
d. Hospice
e. Clinical Research

9. A typical 65 year old man can expect to live for how many more years?

a. About 10 more years
b. About 15 more years
c. About 20 more years
d. About 25 more years
e. About 30 more years

10. If you purchase a bond and the interest rates rise, what will happen to the price of the bond?

a. Rise
b. Stay the same
c. Fall

11. What is the latest age to which you can defer Social Security benefits to receive an increased benefit?

a. 62
b. 65
c. 66
d. 70

e. 72

So? How'd you do? Pretty confident in your answers or were you baffled like many people?

Here are the answers:

1. b. 3 -6 months.

The general rule is you should have three to six months of living expenses in your emergency fund. This money should be easily accessible in case you need it, if you lose your job or are unable to work for a while, your emergency fund can help you ease the strain on your wallet and keep you from going into debt.

Don't save too much though, because you'll want to take full advantage of tax-deferred (or tax free) savings opportunities.

2. c. $750,000

One risk with Life insurance is purchasing more than you need. In general, to calculate how much life insurance you might need, add up all your long-term obligations and subtract your assets. What's left is debt that you don't want to burden your family with after your death as a minimum.

Decisions about life insurance are highly personal and depend on many factors such as mortgage debt, marital status, dependent children or other family members, where you live and many other life circumstances as well as whether you plan to leave a legacy beyond paying off any obligations.

As a general rule, 10x your annual income is a good starting point, but add another $100,000 per minor child for college expenses.

3. c. 8%.

On average, college tuition has increased about 8% a year for the last decade, more than double the average increase in typical inflation per year. Based on that calculation you can expect college tuition to double about every nine years or so.

Source: The Smart Student Guide to Financial Aid

4. b. False

Regardless of your net worth, it's smart to have at least a basic estate plan. An estate plan will ensure your assets are inherited by the people you want them to go to, your finances are handled by someone you trust instead of the court and that your estate avoids costly probate.

Here is a list of items every estate plan *should* include:

- Will/trust
- Durable power of attorney
- Beneficiary designations
- Healthcare power of attorney
- Guardianship designations

5. e. Over $40,000

At a 20% annual interest rate, and after not making any payments at all, the loan amount will have doubled in just over three and a half years. At the end of four years, the amount you'd owe would be well north of $40,000.

6. c. It depends

First, if you're one of the diminishing number of people entitled to a pension, consider yourself lucky. However, like winning the lottery, the decision to take a lump sum or a monthly stipend is one of the most important financial decisions you might ever make. And the answer depends on a host of both personal and financial situations.

There are pros and cons to both ways.

The pros of taking a lump sum include the flexibility to invest in a wider range of investments and the ability to pass on those assets to your heirs.

The biggest con to taking a lump sum is the potential for losing it all with bad investments (like most lottery winners).

The pros of taking a lifetime of monthly payments include a (supposed) guarantee of income for life, sometimes through an annuity.

The risk of taking a monthly pension check is two-fold:

First, that the pension was funded correctly to begin with. As of 2024, State and local government pension plans had unfunded liabilities to the tune of $1.5 trillion dollars. Meaning, the likelihood that someone won't get paid the full amount they're due sometime in the future is uncomfortably high.

Second, if the pension is from a private sector business and isn't guaranteed through an annuity issued by an insurance company, the risk of loss over time is even greater. Gone are the days when companies could guarantee a lifetime income simply based on their history or their bottom line. Whole industries could be at risk of disappearing in the blink of an eye when new technologies are introduced that we've never imagined.

7. e. $266,000

Granted, costs varied greatly by couple based on a number of factors, but back in 2017 the average 65 year old married couple should have planned on spending around $266,000 on health care in retirement even if they are covered by Medicare Parts B, D and a supplemental insurance policy.

Today (Q4 of 2024), healthy 65-year-old married couple can expect to spend upwards of $395,000 on healthcare costs in retirement, according to the 2024 Retiree Health Cost Index from Milliman and no one really expects healthcare costs to go down in the future so that will require a well thought out strategy to have the money available when it's needed.

8. b. Dental care

Don't feel bad if you're under 50 and missed this one. AARP hasn't started sending you stacks of mail that contain all sorts of information on Medicare.

Medicare Part A covers home health services, hospital care, nursing home and skilled nursing facility care, and hospice care.

Part B covers things like getting second opinions before surgery, ambulance services, medical equipment, mental health services and clinical research.

Services that aren't covered by Medicare Part A or B are things like eye exams, hearing aids, acupuncture, foot care, cosmetic surgery and dental care.

9. c. About 20 more years

A 65 year old man can expect to live to just over 84 years old, on average, according to the Social Security Administration. Insurance companies now provide projections, called "illustrations" in insurance parlance, going out to age 121 because one never knows what medical breakthroughs might happen in the next quarter century or so, meaning it's critical to plan ahead so you don't outlive your savings.

10. c. Fall

Bond prices and interest rates have an inverse relationship, meaning when one rises, the other most often falls. So, typically (but not always), if interest rates go up, bond prices go down.

11. d. 70

Age 62 is the earliest that you can file for Social Security. Each year you don't claim it, the benefit grows slightly until age 70, which is the latest you can defer your benefit to receive a higher amount.

Feel any smarter? You should. You now have a better understanding of some financial concepts than the average retail investor.

Here's the thing: When it comes to your finances, any financial planner worth their salt will tell you that poor decisions you make today can cost you for the rest of your life.

You can always make more money, but you can never get back time that you've lost. And throughout this book you'll get drilled into your head that combining time with money is the tool we'll be using to make you financially secure.

Chapter Two

It's not your father's retirement plan.

Your parents may remember a 1988 Oldsmobile TV commercial slogan "It's not your father's Oldsmobile". You may remember that Buick used a similar marketing message mentioning "Grandpa's" Buick. General Motors used both to separate the old from the new. Retirement plans are different now too.

Depending on your age, your father or grandfather's retirement plan consisted primarily of at least one, or a combination of these three things:

A. A lifetime pension that may have even included lifetime health benefits from the likes of IBM or GM or US Steel.

B. Some form of self-directed investment in stocks and bonds, mutual funds, etc.

C. A 401(k) or IRA

And following those, to a lesser degree, insurance-based savings products like annuities.

Good old-fashioned fixed annuities made a startling comeback starting in 2012. Prior to that, they were your great granddad's Studebaker to most people, but when interest rates dropped down to levels not seen since the 1930's and 40's, products like fixed annuities were "reinvented". With guaranteed interest rates higher than what banks could offer in savings accounts, the insurance market dusted off an all but extinct product, put a fresh marketing spin on it and made millions.

So, what's wrong with that setup?

Nothing's wrong with a well-funded pension if you have one. But lately, finding companies that offer one is akin to finding Bigfoot.

What's wrong with a nice, well diversified, portfolio of stocks and bonds, and/or other commodities like precious metals? Again, nothing, if you *actually* know what you're doing and you're well prepared for any unexpected market downturn, which, face it – even experts never are, or they'd all be warning us well in advance.

Here's the dirty little secret that even fee-based investment advisors will never tell you, they *want* you to risk your money. The more you risk the more they might gain.

If you already have a financial advisor, have you ever asked him or her how much you pay them each year? They might tell you that they get a small amount from the funds in your account. Or maybe they'll tell you that they get a small percentage of the amount of money they manage for you. Either way, it's a pretty vague way of explaining how they are compensated and if there's anyone who should know the cost of their advice to your portfolio, it should be you.

Most investors know that their financial advisors take a percentage for managing their portfolios, but unbeknownst to investors, the mutual fund industry is also giving these advisors commission for pushing specific equity mutual funds.

And I'm not talking about the front-end load fees that the client pays. I'm referring to commissions and bonuses that financial planners get after they put their clients into these funds.

The investment industry and the SEC call these payments "commission" but, in reality, they are simply a form of cash incentive for financial planners to heavily push specific equity funds, even if they are not in their client's best interest. This payment structure raises ethical and legality concerns regarding whose interest is being best served: the financial planner or the client.

What's worse is that most investors don't realize what is happening. And the conflicts of interest run deep and wide.

In many cases a financial advisor can look you straight in the eye and say that you're not paying any commissions on the stocks, bonds or mutual funds he just sold you. You're not, but some other organization might be, which in turn raises your fees in the long term. In other cases, there may be no commission paid at all, but you're paying a "mark-up" or "spread" on the price of the security that goes straight into the pocket of the advisor.

This structure of behind-the-scenes payments to financial planners was hidden behind a smokescreen covered by layers of payments through multiple sources. First going to the brokerage houses, then passed along to the brokers themselves.

This hidden-fee structure was mostly addressed in the Dodd-Frank reforms, which went into effect on January 1, 2014. Under Dodd-Frank, disclosures for "commission" or "kick-back fees" (in this context, a kickback is any payment to a recipient as compensation or reward for giving favorable treatment or services to another party. A kickback may be in the form of money, but gifts, credit or anything of value may be viewed interfering with a financial advisor's ability to make unbiased decisions) are now required for pension and 401k retirement accounts, but accounts that aren't regulated by the Employee Retirement Income Security Act (ERISA) were excluded from the new law. Meaning most personal investment accounts are still unprotected.

Later, in the final days of the Obama administration, the Department of Labor implemented something called the "fiduciary rule," which was supposed to hold all financial advisors to a higher standard. When the rule (which still only really affected retirement savings) took partial effect in June 2017, it was thought to be a big win for consumer advocates, who wanted to thwart unnecessary, expensive and fee heavy financial products from being foisted on an unsuspecting public, especially those nearing retirement.

However, a federal court ruling in early 2018 put the kibosh on the rule by finding that the Labor Department was not authorized to make the regulation. The case will likely go on, perhaps eventually landing before the Supreme Court. And while the courts decide, the Labor Department announced they would not enforce the rule as the new standard by which all advisor behavior should be judged.

At the time, many retirement savers took the news as confirmation of what they already knew – that you're on your own in looking after your retirement savings.

At the heart of the debate is something most people probably don't think is all that debatable. The fiduciary rule set a new standard that simply said that any financial advisor has to put their clients' interests above their own.

For example, let's just say you want to invest in a mutual fund with a specific goal in mind, maybe it's aiming at growth, and there are two good options to choose from. One has more fees than the other, but the more expensive one also seems to be the best performing of the two, with the greater potential for long term net gain. Under the fiduciary standard, a financial advisor would have to recommend the fund with the fewest fees (because it can be argued that fewer fees are in your best interest, since there's no guarantee that the more expensive fund will perform as well in the future as it has done historically), especially if the advisors would pocket more money if you chose the more expensive fund.

Put a different way, an advisor adhering to a fiduciary standard might recommend investing in low-cost mutual funds for a fixed fee instead of comparable funds that charge more in commissions. He would also have to promise no hidden fees that might surprise you later.

And, if he had any conflicts of interest that might influence his recommendations about which investment would be best for you — for example, a 10-day, all expenses paid trip to Europe, paid for by the carrier that he'd get for selling you (and a host of others) a particular product — he'd be required to inform you.

In the past, savers had few options other than commission-based advisors who might not be fiduciaries. To keep their licenses, these advisors are only required to make investments on your behalf that are only "suitable" for your needs, not necessarily in your best interest. That means that while the investments your advisor chooses could be *appropriate* for your financial goals, there might be other options that are significantly better for you, and you could end up paying more money in commissions and other fees than if you had hired a fiduciary.

The thinking behind imposing a fiduciary standard being that too many investment advisors would otherwise recommend what will pay them best rather than what's best for the client.

The Obama administration watchdogs estimated that removing these conflicts of interest would save consumers $17 billion annually.

However, opponents of the standard, like pro-business groups such as the U.S. Chamber of Commerce, are vehemently opposed to the rule because they claim that requiring financial advisors to pick the least expensive option for their client would not guarantee the best long term results, would be too costly to implement and enforce, and would lead to less financial advice availability for lower-income savers.

Looking back, making the fiduciary rule into law has been in a quagmire ever since it was introduced.

"But wait", you say, your guy is fee-based and only makes money when you do?

Wanna bet?

You may have seen that Fisher Investments commercial comparing their services to other brokers and noticed the voice over says *"...and while some advisors are happy to earn commissions whether you do well or not, Fisher Investments fees are structured so we do better when you do better"*.

Well, duh...of course they do better if you've got more money in your account this year than the year before. They get a percentage of your Assets Under Management (AUM for short), so if your account value increases so does their fee amount. But do you get your money back if you lose your shirt on their advice? Or not pay a fee when your account value goes south? Nope.

Most advisors today actually operate as "fee-*based*" advisors. Not to be confused with a "fee-*only*" fiduciary advisor, a fee-based advisor can charge clients under either the commission structure or fee structure. Depending on the client and situation, a fee-based advisor can choose whichever payment structure he or she would like. In other words, *they* can choose how much they take from you, not you. Don't assume that just because your advisor says they're fee-based, that it means they legally must put your best interests ahead of their own. They don't.

How can you tell if your advisor can charge commissions on your investments? Ask them if they are a registered broker-dealer. If the answer is yes, then your advisor may not be obligated to act as a fiduciary to some or *all* of his or her clients. True fiduciaries and fee-only advisors don't receive *any* commissions for the advice they give you.

And naturally, if his fees are based on the size of your portfolio, of course he makes more when you make more. That makes sense, right? These fees are commonly expressed in a percentage as 'expense ratios.' And while something like a nominally small average annual fee of 1.02% may sound good at first glance (according to a study by Advisory HQ News Corp, the average financial advisor fee in 2021 was 1.02% for $1 million AUM, but 1.18% for AUM of $50,000), it adds up to big money on a significant nest egg — equivalent to a whopping $5,100 each year on $500,000 portfolio. And so, in many cases, he or she has you somewhere that they think is going to consistently grow, the bigger the better.

If it does, that's great. Especially if it grows to a point that you won't care about all the taxes you'll pay on the gains. But what if it doesn't? What if he's wrong?

When the S&P lost 38.5% in 2008 and generally, everyone's portfolio took a bloodbath, did your investment advisor refund any fees to his clients? Or did those fees stay the same despite the fact that, on his/her advice, they lost over 38%? And when the market was tanking by double digits for 3 years from 2000 through 2002, ask your investment advisor if he or she gave clients back any money while their portfolios shrunk year after year? Or were they still charged the same percentage fees based on the fact that he or she "helped them avoid further losses".

Come on. Seriously? You're going to charge me for your advice to get out of an investment that you put me in that's losing money hand over fist and call it "saving me money"?

And their pat response is that "There's always a risk in any investment".

Um...no...there's not.

So, what kind of investment has a guarantee of no loss...ever?

Investments that aren't traditional "investments", meaning they aren't sold by securities brokers. Like what? Fixed annuities for one. But annuities have a downside in that a substantial portion of your money is basically inaccessible for a specific amount of time and the average gain is generally looked upon as lower than a well-managed portfolio of securities, even with an occasional cliff drop in the market. And then there's that word "fixed" which means you're locked into some (typically low-ish) interest or crediting rate that may not be suitable for the long run.

We'll talk about annuities in more detail later, but for now, let's not get too far off course.

Here's the first step you'll want to take. If you plan to use a financial advisor for advice on your investments, the first question should be whether or not they are a fiduciary. If the answer is anything but a straightforward "Yes", if they waffle in the slightest, run for the door.

Instead, (preferably) look for someone who is a Registered Investment Advisor (RIA). An RIA is licensed with either the SEC or the State in which they do business (or both) and is required by law to adhere to fiduciary standards. Note that an RIA can have additional designations like being a CFP (Certified Financial Planner) or ChFC (Chartered Financial Consultant) or a host of other credentials, however, individuals may have all sorts of various initials after their name, but they may *not* be a Registered Investment Advisor.

Choose a financial planner who charges a fee for their services; has RIA and other credentials to back up their expertise and has no problem sharing their own investment strategy.

Ideally, if your financial planner has his or her cash firmly planted in the same investments that they're recommending to you, then you can be confident that he/she believes in that investment strategy, otherwise, they wouldn't risk their own capital. But that scenario is often not the case. Don't be too alarmed, though, if your advisor's portfolio doesn't match your own since he or she may have a completely different set of short or long-term financial goals than you do, meaning their own strategy might be quite different from yours.

The goal is transparency.

Lastly, find a "pay-for-performance" financial planner. Meaning, your advisor only gets paid if they make you money. If your portfolio loses money, he or she doesn't get paid a dime. And yes, they do exist. Under this structure, there is no way to hide the fees, commission or "kickbacks" that an advisor receives from the financial industry.

But there is a much broader point for you to consider here.

If you do *any* investing outside of the Money Tree strategy presented in this book (or in addition to it), you'll need to develop an approach to retirement planning that includes careful monitoring, whether by you or an advisor. Don't blindly trust anyone. Google Bernie Madoff if you're prone to handing over your hard-earned cash without a guarantee against loss. Inspect what you expect.

It may sound like I distrust the financial advisory industry in general. I can assure you that is not the case, nor should you. A good financial advisor, meaning one who truly has the knowledge and advice to help you substantially grow your wealth to meet (and exceed) your goals, is worth every dime you'll pay them. But shop around. Interview a dozen or so before you decide who to use. And remember, they don't have to be next door. Leverage technology.

In addition, when working with a financial advisor who concentrates on helping you grow and then (eventually) spend your savings after you retire, you'll hear about all the positive steps to take, such as contributing to an employer-sponsored retirement savings program (if it's available to you), diversifying your investments and always seeking low fees. All are good things to do for some people, but your life is not one-size-fits-all. Neither should your savings strategy.

Most advisors will also talk to you about asset allocation, probabilities and market averages until your head explodes, if you let them. They'll encourage saving but likely won't discuss the best ways to convert those savings to a steady income unless you ask them to. Instead, when advisors give guidance on how you should plan to live in retirement, the standard practice being to simply spend down your savings after you retire, so, unless you're already an entrepreneur with your interests in various businesses, they usually mention investing more in fixed income investments (like bonds), and probably downsizing your budget to make your savings last longer.

With this "spend-down" strategy, you are taking 100% of the risk, whether from market volatility or from simply by living too long.

Instead, ask your advisor about strategies that incorporate the most obvious "income" vehicle that will reduce your risk and your taxes after you retire: an income-for-life annuity. Or even better, some other passive form of income (rental properties are a good example). We'll discuss more ideas for passive income later.

The key is to look carefully at your future. Pensions are a thing of the past, and Social Security funding is under constant threat. So, it's totally up to you to ensure that your investment advice comes from a competent and reputable advisor, to make sure you're not being taken for a ride.

There's an old saying: "The rich plan four generations, the poor plan for Saturday night".

The decisions you make now could have an ever-lasting impact on not just your financial future, but that of your grandkids and future generations, so it's never been more important to get into the nuts and bolts of your retirement income requirements and create a well thought through plan to achieve those goals.

If you're hoping some Robo-advisor will do it for you, or some other novel use of AI (artificial intelligence) will guarantee a great return on all your investments, I hate to break it to you, that might be a possibility for your kids, but not for you. That's more likely a first-class ticket to Poorsville. Money is a tool. Learn to use that tool to plant the seeds of your Money Tree now and you'll reap the harvest later.

One final note to this chapter, the only constant…is change.

As I was compiling this book in mid-2019, the SEC adopted a new rule establishing a stricter standard of conduct for broker-dealers and anyone associated with (meaning seller via) a broker-dealer whenever they make any recommendation to a retail customer of any securities transaction or investment strategy involving securities.

This new rule, aptly titled "Regulation Best Interest" enhances the broker-dealer standard of conduct beyond the existing "suitability" obligations, and better aligns the standard with retail customers' reasonable expectations by specifically requiring broker-dealers, among other things, to: 1) Act in the best interest of the retail customer (you) at the time the recommendation is made, without placing their financial (or any other) interest, or that of their firm's, ahead of the interests of the retail customer; and 2) address any and all conflicts of interest by "*establishing, maintaining, and enforcing policies and procedures reasonably designed to identify and fully and fairly disclose material facts about conflicts of interest*", and in instances where the SEC has determined that any disclosure is insufficient to reasonably address the conflict, they will then be required to mitigate or, in certain instances, eliminate the conflict.

Importantly, this new standard of conduct cannot be satisfied through disclosures alone. Meaning they can't just hand you a pile of pages and expect you to read all the fine print before you agree to anything they recommend.

In other words, if they stand to win an all-expenses paid trip to China for selling just one more client into the Thingamabob Fund and you happen to be the next one in the door, if they recommend the Thingamabob Fund to you: a) It had better be in your best interest to buy into that instead of something else; and b) He/she has to make sure you fully understand his or her motivation (and probably the trip's actual value) for recommending it at all, otherwise they stand to lose their license and/or be fined out the wazzoo.

The Regulation Best Interest standard of conduct draws from key principles that are the underpinnings of fiduciary obligations, including those that apply to investment advisors under the little enforced Investment Advisers Act of 1940 which underscores the fact that any recommendation must put the client's best interest before the firm's.

Meaning, it looks as if they're finally going to actually start enforcing existing law for everyone, not just bad actors.

There are various record keeping and other changes associated with the new standard of conduct rule as well, so the SEC generously gave broker-dealers a year from the date it was announced to get their house in order, with the deadline for implementation of the SEC's new rules being June 20, 2020. And, despite it being in the midst of the CoVid-19 outbreak, the SEC stuck to its guns and confirmed that date in early June. At least as an aid to further transparency for investors, it appears that the road is being paved in the right direction.

Chapter Three

What's wrong with these kids today?

The millennial generation – as defined by the U.S Census Bureau, those born between 1982 and 2000 – is now the largest generation, numbering some 83.2 million. Millennials can expect a higher life expectancy than ever before, lower income replacement from Social Security, and are far less likely to have a traditional "**defined benefit plan**", aka a pension, in retirement. This means Millennials must save significantly more than previous generations to maintain their standard of living when they leave the workforce.

Additionally, this generation has already faced a harsh economic landscape of depressed wages, high unemployment, and some major structural changes in the American economy as they entered the American workforce. Millennials also are the most diverse generation in the history of the United States, and unfortunately, the now 'default' retirement savings vehicle – the defined contribution retirement system (401(k)s, IRAs, 403(b)s, etc.) which favors high-income workers and many claim exacerbates disparities along gender, racial and ethnic lines, makes achieving a secure retirement an uphill climb for most Millennials.

An elephant in the room is that Millennials will have to save more than their parents and earlier generations to address a set of unique challenges as they age if they expect to live comfortably in their golden years.

If you're a millennial, you already know you're as much maligned as any generation…ever. Here's a good example, from one of your own. Note the 2nd tweet in the small print at the bottom.

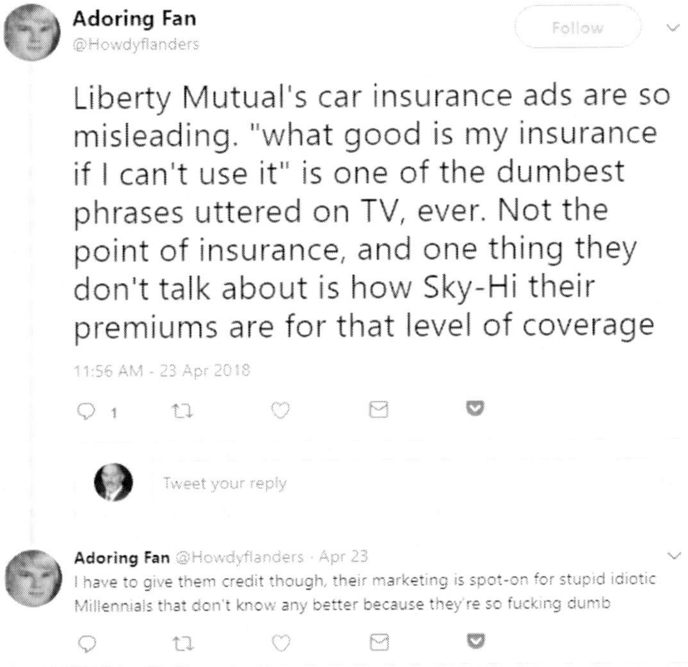

Even early GenXers often still look at Millennials as "just kids" and most parents just raise their hands in dismay when their 30+ year old millennial 'kids' start telling them how they ruined their chances at the American dream. Of course, they didn't *really* ruin it. Your life is what *you* make it, and every generation has its own unique set of challenges, but for Millennials (and now GenZ) it is significantly more difficult for a lot of reasons that could have been forestalled and/or corrected a generation ago. Few will argue that point.

Depending on whose study you read, Millennials are either self-absorbed, job-hopping radicals that spend more time looking at a small screen in their hand than at each other and have no plan for the future because they think the future will accommodate them; or they are responsible savers, far out-pacing their GenX and Baby-boomer counterparts, who have a personal vision of a well-balanced work/life future that includes investing in passion-based give-back projects even though they are starting out as the most heavily indebted generation in history.

Conflicting information is everywhere. Depending on what you read, you'll get a lot of conflicting data on the spending and saving habits of the largest generation in history as to whether they're on-track or off-track.

Yet the one thing that's consistent across the board, regardless of your source, is the amount of student loan debt Millennials are burdened with. The average college graduate with student loans starts out about $33,000 in debt (according to the U.S. Department of Education's 2019 Federal Student Loan Portfolio), and there are a greater number of students borrowing to pay for college almost daily. So certainly, in terms of the debt that they're coming out of school with, it is greater than any generation before them.

As far as saving in general, more studies than not show that they're doing pretty good, but they're not investing those savings in the stock market, the most common reason being because they're very leery for the future of the economy in general. One good reason could be because they lived through the dot-com bubble and the 2008 financial crisis, so they're well aware that the market doesn't always go up.

But there are other reasons.

Millennials are at the epicenter of changes in what can be best described as the employee/employer social contract. Much of it being driven by technology. Many entered the workforce during one of the worst economic downturns of the century and have struggled to launch their careers. And, many approach work with a spirit of experimentation over stability, meaning the old assumptions about education, work/life balance and retirement no longer apply for themselves and their children.

Millennials don't share the confidence of baby boomers and GenXers who believe they'll be financially better off than their parents, according to a study commissioned by Prudential Financial, Inc., findings of which were released in early 2018. Are the findings still valid now seven years later? You be the judge.

In that study nearly nine out of ten Millennials (88%) believed that anyone who was in their 20s and 30s in 2018 will need to work a decade or more longer than previous generations did to retire with the same level of financial security. Even if they work past the traditional retirement age of 65, 79% believed that by the time they reach 80 years old, comfortable retirement for the common worker will be a thing of the past.

Seventy plus percent said that's because it's impossible to save as much money each year as is calculated by then current retirement planning apps. Not much has changed in that regard.

I share that concern unless they (you) learn how to manage money effectively and start as early as possible.

Decades ago, Social Security and pension plans were enough to last the ten or so years that people lived in retirement. But thanks in part to some miracles of science, Millennials' futures will likely look nothing like that. People today are working well into their 70s, either continuing their full-time jobs or switching to part-time to supplement their retirement income. It's not hard to imagine people in their 20s and 30s today living vibrant healthy lives well into their 90s. If that's the case, retirement won't be just a few years anymore, it might easily last three decades in the future - potentially a third of your lifetime or longer.

Almost two-thirds of respondents agreed with a statement that in the future "traditional full-time employment will largely disappear, and freelancers will make up 75% or more of the U.S. workforce".

And nearly two-thirds of Millennials were extremely or somewhat nervous that people will need to learn to work with and adapt to robots and artificial intelligence to do their jobs.

Most Millennials (72%) were nervous that employers will eventually stop offering health care and retirement benefits altogether. One-third said they are "extremely" nervous that employer-provided health care and retirement benefits will disappear.

The survey also found that there is deep concern among Millennials about the decline of government benefits. According to the survey, 83% of Millennials said they're extremely or somewhat nervous about "a future where Social Security and other government-provided social safety nets may provide considerably less financial benefit than they do today".

Millennials' concerns about government benefits are part of a prevailing attitude of doubt and anxiety for the future, according to the Prudential report. Most Millennials expected their future economic lives to be even more volatile than in the recent past. The survey reported that 77% of Millennials thought it's probable that there will be a global recession in their lifetime that will be more disruptive than the Great Recession.

From an investment standpoint, 68% of Millennials thought it is somewhat or highly likely that investments will become completely automated, based on personal data and preferences. Although 58% still preferred receiving financial advice from a licensed professional.

And 71% of the more than 1,000 Prudential survey respondents thought it was likely that the next generation will live in a world without cash.

Apparently, many are without cash right now.

According to a 2024 GOBankingRates survey of more than 1,000 adults found that 66% of people between the ages of 21 and 32 had absolutely nothing set aside for retirement.

Zero. Zip. Nada. For all Americans that number was 28%. Thirty-nine percent aren't contributing to any retirement fund and another 30% don't think they'll ever be able to retire.,

And, the situation is far worse for working millennial Latinos, of whom as high as 83% have nothing saved for retirement.

In addition, the report found that while two-thirds of Millennials work for an employer that offers a retirement plan, only slightly more than one-third (34.3%) participate in their employer's plan. Their reasons have little to do with procrastination but a lot to do with access. More than four out of ten (45%) of Millennials cited that eligibility requirements set by their employers, such as working a minimum number of hours or having a minimum tenure on the job (vesting), prevented them from participating in a plan.

However, the landscape of retirement planning in the United States has undergone some significant changes in recent years, and things have only gotten worse. According to a survey of 1,000 people aged 25 and over, done by Allianz Life Insurance Company of North America in February and March of 2023, factors such as inflation, market volatility, financial crises, and concerns about bank failures have created a 'new' reality for retirement that has long-term implications for many Americans.

These challenges have led to a fundamental shift in how individuals of all ages approach their retirement plans.

One notable trend is that a considerable number of our under 50 population are sacrificing their long-term financial security to meet their immediate needs. For instance, in response to recent financial crises, 46% of respondents in the Allianz survey said they have reduced or entirely halted their retirement savings. Worse yet, they don't anticipate increasing their savings levels at all in the foreseeable future. Obviously, this can have significant consequences for their retirement spending abilities.

Additionally, the rising cost of living is now a major concern for many of us. Around 49% of survey respondents stated that the escalating everyday expenses pose a significant risk to their retirement income. This represents an increase from 44% in 2022 and 38% in 2021. Such a high percentage indicates the growing apprehension about fulfilling basic expense needs in retirement.

Disturbingly, close to 40% admitted to having already derailed their retirement strategy and are uncertain about how or when they can get back on track. This highlights the pervasive challenges individuals face in maintaining a secure financial future. In fact, 56% of Americans now consider "financial crises" as a permanent component of their retirement planning, suggesting a lack of confidence in achieving any form of stability in retirement.

A remarkable 61% of Americans express more fear about running out of money in retirement than they do about death itself. Yet many are not taking any of the necessary steps to establish a strong financial foundation for their retirement years. Overall, the evolving dynamics of retirement planning have forced most Americans to confront various financial risks and often make difficult choices as a result.

In the 2024 National Institute on Retirement Security survey, when asked if the nation faces a retirement crisis, 79% of Americans agree there indeed is a retirement crisis, up from 67% in 2020. More than half of Americans (55%) are concerned that they cannot achieve financial security in retirement. When it comes to inflation, 73% of respondents said recent inflation has them more concerned about retirement.

So why does the largest, best educated, and most diverse generation in the history of the U.S. seem to have so little tucked away for retirement? Well, not all 83 million Millennials are behind.

About one-third are saving for retirement. Most have less than $20,000 but some have much more. According to Fidelity Investments' retirement analysis released in the second quarter of 2024, the average 401(k) balance for Millennials (born between 1981 and 1996) was around $62,000. This represents a 22% increase compared to $48,300 in 2023. That's also a record high savings rate for Fidelity's 410(k) account holders, however, it's worth noting that these figures are based on Fidelity's data and Fidelity's clientele tends to be on the higher end of the economic scale than the general public overall. For the others, it's not necessarily that they don't want to save — it's a question of whether they can.

According to a Willis survey, 60% of (all generations of) working men put retirement saving at the top of their priority list, while just 44% of women thought the same way. In fact, in general, women considered saving for retirement in fifth place, while paying daily living expenses and paying down their debt were their top two, at 64% and 57%, respectively.

With the exception of married women with no children under the age of 18, who also put saving for retirement at the top of their list.

Back in 2020, CNN did a report after speaking to dozens of Millennials about why they have little or nothing saved and most simply believed they'd be better off putting their money elsewhere.

Some wanted to pay off student debt. Some were trying to create or expand their own business. Many had graduated during the recession and had worked low-wage jobs for a few years, then went back to school to improve their job prospects.

For others, there were more immediate day-to-day expenses that took priority, like childcare and rent. That group found it hard to build up even a small emergency savings cushion and the idea of putting money in an account they wouldn't be able to touch for 30+ years didn't make a lot of sense to them, despite the seemingly magical properties of compounding interest. Little has changed since then.

If that sounds like you, don't sweat it. Keep reading. Later we'll discuss how to cover your bills *and* fund your future without losing sleep over it.

However, for some, there was even a more troubling reason than a current lack of cash flow: many Millennials in that study may honestly feel that they don't see a future for themselves in our current economic system.

CNN's article about Millennials' lack of retirement savings was quickly widespread on social media, especially on X (when it was still Twitter), partly because many Millennials saw humor in how it missed how many of them truly felt.

"RT if socialism is your retirement plan," read one Tweet.

"My retirement plan is death" read another.

The 33rd Annual Retirement Confidence Survey conducted by the Employee Benefit Research Institute (EBRI) and Greenwald Research, conducted in 2023, gathered responses from 2,537 Americans aged 25 or older. The main finding is that all Americans' confidence in their ability to have enough money for a comfortable retirement has declined compared to the previous year, with confidence levels returning to those last seen in 2018. And in a Harris Poll, more than a third of Millennials surveyed said they don't see the point of planning for retirement because anything can happen between now and then.

Of course, many Millennials are not even in a position of considering retirement savings, much less having options when it comes to work or life decisions, according to a Pew Research poll completed in late 2017, which noted that "5.3 million of the nearly 17 million U.S. households living in poverty were headed by a Millennial".

Granted, quips about being unable to retire and predictions of absolute social change by their retirement age were blazing around the internet long before CNN's article was published, but I was personally struck by the world-weariness and capitulation displayed by many of the comments.

Older generations, and even those Millennials who are better off and who have managed to achieve some semblance of economic freedom (especially those who market researchers refer to with the acronym of HENRY – High Earner, Not Rich Yet), find such sentiments unimaginable or simply ignorant. And yet, reaction to that CNN piece uncovered large blocks of Millennials with a lack of confidence that capitalism as we know it would even exist by their retirement age and that alternating climate and governmental crises, increases in the concentrations of wealth, and privatization of social welfare programs would doom their chance at financial survival.

It's clear that some don't have faith in our current form of governance and expect a total apocalyptic breakdown of industrial society or at the very least some ideal utopian model where all basic necessities are magically abundant and free, everyone works just a few hours a week at the necessary "chores" of society (like machine maintenance — since ugly work like garbage collection will all be done by AI driven robots) then has the rest of their lives free to pursue whatever projects they desire, be they art, leisure, or industry or science.

In many cases, that kind of uncertainty and attitude of fait accompli can be chalked up to youthful inexperience and/or a lack of historical knowledge combined with belief in too many less than credible news sources on the internet. But that utopian hope, that we could morph into a global, fully-automated, post-work social democracy isn't just being spouted by extremist crackpots.

However, until that happens, we should *all* be expected to fend for ourselves.

Studies show that many Millennials are doing just that, but as mentioned before, considering the risks some of this generation takes with snowboarding down near vertical mountainsides, wingsuit base jumping and extreme sports, where and how that money is being saved is certainly not unconventional. In fact, most will just put their money in banks. Or in investments they feel are *extremely* safe like CDs and Treasuries. What they are not doing, as a whole, is going out and buying a hyped-up "the next Netflix" stock, or for that matter buying *any* stock in particular and sticking with it.

Naturally, when it comes to investing, many are turning to artificial intelligence. Automation in the form of robo-advisors and automating savings mechanisms like Qapital, which rounds up the spare change of purchases to the nearest dollar and automatically moves it into an interest-bearing savings account and/or automatically moves money from your paycheck to investments based on goals you set. Or Acorns which helps you figure out an investment plan based on your income and goals and (like Qapital) draws that money from the "spare change" of purchases made by a specific credit card (or a specific amount deducted from your bank account at regular intervals – like on payday) and invests it into one of five diversified portfolios of stocks that match your risk tolerance.

Qapital's website cites over 2 million users, with over $3 billion saved since its start in 2013. Acorns boasted over 6.5 million users in Q1 of 2023, up from 2 million in 2018. Most are Millennials, and more than 90% are under the age of 54. Another robo-advisor, Betterment, has several different offerings based on your situation.

Betterment, which was founded in 2008 as one of the pioneers in automated digital-only advice platforms and reported a 775,000+ customer count as of the end of 2022, ranging from Millennials to 85-year-olds, with an average age of 37 and an overall average balance of about $44,000.

With more than $36 billion in assets under management as of the date above, the firm lays claim to being the largest independent online financial advisor. And its high-net-worth offering has indeed been embraced by investors with accounts ranging from $100,000 to many millions, according to inside sources.

Its website claims that Betterment's "approach to long-term investing can help you earn 2.66% more than a typical investor" through its technology, which, the digital advisor says, makes lower taxes and fees possible, and encourages "better investing behavior".

Other robo-advisors like Wealthfront (now owned by UBS), Personal Capital (recently renamed Empower after being acquired by Canadian company Empower Retirement), and Stash, and now Sofi, Fidelity and the FIRE (Financial Independence Retire Early) community's ETF 'go-to' Vanguard offer similar services so it's clear that some folks are putting at least regular micro-amounts of money into play.

However, you should be aware that companies that let you buy and sell stocks for free aren't always acting in your best interest. In general, most everyone realizes that when you get anything "free", the actual product the company makes money on is you. What you do on their website is captured and sold to other companies hungry for that data.

Robinhood, for example, is making millions of dollars selling users' data to high-frequency trading firms that actually work against you – a controversial industry practice known as payment for order flow. High Frequency Trading (HFT) can be defined as using an automated computer driven trading system that uses complex algorithms to scan markets for even the smallest of opportunities, then execute millions of orders at speeds faster than any traditional market participants. They get this data by being an intermediary stop between the buyer or seller (you) and the brokerage firm that eventually executes your trade. Such side stops are unnoticeable to you because they take just milliseconds to scan your data, and these firms often make only a small profit on each transaction but by being super-fast and placing vast amounts of orders ahead of yours, they nonetheless generate large returns.

Although Robinhood isn't the only company to use this kind of practice, they are (at least as of this writing) the only one to get significantly fined by FINRA (the Financial Industry Regulatory Authority Inc., a private corporation that acts as Wall street's self-regulatory organization) for wrongdoing related to it.

In December of 2019 FINRA fined Robinhood $1.25 million for sending customer trading orders to four broker dealers without guaranteeing the best price.

While it should come as no surprise that any investment company might sell or otherwise trade in information related to its customers' demographics and purchasing preferences, what's insidious about this practice used by Robinhood and others, is that they frequently tout their zero-commission trading options as going against the grain of the typical Wall Street brokerages. In reality, Robinhood Financial (the parent company of the app) at least, according to an SEC filing, sells users' order details at 10 times the rate of what other financial companies charge HFT firms.

That $1.25 million is a slap on the wrist to Robin Hood, which was worth about $9 billion in 2019. In a statement afterward, Robin Hood said settlement "does not reflect our practices or procedures today". However, Vlad Tenev, Robinhood's co-CEO, defended the practice of payment for order flow in an interview by CNN business shortly after the sanctions were levied, saying:

"Rebates from market makers and trading revenues are one of the ways that Robinhood makes money," Tenev told CNN. "It's how the market works in the US. It's a common practice that is pretty much ubiquitous".

I love the flippant use of the word "rebates" that shows the true marketing spin they're trying to put on this to avoid a negative backlash. The definition of 'rebate' being a partial refund to someone who has paid too much money for something. You certainly can't call it a rebate if you're the only side of the transaction that gets paid. Let's call it what it is — a payment for the data (your trade data) they provide. I'm sure you'll agree that just because 'everyone is doing it' doesn't make it the right thing to do.

Adding Murphy's Law into the mix, on March 2, 2020, when the Dow, S&P 500 and NASDAQ all rose by 1,294, 136 and 384 points respectively, in what was then the biggest ever point gain in a single day on record, Robinhood's trading platform was overwhelmed and crashed, being completely inaccessible and unavailable to all of its customers the entire day and now faces lawsuits as a result.

So, buyer beware.

Changing the subject to long term planning, a sometimes too commonly bandied about statistic is that anyone who starts diligently saving for retirement at age 25 can have in the neighborhood of $1 million plus *more* set aside in retirement savings at age 65 than if they wait to get started at age 35. The time value of money is undeniable. The more you put in, the more you end up with in interest and appreciation the longer you let that compounding percolate, and often, that money deposited in that first decade can seem like it has worked miracles over 40+ years.

However, while the numbers are right (saving $1,000 per month with a consistent 6% annual ROI), that statistic assumes no roller coasters of market returns or life events that might sidetrack or potentially derail your retirement savings plan. The critical component of that method is putting your money somewhere that will deliver an average 6% return without fail, regardless of what happens in that timeframe. In today's financial environment, how many investments do you know of that can guarantee that?

On the topic of auto-enrollment in things like 401(k)s, the clear majority are smart enough to realize that the company match is free money, so they're at least putting in enough to get 100% of that match.

We'll discuss the pros and many cons of 401(k)s in the next chapter.

Something else that it appears that Millennials have a leg up on is creating a budget for themselves. But face it, with too numerous a list of good budgeting apps, it's as easy as taking a snapshot of your receipts in even the most un-tech-leveraged app. And anyone who can build a basic budget would quickly realize if they would buy just a few less Starbucks Ventis or 12-ounce Red Bulls a week they've found enough money to put away month after month that given 30 to 40 years in the right vehicle will create a lot of dough.

How much? Well last time I checked, a Starbucks Venti (just straight up coffee sans all the fancy additional goodies) and a 12-ounce Red Bull cost about the same - $2.50. Saving that much money just on weekdays adds up to $12.50 a week, or $50 per month. Stashing aside just that extra $50 a month into some form of tax-free retirement plan with an average investment return of just 7% adds up $129,113 over 40 years. Do I have your attention yet?

Can't live without your caffeine boosts? Fine, but there's bound to be something else that you can easily shed or simply replace with something less expensive like bagging your lunch occasionally instead of eating at the local food truck every day.

The problem is, too many haven't yet been exposed to feasible methods to get there that don't include the risks of stashing that cash in traditional investments, and without what seems like a secret knock and password, many never get through that door to enlightenment to learn the methods that rich people use without having a fat wallet, just yet. We'll solve that in this book.

So how are Millennials doing in terms of overall finances?

Go to school, get a good job, pay your bills on time, have cash set aside for emergencies, and invest your money for the future. Those are the rules that everyone who's anyone says people should follow if they want to build wealth. Pretty straightforward advice, but for too many people, one or more of these milestones can seem out of reach.

Millennials are slowly finding their financial footing. The good news is that those that *are* saving, are saving at a rate that will put them in reasonable territory down the road – if they stay on track. They are embarking on the next phase in their lives, which will have a growing focus on career and family. They are planning a financial future in an economy that has rebounded from the Great Recession — but most see a world that feels more volatile, uncertain and complex than ever before.

In terms of financial literacy, a January 2023 report from the National Financial Educators Council showed that 38% of individuals in a survey (conducted Oct. 23, 2022 through Dec. 5, 2022 among about 3,000 adults across the country) said their lack of financial literacy cost them at least $500 in 2022, including 15% who said it set them back more than $10,000. That's up from about 11% in 2021.

The majority (68%) of respondents said poor financial literacy cost them somewhere from zero to $499.

But the average cost was $1,819, according to the survey. That 2022 figure is nearly $500 higher than the average $1,389 in 2021.

Here are some of the prevailing trends that the NFEC survey and other similar recent reports pointed out:

- 27% of U.S. adults are not confident that they're saving enough as of 2019.
- 19% of Americans say they are very uncomfortable with their level of emergency savings.
- 6% of American adults didn't have bank accounts in 2021. Hispanic and Black respondents were less likely to have a bank account compared to American adults overall.
- 11% of American adults with bank accounts paid overdraft fees in 2022.
- 17% of American renters were behind on rent at some point in 2022.
- In 2021, 12% of those with student loans were behind on payments.
- 64% of Americans report that money is a significant stressor in their life.

- Credit card debt in the US surpassed $1 trillion for the first time in the second quarter of 2023, thanks to inflation and rising interest rates.

Young people are struggling. Less than 30% of Americans have an emergency savings account that equals 3-6 months of household income. Of those people, only 19% of Generation Z (after Millennials) has saved for a rainy day, followed by Millennials (20%), GenXers (28%), Baby Boomers (37%) and World War II/Greatest Generation (40%).

While almost half of states require either a personal finance or economics course to graduate high school, in 2021, 34% of U.S. adults reported that "just getting by financially" describes them completely or very well.

Unsurprisingly, people who have higher net incomes save a larger percentage of their pay and on a more regular basis. People in the bottom 90% of the income scale save relatively none of their pay each year (which includes the vast majority of Millennials), while those in the top 10% save in the range of 15%.

Needless to say, depending on the focus of the study, conflicting numbers abound.

In a PGIM Investments survey, when asked their level of retirement preparedness, pre-retirees gave themselves an average grade of "C," but that survey of 1,500+ people included an unknown number of GenXers and Boomers.

What can be quantified confidently is that the vast majority of us are not doing everything we can to prepare for retirement, including meeting with a financial advisor to devise a plan (or reading about how to set one up on our own), researching Social

Security or even talking to friends or family about short term vs. long term planning. Even more importantly, 21% of all Americans are "not at all confident" they will be able to reach their financial goals, meaning they'll either work until they die or die broke.

Parents plan more than non-parents. It is a more than reasonable assumption that people with children have more demands on their money, and therefore are more inclined to think ahead and follow budgets, contribute to college savings and retirement accounts and hire, or at least speak to, a financial advisor to help them create a budget and plan based on their circumstances and goals.

Those who don't have kids likely don't have as many competing demands on their money but still aren't as practical about following any real financial plan. Only 33% of Americans have a written financial plan, according to Schwab's 2021 Modern Wealth Survey. Of the rest, almost half said they didn't have enough money to make a documented plan worthwhile. Others said it was too complicated, or they didn't have time to develop a plan. Just as bad, only 26% contributed regularly to a retirement account.

Other recent studies have also confirmed that most Millennials, as well as consumers in general, at least have some semblance of a budget. But only one in three Americans prepare a detailed written or computerized household budget each month that tracks their income and expenses. A large majority do not. I get it, keeping track of every dime you spend is not exactly entertainment. As little as 10 years ago, most people still wrote them out on paper. And while technology has made keeping track of your spending light-years easier today, most still need to be more motivated to do so.

Those with at least some college education, and interestingly, those with conservative and independent political leanings, as well as those making $75,000 a year or more are slightly more likely to prepare a detailed household budget than are their lesser educated, lower income or liberal leaning counterparts, says a Gallup study.

Go figure.

In terms of use of credit cards, Millennials are no different than most Americans when it comes to credit card debt, with four in ten carrying forward some debt month to month. The average balance on a credit card was $2,573 in June 2023, up 6.5% from 2022, according to credit scoring company FICO. Even more telling is that the percentage of accounts past due by one cycle increased 42% in the past two years — that is the highest level since September 2017. How do you save and invest if you can't pay your bills?

At the same time, according to Bankrate, the average annual percentage rate on credit cards was 20.60% in September of 2023 when the revisions on this book were made, the highest since 1985, the year Bankrate first started tracking that data.

And while Millennials are typically saving more than adults over 35 (36% of Millennials compared to 22% of older adults), a recent study by the National Foundation of Credit Counseling (NFCC) showed they are twice as likely to have made a wide variety of credit card blunders in the last twelve months, including overspending their limits and paying late.

However, the real burden for Millennials is college debt. More than any generation, those who have it shoulder a debt that will take them nearly as many years to pay off as a 15-year mortgage.

In fact, in the most recent (2019) Survey of Consumer Finances by the Federal Reserve, it showed that Millennials held an average of $128,000 in total debt. That's nearly twice the average debt balance of $67,000 that Generation X carried when they were the same ages in 2001. Much of it is tied to the increase in student loan debt.

It's also much higher than the $48,611 average (as of September 2023) debt of Millennial subscribers to online credit monitoring company Credit Karma, but that difference can be attributed to the fact that Credit Karma members are far more likely to be actively managing their debt than non-members.

According to a 2023 study by Self Inc. using Federal Reserve data, in 1998, the American population under 40 years old held 13.1% of America's total wealth. Today, those under 40 hold only 5% of the total wealth. This means that Millennials own less than half of the wealth that older generations owned when they were the same age.

Some of what they found includes that in 2016, wealth of the median family headed by someone born in the 1980s was 34% ($12,000) less than the wealth benchmark levels that were determined by the experiences of older generations at the same ages.

While the report noted that Millennials have the potential to be the "highest-earning-group ever," in general, young families today typically have truly little wealth. If you're a millennial and you entered adulthood saddled with student loans and other types of debt, such as credit card balances and auto loans, your total net worth could easily be negative.

What's worse is the debt situation in which many Millennials find themselves has long-term impacts.

According to a 2018 report from some researchers with perhaps a vested interest at Morningstar who crunched data from the Federal Reserve, every dollar in student loan debt decreases your retirement savings by 35 cents. That means for a couple with $100,000 in student debt, that's a $35,000 setback.

Due to the way compounding works over time, the first 10 years of a person's working life, meaning their ability to create an income large enough to contribute to a retirement fund of any kind during that period, is probably as important as anything they might do after the age of 50. Student loans often rob people of the opportunity to contribute fully to their future during those important earning years.

The report also found that relationship holds true no matter how old you are or how much money you're earning,

Naturally, part of the ongoing problem is the continually rising cost of a college education. The other part is the reality that a college education is often a requirement to get a decent paying job.

As a result, many Millennials find themselves stuck between a rock and a hard place.

Their liquid capital stance doesn't fare much better. Typically, Americans don't carry much cash on their person on a daily basis to begin with, two-thirds carrying less than $99, most at around the $25 level. But the NFCC study showed that young adults are more likely (24% to only 11% of adults 35+) to have to sell something they own if they find themselves in need of a quick $400 for an emergency.

So, if you're not a HENRY…or even if you *are* a high-income earner and you're part of that 49% of those earning more than six figures who find themselves stretched so thin (according to Q3 2022 Lending Club report) that they reported living paycheck to paycheck (a jump from the previous year's 38%) and you struggle to pay your bills month to month and/or you find it impossible to consider setting aside the 15% or so of your net income that pundits prescribe and still have a life, how do you create a realistic plan to move forward?

First let's look at what those pundits and financial gurus are pointing you toward and exactly why much of it should be ignored. Then I'll lay out a blueprint that will work for anyone…HENRY or not. Fair enough?

Chapter Four

401(k) plans suc(k)

You've heard it too many times. Experts in the financial services industry have long advised anyone who pays taxes to save money for the future via a tax-deferred savings plan. And for good reason, for decades, tax-deferral planning for retirement was the *only* game in town. Everyone who is anyone still tells you to max out your 401(k) from day one and reap the benefits of tax deferral until you're forced to take that money out by government requirements at age 73. By that time your money will have grown into the multi-millions, they claim. And in an ideal world, they would be right.

First question: Do we live in an ideal world?

Next question: Do you expect the next 30-50 years to be economically ideal?

The answer to both is of course not. And as Hamlet said, "Aye, there's the rub".

Let's take a brief trip back in time.

For anyone born after 1970, we tend to think of 401(k) plans as the foundation of any good retirement savings plan...*if* one is available to you. But history tells us that these plans, plainly named after the section 401(k) in the Internal Revenue Code, were actually developed more by accident than by design.

When lawmakers created the Revenue Act of 1978, the purpose was to limit top executives at some companies from having unfettered access to the incentives of cash-deferred plans. That, in and of itself, is a paradox since going back to the 1950s, big corporations had been fighting with the Internal Revenue Service to allow more money to be squirreled away in such plans as an incentive to keep key executives from defecting to other companies offering higher traditional compensation. The sentiment at the time in the Congress and Senate however (much like today), was not with already highly paid executives, it was more geared toward the little guy, the working stiff, average Joe.

As a result, the almost accidental birth of the 401(k) plan as we know today can be credited to a benefits consultant by the name of Ted Benna. In 1980, Benna used his interpretation of the law to create a 401(k) plan for his own employer, The Johnson Companies, which allowed all full-time employees (the little guy) to fund accounts with pre-tax dollars, as well as employers to make contributions of the same or similar value to the employees' accounts as an added incentive. Benna then lobbied the Department of Treasury official, who was writing the 401(k) regulations, to allow the employer matching and employee pre-tax salary reduction contributions. New regulations issued in the fall of 1980 permitted both which quickly led to the widespread adoption of 401(k) plans by most large employers in the early 1980s.

Back then, no one, including Benna, expected it to morph into the primary vehicle for retirement savings that it is today for people in most companies with over 500 full time employees.

In the early 1980s, before the advent of a personal computer on every desk, 401(k) plans were far more complicated to set up and administer and were only available to a handful of large companies, such as Johnson & Johnson, PepsiCo and Honeywell. The latest data from the Census Bureau suggests that still only as few as 14% of all employers offer a 401(k). Yet, as of 2020, roughly just over half of the entire U.S. workforce had access to a "**defined contribution plan**" (big difference from a defined *benefit* plan, the academic term for a pension) like a 401(k) according to the Department of Labor. How is that possible?

The easy to guess answer is that large companies that employ high numbers of workers are the most likely to sponsor retirement plans.

Over 91% of businesses with more than 500 employees offer a 401(k) plan (yet 89% of 401(k) plans have fewer than 100 actual participants, meaning many don't contribute even when it's offered), just over 35% of businesses with over 100 but less than 500 employees offer one and only 12% of businesses with less than 100 employees offer a 401(k) according to 401(k) administrator Human Interest.

A survey done by payroll company SurePayroll Small Business Scorecard showed that 42% of small companies who do not offer 401(k) plans say they do not see the value in it. What does that tell you when almost half of small business owners don't see any real value to themselves or their employees by implementing a 401(k)? Thirty five percent say the fees are too expensive, and 23% say they don't have enough knowledge in how to manage a 401(k) even with all the advanced technology available today.

Small businesses (those under 500 employees as defined by the government) make up more than 99% of the employers in the US so that 42% that doesn't see the value represents more than 12.6 million businesses, most of whom have a far different tax structure than large businesses where a 401(k) impacts the bottom line in a far different manner.

If you don't already know, at its most basic, a 401(k) plan is a retirement account that you can only access through an employer. You contribute a portion of your pre-tax salary to the plan, and if you choose to put that contribution in a traditional 401(k), it isn't taxed *until* you withdraw the money, which allows your investments (chosen by you, not the employer) to grow over time without being taxed, but you will pay substantial penalties if you take your money out before age 59 ½. And, as an added bonus, your employer may also offer to help you save more. Close to 95% of 401(k) plans provide matching contributions, and the average company contribution is 2.5% of an employee's pay. Contribution matching guidelines among 401(k) plans differ greatly depending on the company, but the most common is a dollar-for-dollar match of up to about 6% of an employee's pay.

Starting in 2025, all new 401(k) plans — those established after Dec. 29, 2022 — must automatically enroll eligible employees unless they opt out. If you work for a company with fewer than 10 employees or a business under three years old, your employer is exempt from the automatic enrollment requirement. Government and church plans are also exempt.

Up until 2024, you had to work at least 1,000 hours in a year or 500 hours over three consecutive years to qualify for an employer's 401(k) plan. But starting in 2025 the three years has been reduced to two, making it quicker for part-time workers to become eligible. That change could certainly benefit you if you have multiple part-time jobs rather than just one full-time job.

Keep in mind, however, that if you work two jobs and enroll and contribute to two separate 401(k) plans, you have to keep your total annual contributions to no more than the yearly limit. For example, in 2025, the 401(k) contribution limit is $23,500 (up from $23,000 in '24). So, if you contribute $15,000 to Plan #1, you can only contribute $8,500 to Plan #2.

By any standard, the current 401(k) stats are impressive. As of the end of March 2023, 401(k) plans held an estimated $9.8 trillion in assets and represented more than 27.6% of the $35.4 trillion in US retirement assets, according to Investment Company Institute reports. That's more than 300 times the $92 billion in assets held in 1984, the earliest data available from the Department of Labor.

Benna, often called the "Father of the 401(k)," has been critical of his creation, noting that there are too many investment options available today and that complexity has a negative impact on 401(k) plan participants.

The original 401(k) plan was called a "salary reduction plan" because it reduced the taxable salary for highly paid executives without reducing their overall compensation. It only had two investing options: a stock fund and a money market fund, and virtually no risk. Eventually, Wall Street saw an opportunity and started offering the administration of these plans and offered funds with higher potential growth, but with the trade-off of more risk. The typical 401(k) now offers a dozen or more funds and the onus is on you to figure out which is best for your particular situation. Most end up picking just one or two based on a coworker's advice.

Here's a fun (read that as 'scary') fact, a 2014 survey of 401(k) plan participants, commissioned by Schwab Retirement Plan Services, showed that the average 401(k) participant spends more than twice as much time researching options on a new car they plan to buy or their next vacation (about two hours) than they do researching the investment options in their 401(k) (about one hour). Chances are fairly good that hasn't changed much since then.

As 401(k) plans have thrived, traditional pension plans in the private sector have waned. According to the Department of Labor, from 1975 to 2016, the proportion of traditional (defined benefit) pension plans fell from 38% to just 6%. Today that number is likely closer to 4%. Meaning, if you don't work for the government, chances are slim your company offers one.

For employers, 401(k) plans are a far more enticing option because they cost less than traditional pension plans, and they don't carry the same accounting liabilities and investment risks. Many 401(k) critics say that workers would be better off in traditional pensions even though pensions carry the same risk of loss.

Here's the big difference – in a 401(k) plan the burden of choosing the right investment is on you, not the employer. That's a ***huge*** transfer of investment risk. The financial crisis of 2008 laid bare that vulnerability in the defined contribution retirement system as Americans who had done everything according to plan watched the value of their retirement plans plummet when the financial markets crashed and trillions of dollars of household wealth disappeared in the blink of an eye.

That financial debacle saw combined asset values in all kinds of retirement accounts fall from $9.3 trillion at the end of 2007 to $7.2 trillion by the end of 2008. The crash also triggered a dramatic reduction in total contributions to 401(k) retirement accounts because many employers stopped matching employee contributions for some (then indefinite) period of time.

Pensions, however, were never as widely available as 401(k) plans. Even in the 'good old days' when supposedly 'everybody' had a pension, the reality is that most workers in the private sector did not. Even among those who did work for an employer that offered a pension, most weren't working long enough with a single employer to accumulate the service levels needed for a full pension. Today, just over 41% of the American workforce has no access to any company sponsored retirement plan, 401(k) or otherwise.

Despite the growth of 401(k) plans, there's an estimated $6.6 trillion deficit in what Americans currently have in savings compared to what they will actually need in retirement, according to an analysis by the Center for Retirement Research at Boston College.

This shortfall should make maximizing retirement accounts, like a 401(k) plan, a priority but most people ignore it. As of 2024, you can defer up to $23,000 from your paycheck into a 401(k) plan, up from $19,500 in 2020. Those age 50 and older can save even more by making what's called a "catch-up" contribution. That's limited to an additional $7,500 a year in 2024, for a total of $30,500. However, Under SECURE 2.0, if you are at least 50 years old and earned $145,000 or more in the previous year, there's a catch. You would have to make those extra contributions on a Roth basis, using *after-tax* money.

These limits don't include the matching contribution you may receive from your employer, but they also apply to 403(b) plans and the federal government's Thrift Savings Plan.

Experts tell you that if you're not maxing out your 401(k), you should consider boosting your contribution by 1% every six months. For most of us, that's about $20 to $50 per paycheck, which you probably wouldn't miss all that much. And since most employers will automatically deduct a 401(k) contribution from your paycheck, it makes the extra savings easier to stomach because you never get your hands on it.

So, all that sounds pretty good, right? What you read so far about 401(k) plans was mostly informational, with a few good news/bad news tidbits interspersed. Then you might ask why this chapter is titled 401(k) plans suck? Here's a clue:

Unfortunately, according to Vanguard, only 12% of Americans make the maximum contribution annually to their retirement account. And let's consider the plight of those folks that the IRS calls HCPs (Highly Compensated Employees). You might already be one, if so congratulations, or you might very well become one 20 years from now. The problem will be the same if you don't act.

For illustrative purposes, let's imagine an executive earning $220,000 who has maxed out his $23,500 401(k) contribution. Smart, but that's just barely over 10% of his gross income going to his retirement savings, so he also wants to make an additional after-tax contribution to his retirement savings of at least $10,000 (totaling 15%). He could contribute into a traditional IRA, but his annual income exceeds the eligibility for a Roth, so growing his leftover money will most likely mean putting 100% of it at risk in another eventually taxable bucket or the stock market or some other asset class with an equal risk of loss.

If you plan to go into a highly paid profession, you should be planning your retirement savings strategy the day you start, not wondering 20 years later how to keep from losing money to the tax man or market downturns. Statistics aren't in your favor.

Study after study has shown that after 40+ years of this 401(k) 'experiment' that people do worse in 401(k)s than they would have if their money was in a traditional pension plan or if it was in a plain vanilla retirement account managed by a professional.

The general public does a poor job of picking the right funds for their specific needs, checks them less than they should, re-allocates them next to never and suffers massive losses when the markets go down.

Worse yet, 401(k) plans are rife with fees charged by their sponsors that are rarely disclosed to you in any conversation about the actual internal costs. These fees used to be so hidden, so deep in the fine print of the fund's prospectus, that only the nerdiest amongst you would ever find them. Even now that they are required by law to be disclosed separately from the fund's prospectus, plan administrators bank on the fact that you'll never read them and if, in the rare chance you do, they're described in such complex industry jargon it'll make your head explode.

Remember that a 401(k) is nothing more than an assortment of securities that go up and down with the market.

And beyond a shadow of a doubt, investor *unawareness* is so rampant that millions of people never stop to ask how much the 401(k) plan provider or administrator, or the mutual fund company that created the basket of securities into which you choose to park your cash – is generating off the money you trust them to invest.

One study done by AARP way back in 2011 showed that 71% of participants thought that they didn't pay *any* 401(k) fees — something that simply isn't true. Their services aren't ever free. And although most people nowadays understand it isn't free, they likely have no clue what they're paying or why.

Your 401(k) administrator collects a fee (or fees) every month. In a very legal (but unsurprisingly next to impossible to find any public documentation on) arrangement, 99% of plan providers accept payments from the mutual funds they offer in your 401(k) plan. This is called 'revenue sharing' or when money is exchanged for specific services or the privilege to engage in certain activities. Sometimes referred to as "Pay to Play". Naturally, the list you have to choose from includes the funds that pay the provider the highest amounts — rarely the best performing, and certainly not the lowest in cost. The cumulative amount of those fees can dramatically change your long-term returns.

Additionally, many providers restrict the low-cost funds that are available only to plans that exceed a certain amount of assets, meaning that employees of smaller companies are forced to invest in funds with higher fees. And seeing that the providers don't make much of a margin on the lower-cost funds they serve up, they then charge a significant markup. One major company offers an S&P 500 Index fund for more than 1% annually, when the actual cost is 0.05%. That translates into more than a 100% markup. Where does that money come from? Your investment.

On that subject, one CNBC writer wrote "*Imagine walking into your favorite clothing store, where — curiously — not a single item has a price tag. You grab what you want, but when you reach the register, the cashier refuses to tell you the price.*

Instead, he grabs your credit card and says, "Just trust me.' This ridiculous example illustrates the essence of how the multi-trillion-dollar 401(k) plan industry operated for decades".

There are a host of different charges that can seriously eat away at your nest egg, even though they may not sound burdensome on the surface or be obvious on your statement. Over time, those fees can cost a single plan participant hundreds of thousands of dollars. For example, let's say you save $10,000 a year for 30 years in your 401(k). If you average 7% returns annually and pay 0.5% in annual expenses, you'll finish with about $920,000 saved. However, with 1.0% in annual fees, that total drops to a little less than $840,000, and if you have 2.0% in annual fees, your finishing total is just under $700,000.

I don't know about you, but I'd feel ripped off if someone took $220,000+ out of my pocket, even if it was just a little bit at a time.

For nearly 30 years, the 401(k) plan industry wasn't legally required to explain exactly how much it was charging investors. It wasn't until 2012 that the feds finally forced 401(k) providers to make detailed disclosures of how much they were extricating from your hard-toiled savings.

Making matters worse, 401(k) plans typically come with just a set menu of funds, and good or bad, you're stuck using the list of funds from provider your employer has chosen. Additionally, sitting atop all those funds could be expensive administrative fees that are determined at the plan level, and are totally out of an individual employee's control. Meaning, there's just nothing you can do about them.

As pervasive as they are in large companies, not everyone who's offered an employer-sponsored plan takes advantage of it. Of that 59% of working Americans who get the choice to fund a 401(k), more than one third opt not to contribute. As such, only about a third of the total American workforce is saving in a 401(k).

Even those who participate in 401(k) plans aren't funding their accounts adequately. Obviously, amounts in 401(k) plans will vary with age, but we can get a good feel for what's going on with the typical investor by looking at the averages, and more precisely, at median amounts. For example, in the 2nd quarter of 2023, the *average* American's 401(k) balance was $112,400, according to Fidelity Investments. Apparently, 2022 took a toll on most 401(k)s since that's down just shy of 5% from the $118,100 that was the average in mid-2020, when I published the first edition of this book. While that's a pretty big leap from the $96,288 average in 2017, five years ago, it doesn't reflect reality for many.

If that balance still seems high to you, that's because it is. Averages tend to be skewed by outliers, and in this case, that number is being propped up by those rare millionaires. The median, which represents the middle balance between the highs and lows, was $23,700 in the second quarter of 2023. Much closer to the modest average of $44,900 held by Millennials according to Fidelity's Q2 2023 data.

But what does that tell you? Not a whole lot if you don't know the age of the median 401(k) investor in the Fidelity study. One would hope that's an amount for someone with a long horizon before the sun sets on their career, but unfortunately that's not the case.

For those closest to retirement, ages 55-64, the median was a paltry $71,168, up 12% from the $62,700 median for that age group when I first wrote this book in 2020, but nowhere close to the "401(k) millionaires" I continually hear about.

In the first edition of this book, I pointed out that workers with 10 straight years in the same 401(k) plans administered by Fidelity saw their average balance rising to $266,100 by mid-2017. Ten years prior, the average was about a third of that amount, $78,800. Even still, of those with plans managed by Fidelity, as of July 1st of 2023, the <u>*average*</u> 50 to 59-year-old's retirement savings of just over $189,800 (and just $800 higher than the previous year) is nowhere near enough to provide a steady stream of enough income to live on in retirement, even assuming it grows significantly between now and then. Similar studies done by Vanguard, MassMutual and the Federal Reserve all have comparable results. And you should also take notice that those aged 65 and older had an average balance of $203,000 according to that Fidelity assessment, $209,984 according to Vanguard the median was $70,620!

Let that sink in for a minute. Discounting that the median is the actual number in the middle, let's think positively and look at the higher average number, $209,984 saved at age 65 and we'll even round that up to $210,000 to make the math easier.

At the commonly suggested spend-down rate of 4% annual distribution, that's $8,400 a year or $700.00 a month. Oh, wait a minute, we forgot something. The typical 401(k) is not tax exempt like a Roth, they're tax *deferred*, meaning Uncle Sam is going to want a piece of the pie before you get a dime. And an income of $210,000 is going to hit you for $37,104 - plus 32% of the amount over $182,100 (using 2023 tax tables for individuals or married people filing separately), meaning another $8,928 – totaling $46,032. Given that, even if you live in a State that has no income tax, that still reduces your nest egg to $163,968, so again, using the 4% annual distribution rule of thumb, that's $6,558.72 a year, $546.56 a month. Add that to the average monthly Social Security payment for retirees of $1,885 in 2024 (before taxes – yep, that's taxed too) and that's a grand total of 2,431.56 a month. Rounded up that's $29,179 a year. Not even ten grand over the US poverty line for two people of $19,720.

Now, granted, in this day and age both spouses might have had a career and both had their own 401(k) so let's double that to just under $60,000. Can two people live off that? Well, technically it'll turn out to be more like $55K after you pay taxes on the Social Security income, but yeah, sure they could…today. But what's that income going to look like 10 or 20 years from now? Considering prices on nearly everything tends to double every 20 years or so, that's certainly not very much in the grand scheme of things when you talk about funding retirement until death, especially when you consider the fact according to data compiled by the Social Security Administration, a man who is 65 years old today can expect, on average, to live until age 84.3. A woman turning age 65 today can expect to live until age 86.6, twenty years longer than what the life expectancy was when Social Security was first introduced.

Compare that to their life expectancy at birth (in the United States) which was only around 77 for men and 79 for women.

And those are just averages.

Today the Social Security Administration says that about one out of every four 65-year-olds today will live past age 90, and one in ten will live past age 95.

That means that you could be living from one quarter to fully one third of your life in "retirement," meaning after you start to receive Social Security benefits, whether you eventually quit working or not.

And medical advancements happen daily. I joked with my 31-year-old son that I'll live to 150 because in 25 or so years I'll likely be able to walk into Walgreen's and buy any new bodily organ made from my own stem cells.

How long will someone with only about $164,000 in retirement live after their money is gone, let alone the real median of $70,650 (less taxes on that number too remember)? That depends on the individual and their unique circumstances, but let's get an idea of how long that slightly rounded number of $164,000 will last by estimating the cost of something really easy – like feeding yourself and your spouse.

That equation looks like this: 2 x 3 x __ x 365 x ___= _____

We'll assume by the time you retire, all your kids have left the nest and you only have to feed yourself and your spouse. So then, it's 2 people times 3 meals a day, times whatever the average cost of your meals are, time 365 days a year times however long you expect to live.

Do the math. If you retire at 65 and expect to live to at least 90, and your average cost of a meal is only $5 dollars apiece (not exactly living high on the hog considering what inflation will do to the cost of food between now and then), the cost to feed just you and your spouse for that 25 year time period is $273,750. And that's just super cheap food – nothing else!

Now consider another research report from the NIRS in 2018 entitled *Retirement in America: Out of Reach for Working Americans?* provided details of an analysis of U.S. Census Bureau data which revealed that overall, four out of five working Americans have less than one year's income saved in retirement accounts and the latest data from the 2022 Northwestern Mutual Planning and Progress study shows that figure hasn't changed. Studies from Personal Capital and U.S. News indicate that 41% (more than 100 million) of working age individuals don't own <u>any</u> retirement account assets in any employer-sponsored pension, defined contribution plan (401(k), etc.), or any individual account, and of those that do have access (59% of American workers), only about half (32%) actually use them.

That should give you some idea of the crisis your generation is facing in how to support the soon-to-be burgeoning population of the unprepared. Keep that in mind for later when we talk about the possibility of your taxes going up.

Another problem with 401(k) plans is that you're being taxed on the harvest, not the seeds. Meaning, the money you put into it is not taxed until you take it out.

Think of yourself as a farmer. Would you rather pay taxes on the low cost of the seeds you buy to plant your crop or the taxes on the much higher value of the crop at harvest time? That's how the government tricks you into thinking you're getting a good deal by buying into a 401(k) plan. Remember, that tax savings isn't a "gimme," you'll still pay taxes on that money *and* all the growth it accumulates down the road. They're counting on you not to understand the math that you'll be paying far more in taxes later (even if taxes go down some, because you'll be paying on a much larger amount) than if you paid taxes now and grew the money in a tax free account.

Conventional wisdom says that you'll scale down in retirement and since your income is reduced, you'll pay less in taxes. What that assumes is two things: a) that you'll truly want to reduce your standard of living significantly; and b) taxes will not have increased.

Will you really want to reduce your standard of living at retirement?

Most are forced to; they don't do it by choice. Wouldn't you like to *have* that choice?

Secondly, will taxes go up or down in the next 30 to 40 years? Your guess is as good as anyone's, there's no crystal ball, but there's also no guarantee that even if you make less money, you'll pay less overall in taxes on the deferred money you're literally forced to take from your plan after age 73, called 'Required Minimum Distribution' or RMD.

Let's do some easy math. Let's say that you start a 401(k) tomorrow and immediately max it out every year at $22,500. You won't of course, but the contribution limit will rise over time so it'll even out the equation a little better. And in this example, you invest that amount in your 401(k) in a good growth mutual fund that gives you an average gross return of 7% annually for 30 years (naturally, we assume there are years where you make a lot more, but there are also years where you lose a bunch, so the average rolls in at 7%) making a nice tidy sum of $2,136,572,65. Right?

Wait a second, we forgot to include those nasty (often hidden) administrative fees. Luckily, you only have an average fee cost of .75% (25% *below* the average cost) annually over those 30 years, so your average rate of return is actually 6.25%, making the revised balance of $1,867,226.60. Still not bad, eh?

Oh yeah...remember, you didn't pay taxes on any of that money when you put it in, so it all gets taxed whenever you withdraw it so don't forget to reduce that number by whatever tax rate you expect to have 30+ years from now.

Of course, any good investment advisor will tell you that the only time you'll pay taxes on that *entire* amount is when you withdraw it in its entirety. So, let's say you're withdrawing only the conventional 4%. Then of course you'll only pay taxes on that much smaller amount and the rest will continue to grow. You could easily live off that, right?

Maybe not. Remember, the balance you still have in your investment account is 100% at risk of loss. If another major crash hit, you could lose far more than what you'd pay in taxes. And besides, a better investment advisor would have told you to protect those hard-earned dollars by rolling them into an annuity that guarantees lifetime income. So yeah, you're more than likely going to pay the tax on the whole amount at once.

Even if your tax rate is the same as the 2023 rate of 37% for personal income of $539,901 or more (which you certainly can't count on), further reducing your nest egg by $653,828.47, but you'd then have a little more than $1.2 million in today's dollars for the next 20 to 40 years. Still not so bad, with the exception that we have no idea of what kind of interest annuities will pay out in 30 years.

Gosh, do you know what else we forgot? $1.00 in 1980 had the same buying power as $3.68 in 2023. Annual inflation over that period was just over 3%, and considering the effect that inflation has had on us these last couple years, we certainly don't expect anything will cost the same in the future as it does now. Which means we need to calculate for the inflation rate of about 3 percent annually based on all the historic averages, further reducing the spending strength of your bankroll and making the total actual return BEFORE TAXES more like 3.25% or today's dollar equivalent of $1,116,719 and change. Now subtract whatever the tax rate is in 30 years from that.

Get the picture?

I know. Kinda scary, right? You could do everything the experts tell you to do with a 401(k) and still not have enough to live on for very long.

I will say this however, sometimes the damage to your retirement savings can be self-inflicted.

Because the days of lifetime employment with a single company have given way to job-jumping to greener pastures, the general attitude of millennial workers is that no job is permanent, nor should it be. Maximizing your earning potential often means changing employers and negotiating better pay. Some studies show that if you keep the same job for more than three years, you're losing significant income growth over the typical 30-40 year working life.

A problem arises however, every time you change jobs in that you have to figure out what to do with your old employer sponsored retirement plan. According to a Wall Street Journal survey, 30 to 40% of people cash out their 401(k) accounts when they switch jobs.

But I completely understand. I did the same thing once. The temptation to grab that big chunk of change can be really strong, especially if you have to relocate for a new position. I used it for a bigger down payment on a new house in a new town. It's easy to rationalize the plethora of ways you could use a cash infusion, so why not? Not only do you pay a big penalty to Uncle Sam, but you shoot yourself in the foot — that's why.

If you do that, you are basically restarting your retirement savings from scratch each time you change jobs. As you might be able to guess, that's not a very effective way to meet your retirement savings goals.

Adhering to a disciplined strategy to save for retirement with all the unforeseen financial hardships that constantly move the goal posts is hard enough as it is. Don't compound the problem by starting over on purpose.

Now you're saying, *"But what about IRAs and even Roth IRAs that can be separate or even be embedded into 401(k) plans?"* Roth IRAs being paid-in with already taxed dollars, so you only pay taxes on the gains.

You're absolutely right. Guess what? They suck worse.

If your employer doesn't offer a 401(k), or you're self-employed or part of the gig economy, you can contribute to an IRA or Roth IRA to save for retirement. Or, some 401(k) plans have Roth's included as an option. They also have tax advantages, but they have even stricter contribution limits, too. You can only contribute $7,000. Or if you're 50 or older, you can add an extra $1,000, for a total of $8,000 in 2025. Quite a difference from the $23,500 and $31,000 respective contribution limits in 401(k) plans.

But wait…there's more! There's also a restriction on who can use a Roth IRA based on income. For 2024, you can only contribute the maximum amount to a Roth IRA if your income is under $150,000. After that, you'll be able to make reduced contributions until your income hits $165,000. That's known as the phaseout range ($236,000 to $246,000 respectively for those who are married and filing jointly). When your income jumps over $165,000, you won't be able to contribute anything to a Roth IRA. So, if you make more than that, either now or later in life, you don't qualify. Period.

I will note however, that there is a strategy for people whose income is too high to be eligible for regular Roth IRA contributions called a "Backdoor Roth", in which you simply 'roll' (transfer) money from a traditional IRA into a Roth IRA. Since there are no income or contribution limits for a traditional IRA, anyone can convert any amount of money from a traditional to a Roth IRA. However, in doing so you risk a hefty tax bill on the rollover if you have pretax money in the form of either contributions you've previously deducted or investment earnings sitting in any traditional IRAs. 'Complicated' is a generous description of the process if you're a high earner.

Another interesting limitation is that if you're married and file your taxes separately, maybe because you own a business that's yours alone or frankly, for whatever reason, if your modified adjusted gross income (MAGI) is greater than $10,000, you don't qualify. Confusing as all get out, right?

And to qualify for a Roth, you must also have "earned income" in the year you want to make a contribution. So, you can't open one for your kids until they start earning actual income (not allowances). Earned income does not include things like interest and dividends from investments, income from rental property, or pension payments from an earlier career.

So, if your earned income for the year is less than the contribution limit, you can only contribute up to your earned income. In other words, if your earned income is $4,200, you can only contribute up to $4,200.

Basically, the government allows you to save just enough to keep you poor. Or, better yet, forces you to pay taxes on your earnings above those marks until you're dead and gone, then taxes your heirs on what you left them.

Very magnanimous of them, don't you think?

Granted, if you're part of the freelance/gig community, the individual 401(k), better known as the Solo 401(k), is available to anyone who works for themselves, *by themselves*, meaning no employees. Solo 401(k)s work for business owners as well as people with just a side hustle and have more flexibility than employee sponsored plans in terms of contribution limits.

Unlike a traditional 401(k), in 2025, you can contribute up to 25% of your income, tax deferred, as long as your annual contributions aren't more than $70,000. Once you have freelance income, you are then eligible for a Simplified Employee Pension (SEP) IRA — which is a little less complex and less costly to set up than a Solo 401(k) and again, contributions are tax deductible, and SEPs are limited to 25% of your income if running a business, or 20% of your income if you're self-employed.

Not bad until you realize that 100% of that money is at risk of loss in a market downturn and then you're still likely to have to give a third back to Uncle Sam in taxes when you start taking your money out.

Interestingly, the tide may be turning. In the latest NIRS survey more than two-thirds of Americans consistently agreed that pensions are better than 401(k)s for achieving financial security in retirement. And 77% agreed that the unavailability of pensions makes it harder to achieve the American Dream. Eighty-three percent of Americans say that ***all*** workers should have a pension so they can be independent and self-reliant in retirement.

IBM shocked the retirement world in late 2023 by announcing the company would reopen its defined benefit pension plan and end its defined contribution 401(k) matching contributions, a trend that also is occurring in the public sector.

Frankly, I don't find it surprising that the ground is shifting when it comes to pensions. The U.S. now is four decades into the (what I consider to be failed) 401(k) experiment, and it's clear that, unless you're a highly paid worker or executive, these plans just can't do the job alone. Most middle-class Americans are unable to accumulate enough savings to be self-sufficient in retirement without a pension or incredible discipline when it comes to saving and investing.

In addition, Social Security replaces less income than it did in the past. Americans also are dealing with rising costs everywhere, not just in retirement. Housing, healthcare, and long-term care costs are rising sharply, presenting even greater obstacles now than in the past.

Chapter Five

Forget what you think you know

I changed the title of this chapter several times.

In the first draft, it was simply "Traditional investing myths debunked". But quite frankly, while that *does* describe the gist of this chapter, it doesn't come close to a description of the pervasive ruses that you and everyone else for nearly 35 years have been too often blindsided by. What it really boils down to is that most of what you've been told or read about how you *should* invest, while rooted in somebody's best practice somewhere, is so wildly impractical for the average investor that the word "myth" is an understatement. Truly successful investing by following traditional methods spouted every day by too many in the financial services industry is, by far, the exception, not the rule.

To some it may sound like I'm positing about sour grapes, but I assure you that's not the case. The rules of the road to success are good, but so few follow those rules it's pitiful. And it's not that they don't try, it's simply that human nature often works against us and the financial services industry is keenly aware of those flaws and it takes wide and deep advantage of them at every opportunity.

When I started the research for this book, I was pointed to *Dalbar's Quantitative Analysis of Investor Behavior* study. Dalbar's "QAIB" has been the nation's leading investor behavior study over the past 30 years and this annually published study shows just how poorly investors perform relative to market benchmarks over time and the reasons for that underperformance.

The latest study just updates much of the information in previous studies that reiterates that, despite a continuous stream of mainstream and social media rhetoric from "experts" about strategies like "*investing for the long-term*" and "*buy and hold*" investing and other such nonsense like "*dollar cost averaging*", retail investors as a whole, are ridiculously bad at making a profit in the market.

According to the 2024 Dalbar "Qualitative Analysis of Investor Behavior" (QAIB) report over the past 30 years the average equity (stocks) investor earned 5.5% less than the S&P 500 in 2023, the 3rd largest investor gap in the last 10 years.

And of course, that's before taxes and inflation. I will say this though, that's an improvement over the data I had from the same study in 2020 that showed the average retail investor at a lousy 4.25%.

2018 was a perfect example. Dalbar found that in 2018 the average investor underperformed the S&P 500 in both good times and bad. In August of 2018, a strong month for the S&P, the market return was a positive 3.46% vs. only a 1.80% return for the average equity investor, and in October 2018, a bad month for the market, with an S&P 500 decline of 6.84%, the average equity investor lost 7.97%.

When the market showed signs of breaking bad in October of 2018, investors showed signs of panic. The average investor was pulling money from their stock funds at record levels, but they had supremely bad timing. By Christmas of that year, the gap was enormous. And by the end of 2018, while the S&P was off 4.38% for the year, the typical investor more than doubled that decline, taking a beating of just over 9.42%.

Of course, anyone who rode out that market had a loss for the year, but those who got out — meaning Joe Average Investor — had it much worse. Adding insult to injury, investors who were in the population of those who lost more than the market that year found themselves on the sidelines when the market had record growth the following January.

Interestingly, Dalbar's executives noted that while the bursting of the internet bubble beginning in 2000, often referred to as the 'Tech Wreck', and the financial crisis of 2008 were both massive market takedowns, investors were more patient in those situations than during the 2018 mini-meltdown that lasted less than 12 weeks.

In an interview for the Seattle Times, after the 2019 report was released, Lou Harvey, Dalbar's CEO said "[Investors] haven't learned anything. In the last 20 years we haven't seen a gap like this, and we have seen some very real market problems in the last 20 years".

He added "The big loss here was from the investor who sits down, opens a statement, sees the half a million dollars they had in a retirement account is now worth $400,000 and says 'Get me out of here.' The normal reaction is liquidate, just dump it all. They just don't know how much to do, so they don't think 'I'll take out 25 or 50 grand.' They're scared, they just want out".

However, once they bail out, typically, they don't jump back in without the market rising enough to signal an "all clear" and prompt a reinvestment, meaning they're buying high…again.

Historically speaking, since only one in five market downturns lasts longer than three months, meaning that investors who have nerves of steel are typically rewarded for their patience. Sadly though, too few investors really have that kind of fearlessness. Mostly because all true bear markets start as a simple downturn, but again, historically speaking, since 1950, the S&P 500 index has declined by 20% or more on twelve different occasions, or just over six years on the average. The average stock market price decline of those twelve was -33.38% with the length of market crashes typically ranging from about nine to sixteen months.

Before we go any further, let's just agree to dismiss the whole notion that it's even remotely possible for any investor to *consistently* outperform an index over lengthy periods of time by 'timing the market'.

It's not.

And by an index, if you're not familiar with the stock market and investing in it, a market index is an aggregate value produced by combining several stocks or other investment vehicles together and expressing their total values against a base value from a specific date. In layman's terms, a big bunch of securities that have something in common.

Market indexes are intended to mimic an entire stock market, or some sector thereof, and thus track that market's changes over time.

Index values help investors track changes in market values over long periods of time. For example, the widely used Standard and Poor's 500 Index is computed by combining 500 large-cap U.S. stocks together into one index value, essentially guaranteeing diversification. Investors can then track any changes in the index's value over time and use it as a benchmark against which they can compare their own portfolio returns.

Other often cited indexes are the Dow Jones Industrial Average (DJIA), often shortened in reference to just "the Dow", which measures 30 popular stocks traded on the New York Stock Exchange (NYSE) and the NASDAQ. The Dow's companies include premier corporations like Coca-Cola, the Walt Disney Company, Exxon Mobil Corporation and Microsoft Corporation. The NASDAQ Composite index goes further and monitors the daily value of the 4,000 stocks traded on the NASDAQ National Market, where most "tech" stocks reside.

Another index, the Wilshire 5000, sometimes called the "total market index," is a lesser known index that keeps on top of all publicly traded companies based in the United States. All four indices measure the daily performance of large companies. The Russell 2000, on the other hand, monitors 2,000 small companies in the market.

Most investors prefer the Standard & Poor's (S&P) 500 over the other market indices simply for its pulse point accuracy of the economy in general. You'll notice that I refer quite often to the S&P 500 in this book, that's because the S&P is widely regarded as the best single gauge of large-cap U.S. equities. "Large cap" refers to any company with a market capitalization of more than $10 billion. There is over $9.9 trillion dollars indexed or benchmarked to the S&P index, with indexed assets comprising approximately $3.4 trillion of this total. The index includes 500 leading companies and captures approximately 80% coverage of available market capitalization.

The value of the market index is referred to in "points". Meaning that when it is said that the Dow went up 300 points in a single day, it means that its value increased from the previous day's value to the current day's value.

Indices indicate the financial health of an industry in which an investor has invested. So, if the DJIA drops and keeps on dropping over the course of a month, for example, the investor might conclude that some of its companies are in trouble. If he owns some of these stocks, he might reassess his portfolio, sell some of those stocks and look for other better performing companies in which to invest.

Here's the problem. Over time, beating the performance of an index, even if you are a master analyst, is next to impossible. Especially, over lengthy periods of time, like from now to your retirement horizon.

If you think you can magically predict when the market will rise or fall, I hate to break it to you. You can't. You won't. So, if someone tells you they did so by using some secret system they're willing to share with you in return for your credit card number...*please* don't buy it.

Just to give you some sense of reality, in the short two week span between September 15th 2008 and October 6th 2008, the SPDR S&P 500 Exchange Traded Fund (SPY), based on the S&P index, dropped like a stone, 29.7%. In that same time period, the average retail investor trying to time the market lost around 50% of their portfolio's value because they didn't hold <u>all</u> the stocks in the S&P 500. Between October 8th 2007 (the peak before the crash began) and March 2nd 2009 (when it finally bottomed out) the S&P lost 55.9% of its value, meaning if diversifying using an S&P fund or the SPY ETF, even those "buy and hold" strategists lost more than half of their savings. And it didn't matter where you were invested, the NASDAQ lost 60.4% and the Dow lost 49.2% in that same drop. For many who weren't diversified, a lifetime of savings was lost.

Not to mention that indexes do not account for the impact of taxes, trading costs and transaction fees over time. There are also internal dynamics of an index that impact long-term performance which never apply to an actual portfolio, such as share buybacks, substitution, and market-cap valuations.

If you own stocks directly, then anytime you buy or sell any form of equity, especially mutual funds or international stocks or ETFs, you're probably paying a **trading cost**. These costs can range from $0 per trade up to $50 per trade depending on the broker and the type of security. Your trading costs will depend on where you hold your investments (Fidelity Investments, Charles Schwab, etc.). These companies, known as custodians, make some of their money through trading costs so it's important that you work with a custodian that keeps costs low. Note that in October of 2019, Charles Schwab eliminated trading commissions for U.S. stocks, ETFs and options to better compete with fully online companies like Robinhood. Fidelity, TD Ameritrade (before the Schwab acquisition) and other leading custodial institutions quickly followed suit.

Another cost is the internal expense of funds. Pay close attention to this one if you plan to own any kind of mutual fund or ETF directly. Unless you're masochistic and enjoy reading through the fine print of every prospectus (the legal document that spells out all the fees, objectives and performance history of mutual funds and ETFs), then you probably don't have a clue what the actual internal costs of the funds are that you're invested in.

What is an internal cost? It's the cost related to the management and operation of the mutual funds or ETFs that you've invested in. All mutual funds and ETFs have an internal expense. If the internal cost of your funds is anywhere near 1% or higher, you should have a conversation with your advisor about the reason for that. There are plenty of good mutual funds and ETFs with internal expenses between 0.05% and 0.40%, so it would be hard to justify paying more than that.

However, even all those factors don't fully account for the underperformance of investors over time. Quoting from Dalbar's website description of their previous year's (2018) findings:

"No matter what the state of the mutual fund industry, boom or bust: Investment results are more dependent on investor behavior than on fund performance".

For example, the 2019 Dalbar study also showed that as of 2018, the average investor in asset allocation mutual funds (the type of fund that spreads your money among a variety of classes for diversification) earned only 1.87% per year over the last two decades, but factor in that inflation averaged 2.17% a year, and it doesn't take a math whiz to figure out that they actually ended up losing 0.30% (on average) every year for 20 years.

A study done by J. P. Morgan Asset Management released later in 2019 confirmed Dalbar's data and then some.

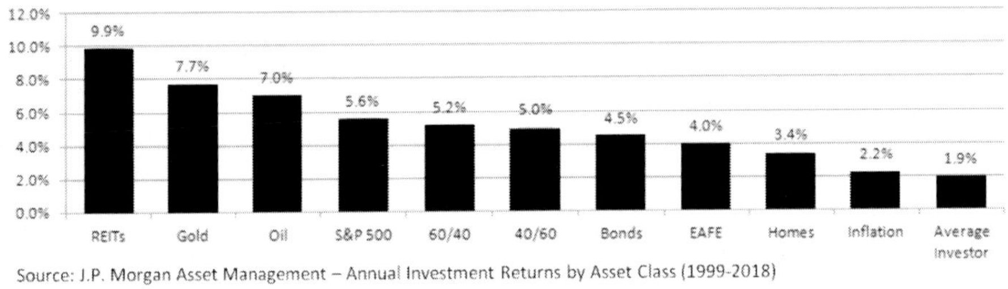

Source: J.P. Morgan Asset Management – Annual Investment Returns by Asset Class (1999-2018)

Looking at that chart, from J.P. Morgan Asset Management's data, which shows 20 years' average annual return of various separate individual asset classes, including traditional retirement savings portfolio asset allocations like 60% stocks/40% bonds and vice versa, **REIT**s (Real Estate Investment Trusts), commodities like gold and oil, the **EAFE** index (The EAFE acronym stands for Europe, Australasia and Far East and represents a stock market index that measures the equity market performance of developed markets outside of the U.S. & Canada), personal real estate (HOMES and considering the national home price index tends to track very closely to inflation, this 1.2% outperformance for that time is pretty good compared to now), as well as the average inflation for that time period. Again, it doesn't take a financial genius to recognize that the average investor, with or without financial advice, when adjusted for inflation, managed to lose money over that 20-year period which has included a record-breaking bull market. If you go online, you can likely find updated versions of this chart showing very little has changed.

Asset managers like J.P. Morgan, one of the largest traditional asset managers in the world (which charges clients between 1.15% and 1.45% of assets under management, based on holdings of 1-10 million dollars, which is mid-range for the industry) are a big reason why robo/digital wealth advisors were created during the last financial crisis. People want to pay lower fees and aren't satisfied with active management results. And with good reason considering even the 60/40 portfolio, meant to lessen the losses during big downturns, didn't outperform the S&P 500 index.

But the biggest losers were those invested in fixed income funds. They managed to eke out an average annual return of only 0.22%, not even close to the rate of inflation and thus, digging themselves deeper and deeper into a hole every year.

The fact that investors sucked so bad in the last two decades relates directly to the well-known psychological behaviors of individual investors, however, as the Dalbar report once again pointed out:

"The results consistently show that the average investor earns less – in many cases, much less – than mutual fund reports would suggest".

Despite ongoing rhetoric about "buy and hold" and "dollar cost averaging", both of which are failed strategies according to Dalbar, the reality is that investor psychology is the biggest impediment to long-term success. In other words, if you try to do it yourself, even if you think you know what you're doing, your odds of being successful are slim.

In addition, retention plays a key role. As noted by Dalbar:

"The retention rate data for equity, fixed income and asset allocation mutual funds strongly suggests that investors lack the patience and long-term vision to stay invested in any one fund for much more than four years. Jumping into and out of investments every few years is not a prudent strategy because investors are simply unable to correctly time when to make such moves".

According to Dalbar's study, over the past 20 years, equity mutual fund investors have rarely managed to stay invested in their funds for more than 4 years. And, in general, the only times they have done so have been during periods of bull markets. Equity fund retention rates surpassed the 4-year mark in 2004, after the S&P rose over 28% in the previous year and stayed there for the 3 years leading up to 2007. Equity fund retention rates are currently back on a streak of exceeding 4 years, starting in 2013 with the S&P surge of over 32%. The latest QAIB study found that over a 20-year period, the average equity investor underperformed the S&P 500 by 4.26% annually.

Also, there are three primary causes for the chronic shortfall for both equity and fixed income investors, shown in the following chart.

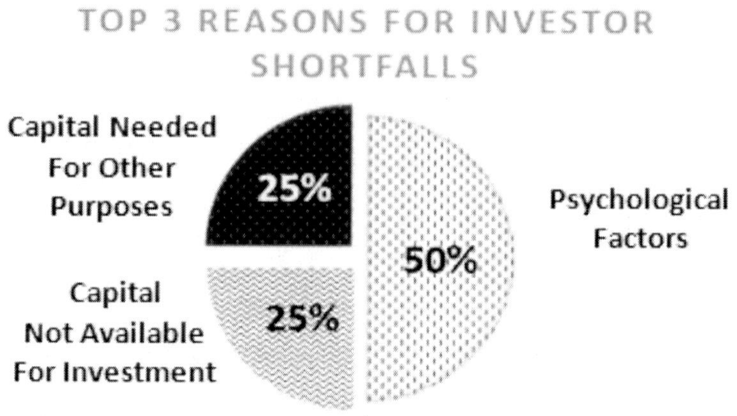

Notice the key issues come down to primarily either a lack of capital to invest or psychological factors. The issue of expenses, meaning both fees and transaction costs, are an important consideration when choosing between two specific investment options, but the emotional mistakes made by investors over time are far more damaging.

While the inability to participate in the financial markets is certainly a major issue, the biggest reason for poor performance by investors who *do* participate in the financial markets over time is behavioral psychology.

You're not a machine. Which means, whether you realize it or not, you have behavioral biases that lead to poor investment decision making and are the single biggest contributors to making less than you would like over time. Dalbar defined nine of these irrational investment behavior biases specifically:

1. **Loss Aversion** – The fear of loss leads to a withdrawal of capital at the worst possible time. Also known as "panic selling".

2. **Narrow Framing** – Making decisions on or about part of the portfolio without considering the effects on the total.
3. **Anchoring** – The process of remaining focused on what happened previously and not adapting to a changing market.
4. **Mental Accounting** – Separating the performance of investments mentally to rationalize success and failure.
5. **Lack of Diversification** – Believing a portfolio is diversified when in fact it is a highly correlated pool of assets.
6. **Herding** – Following what everyone else is doing. Leads to "buy high/sell low".
7. **Regret** – Not performing a necessary action due to the regret of a previous failure.
8. **Media Response** – Overreacting to events in the media, follows the herding mentality.
9. **Optimism** – Overly optimistic assumptions tend to lead to rather dramatic reversions once met with reality.

The topmost of these problems for most people being the "herding effect" and "loss aversion".

These two behaviors tend to function together compounding the issues of investor mistakes over time. As markets are rising, most people (including you) are internally wired to believe that the current price trend will continue to last for an indefinite period.

The longer the rising trend lasts, the more ingrained that belief becomes until the last of the "holdouts" finally "buys in" as the financial markets evolve into a state of what behavioral science calls "rapture".

Then, as the markets eventually decline, there is a too slow realization that *this* decline is something more than a "buy on the dip" scenario. Then as losses mount, the anxiety of loss begins to mount until most people panic and try to prevent further losses by "fire-sale" selling.

The result is most people buy high and sell low.

To give you a real-world example, some years ago Fidelity Investments conducted a study on the performance of its flagship Magellan mutual fund during the tenure of its (then quite famous) manager Peter Lynch. If you're not familiar with that name, bestselling author and money manager, Peter Lynch ran the Fidelity Magellan fund from 1977 to 1990 and delivered an astounding 29% average annual return during that timeframe (which included the historic "Black Monday" crash of October 19, 1987 and the "Friday the 13th" mini-crash on October 13, 1989). Despite his incredible cumulative results while running the fund, the Fidelity case study determined that the average Magellan investor actually *lost* money during Lynch's 13-year stewardship.

Why and how? According to Fidelity, investors would typically exit the fund during periods of poor performance, meaning after they'd already lost money and then flood back in after periods of success, meaning they missed most of the recovery bounce back. Classic buy high and sell low behavior.

But that was a long time ago, right? Technology has vastly improved the way that people can buy and sell stocks, and that little black box we so often hold in our hand - that has more computing power than the entire NASA organization had when they put men on the moon - can certainly alert us to market slides and better predict when to get back in, right?

In your dreams.

Again, using 2018 as a good example, the market seemed to hit a new high just about every month and by the summer, according to a variety of sources, there was about $1 trillion dollars being held in 401(k) and other various retirement accounts. Estimates from Fidelity Investments' quarterly data suggested that by September 2018 about a million people had more than $1 million in their 401(k) accounts, and about 18% of those accounts were held by Fidelity clients. For Fidelity, that was news worth crowing about…then.

Of course, that was when the market's upward drift was still intact and the euphoria when people looked at their statements showing their ever-growing nest eggs was abundant. Then the fourth quarter arrived, bringing with it that hard slap in the face of reality as almost 20% of the value of the Standard & Poor's 500 Index went up in smoke. Several overseas markets had even worse results. From a timing perspective, the last month of 2018 was one for the Wall Street history books — not only was it the worst December for stocks since the Great Depression, but the entire year's gains (and for many stocks, the last 18 months plus of uptick) had disappeared by Christmas eve.

In response, a Tsunami of investors all but gave up on the active managers of their mutual funds. According to Morningstar, in December of 2018, actively managed mutual funds experienced selloffs of nearly $143 billion dollars, their worst month ever. The record exodus brought the yearly outflows to over $301 billion dollars, just shy of 2016′s $320 billion.

As for Fidelity's 401(k) millionaires club? The number of people in that group fell by more than 28% in the fourth quarter of 2018.

And of course, that means they were selling out only after the bottom fell out of the value of their mutual fund – classic 'selling low' behavior.

That market drop may have created lots of fretting and handwringing, but it was also perfectly normal. As I've mentioned before, based on historical data, such volatility is a recurring characteristic of equities markets, not some anomaly. Even so, the December 2018 market retraction led some to speculate that the long string of gains dating back to the end of the financial crisis almost a decade before was in danger. The historically long in the tooth bull market, according to some pundits, was finally ending.

And again, they were wrong.

Despite being in the midst of the longest running government shutdown, U.S. equity markets, fueled by better than expected Federal Reserve announcements and strong job numbers, recovered handsomely in January of 2019. And while that month saw the strongest start to a year for U.S. stocks in more than three decades, many retail investors who had cashed out, watched the rally not from the sidelines, but from outside the stadium.

TD Ameritrade, the Omaha, Nebraska based brokerage (acquired by Charles Schwab later that same year), then the third largest in the U.S., with over $1 trillion in client assets and over 10 million accounts, with clients placing around 600,000 trades each market day. reported that their clients, still jumpy at the start of 2019, further cut their exposure to stock market risk in the first four weeks of the New Year. The firm's Investor Movement Index, which has tracked clients' positioning in the market since 2010, declined for the fourth straight month in January of 2019 to its lowest since July 2012. Clients using TD Ameritrade's platform still bought financial products but focused more on less volatile fixed-income assets, according to the firm. Meaning they traded in stocks for cash equivalent guarantees.

That, as the S&P 500 Index gained almost 8% that January, the best month for the equity benchmark since 2015. The index hadn't seen as big a January rally since 1987, when it soared 13%. Meaning those that did get back in after January, got in too late and missed the biggest gains.

In the end, we are all human. There is no such thing as a totally rational human being. Whether we admit it or not, we are incapable of making decisions that are 100% logical and zero percent emotional. It just comes with our DNA. Despite our best of intentions, it is next to impossible for an individual to be devoid of the emotional biases that inevitably lead to poor investment decisions over time.

This is precisely why all great investors have extremely strict investment disciplines that they follow to reduce the impact of human emotions. Worse yet, for those already in retirement, money taken from portfolios during declining market environments accelerates the reduction of investment principal. Something that never happens in the Millennial Money Tree strategy.

More importantly, while there are many articles that try to guilt investors into the "buy and hold" and "passive indexing" strategies they market (also called passive investing, passive indexing is an investing strategy that tracks a market-weighted index or portfolio. The most popular method is to mimic the performance of an index by buying an index fund like the S&P) the reality is that few will ever survive the downturns in order to see the benefits.

Chasing an arbitrary index that is 100% invested in the equity market requires you to take on far more risk than you will likely want or can endure. Two massive bear markets over the last decade have left many individuals further away from retirement than they ever imagined. Furthermore, all those investors lost something far more valuable than money – the *time* that was needed to reach their retirement goals.

The reality is that the majority of financial advisors are simply not well prepared for a negative impact event to occur. And this is almost always the case in late-stage bull market cycles where complacency runs high.

This complacency can be seen in the shift from active portfolio management strategies to passive indexing which is a trademark of a late-stage bull market. When the next crash eventually occurs, unfortunately, the tsunami of calls to 1-800-ROBOADVISOR for calming messages and a plan to avoid major losses will go unanswered.

I continually see criticism of Millennials who shy away from investing due to the inherent risks in the market. In part, the problem is seen as the idea that Millennials may be putting their future financial security at risk by shying away from stocks on the premise that the S&P 500 averaged a 9.78% return from 2013 through June 2023 (adjusted for inflation and with dividends reinvested). But by comparison, add another 12 years to that, which includes the downturns in 2001-2003 and 2008, then the average annual return for that same calculation is an average of only 4.3%. Not good.

Noting that the biggest drop in the S&P in the last few years happened in October 2022, that year overall was a banner year for bears with a 19.4% loss in the S&P, an 8.8% drop in the Dow, a 21.6% drop in the Russell 2000 and a whopping 33.1% decline in the Nasdaq, as a result I see academics and other financial experts pointing to the risk in the stock market as something that Millennials and Gen Z will have to get used to. One well-known academic said this:

"The risk of the stock market is not the biggest risk in life. Taking risk is not a luxury; it's a necessity. If you look at risk in the overall context of life, you see that we take risk not because we like risk, but because we have aspirations. Aspirations are the engine, the driver of the train, and risk is really one of the cars of the train".

Implying that every time you make a decision — whether it's your career choice, where you're going to live, whom you're going to marry — that decision entails risk. That kind of "advice" makes me cringe. It's true enough that your chosen profession may become obsolete, or you'll choose a partner who isn't right for you and end up divorced. There *are* inherent risks in life but betting your financial future on the risks in the stock market doesn't have to be one of them. Getting over seven percent average annual return using the Millennial Money Tree strategy, with ZERO risk of loss, is not only commonplace, but also conservative.

Worse yet, I continue to see advice from so-called advisors that sounds something like this:

"If you're still young you have more time to save money. So, it makes sense to invest in the higher-risk, higher-return financial opportunities like stocks".

No. It doesn't. Really. What they *really* mean is that you have more time to recover from the dramatic loss you will surely experience at some point so it's okay to take those higher risks. Maybe you'll get lucky.

News Flash: There is no linear relationship between high risk and high reward. In fact, it turns out that it's just the opposite. That old wives' tale was debunked years ago, but it still proliferates. There's even a book on the subject called "High Returns from Low Risk: A Remarkable Stock Market Paradox" by Pim van Vliet and Jan de Koning, but I guess a lot of advisors didn't bother to read that.

To find out whether portfolios of high-risk stocks performed better than portfolios of low-risk stocks over time, the authors used a well-known stock market database consisting of the 1,000 largest US stocks sorted into 10 portfolios based on their risk. Portfolio one (the lowest-risk portfolio) consisted of the 100 stocks with the lowest volatility and portfolio ten (the highest-risk portfolio) contained the 100 most risky stocks at that moment in time. Then they went back in time, back testing each portfolio. Starting in January of 1929, they rebalanced each of the portfolios each and every quarter until 2015, based on the risk profile of the available stocks in that point in time. In doing so, it would resemble a replicable investment strategy of high-risk vs low-risk. If the old saw that higher risks mean higher rewards were true, then you would expect the high-risk portfolio would consistently outperform the low-risk portfolio. No?

Nope. The low-risk portfolio beat the high-risk portfolio, hands down, with much less risk. The lower risk portfolio generated an annual return of 10.2%, while the higher risk portfolio generated a return of only 6.4%.

To give those numbers some perspective, assume that you put just $100 into both portfolios on New Year's Day 1929 and reinvested all the capital gains for the full 86 years until New Year's Day 2015.

The low-risk portfolio's final value would be $395,000, while the high-risk portfolio's final value would only be $21,000. The low risk portfolio beat the high-risk portfolio by a factor of just shy of 19X.

The way to avoid all that stress over what to do when and how to do it, is to implement the Millennial Money Tree strategy. It's automatic and stress free with zero risk of loss. If you didn't know better, you might think I was referring to annuities.

Chapter Six

What's wrong with annuities?

Actually, nothing that's not timing related. But I'm not going to spend a lot of time explaining annuities because they don't need to be on your radar until you're within 10 years of retirement, and chances are that's a ways down the road for you. However, you should know the basics.

An annuity is an insurance product that binds a buyer and an insurance company into a contract whereby the insurance company promises to do something with the buyer's money — like grow it and pay it out over a number of years. If you are looking for a steady stream of income in retirement, it may be wise to invest in an annuity as a part of your overall retirement strategy.

Shaquille O'Neal is known for being wise enough to sock away several million dollars into annuities throughout his career in the NBA. He frequently mentions that strategy as what helped him to never have to worry about money after his basketball career ended, even if he did nothing else. But he would have made more using the Money Tree strategy.

Even though annuity products may come in all shapes and sizes depending on the terms you choose, most work in the following way:

First, you make a lump sum investment in an annuity.

Then, the annuity starts making payments to you on a future date or series of dates that you've chosen. A variety of factors, including the length of your payment (or accumulation) period, determine the size of your annuitized income payments.

The income you receive from an annuity can be distributed to you on a monthly, quarterly or annual basis. Or, it can even be dispersed to you in a single lump sum payment.

Depending on what kind of annuity you purchase and/or your preferences, you can opt to receive payments for the rest of your life (guaranteed, even if you live long enough that your account runs out of money), or for a set number of years.

The amount of income payments you receive really depends on if you opted for a fixed or variable annuity. This means whether it was a guaranteed payout, or a payout stream determined by the performance of your annuity's underlying investments, respectively. Note that the latter can lose money, a fixed annuity will not.

Annuities are helpful in some situations. In general, some of the advantages and benefits include tax-deferred growth and compounding within the annuity contract. Which means you only get taxed on the interest you earn once you start receiving payments, not while it's building up. And there are guaranteed rates of return on your dollars invested and/or guaranteed lifetime payments when you annuitize.

Note that the guarantees are only as strong as the insurance company that issued the annuity. In other words, if the insurance company fails, the promise is no good. While that's a highly uncommon occurrence, you should mitigate this risk by using only the strongest insurance companies out there. That said, because the industry is so highly regulated, so far, no one has ever lost a dime in an annuity.

Then, what's wrong with annuities for building money for retirement?

First, they generally cost too much up front to get a good rate of return if you're looking for real growth. And by 'good' I mean just slightly higher than the rates of interest that banks pay (for fixed annuities). There's that word "fixed" again. In this case, *fixed* doesn't mean "repaired", when you see that word tied to any form of investment or crediting method it means immovable, unchangeable and constant. Sometimes that's a good thing, sometimes it's not. Fixed *indexed* annuities are a better choice, being tied to some of the market upside but with none of the downside risk, but they too cost a lot of money up front and generally don't allow ready access to big chunks of your money without paying substantial surrender fees.

Variable annuities are tied directly to the stock market and can suffer tremendously when the market tanks, beyond having oddly high fees and not being able to pull your money out without some pain.

In general, annuities are not a good option for someone who has little already saved for retirement and can better afford paying into a plan periodically rather than in a large lump sum.

Also, experts are mixed on whether they'd recommend them at all.

Ken Fisher, executive chairman and co-chief investment officer of Fisher Investments (an investment firm with some $72 billion in assets under management), and the author of 11 books on investing, 6 of which are national best sellers, once said that he "…would die and go to hell before I would sell an annuity". His take is that most annuities have "nosebleed-level fees," are difficult to get out of, are "extremely confusing" and are made to benefit salespeople over consumers.

While I don't agree with his assessment in *all* cases, the most comprehensive place I've found to learn about whether annuities will make sense for you and your situation is the website stantheannuityman.com; created by consumer advocate Stan Haithcock, aka "Stan the Annuity Man".

Haithcock is a nationally recognized author, annuity expert and often a harsh critic of the annuity industry and has been a decades long consumer advocate, exposing false claims made by some annuity marketers, calling himself "a walking middle finger of annuity truth".

One of Stan's many trademarked phrases related to annuities is "Will Do. Not Might Do". The meaning of that is that by design, annuities are "fixed" products, purpose driven to be the antithesis of uncertainty and change. When you buy an annuity, you know what you have and what you can expect in the future. Those unchanging characteristics are what make an annuity such an important part of some people's retirement plans, but they also inhibit your ability to respond to change.

So, don't ever buy an annuity thinking that it will solve *all* your challenges during retirement. Even though an annuity producing a guaranteed income for life can be a solid foundation for a retirement plan, it's never a good idea to put *all* your funds into an annuity. It is always wiser to keep some of your assets aside in the event of an emergency and even for an unexpected opportunity for growth.

The bottom line is that annuities can be a valuable tool intended to help you build a secure retirement. However, before you buy one, take the time to make sure you understand exactly what an annuity can and cannot do, and be sure it's the right tool you need, at the right time and can use it to achieve the goals you want to achieve.

My advice? Unless you get a windfall like winning the lottery or a sizable inheritance, (or you're like Shaq) even if they make good sense to you, get an annuity when you get into the retirement "red zone" (five or ten years before your planned retirement date), not before.

Chapter Seven

It's not your fault

Unless you were brought up in a wealthy family, or at least one with parents (or older siblings) that were savvy in the ways of finance, which quite frankly, based on some of the studies we've already discussed in this book, is pretty rare these days, the likelihood that you've been taught anything, or even heard about, using insurance products as a proven method for building wealth is slim to none.

Robert Kiyosaki pointed out in his book "Rich Dad, Poor Dad" that rich people buy assets. Poor people only have expenses and the Middle Class buys liabilities that they only think are assets. For the most part, I agree. Here's why:

Assets can appreciate in value. Liabilities do not. The best assets are those that put money on the plus side of your accountant's ledger consistently, day in, day out, in good times or in bad.

Too many people think a nice car is an asset. Some people look at a *paid off* car as an asset even if it's a piece of junk. And it's true that any accountant, when making a list of your assets and liabilities, will put a vehicle in the assets column – so will the IRS – only because it has "economic value to the owner", which, in the simplest sense, is the definition of an asset. But they don't include the ongoing cost of maintenance in that valuation and eventually, almost any vehicle that's driven regularly will cost more to maintain than it's worth.

Generally, common wisdom will tell you that unless you bought a rare classic car and don't plan to drive it, any four-wheeled mode of transportation will go down in value dramatically the minute you drive it off the lot. In other words, if your strategy is to buy a brand new, even very limited version of a particular automobile for cash, never drive it a mile, house it in a fully enclosed, climate controlled environment and keep it maintained in pristine, drivable condition for 20+ years (bearing in mind the insurance costs, maintenance and shelter for all this time should also be included in the total cost), it might possibly go up in value. I'll wager you're not in a position to sit and wait that long before something you buy appreciates in value.

You'll get my opinion of debt a little later in the book, but auto debt is particularly insidious because the "asset" you're buying so rarely appreciates in value that one astute personal finance blogger did some math and realized his car loan cost him between $2.5 and $5.2 million dollars in lost opportunity cost (if you're not aware, 'opportunity cost' is money or benefits lost by not selecting a more profitable option during the decision-making process). Google

"Why your car loan cost you $5.2 million dollars" by John Cook for the full story. Needless to say, just because something has economic value, that doesn't make it an asset for you the way you need it to be.

An even more relevant example is that most people think a house is an asset. That is often not true except for in the form of the accounting/estate value definition. Unfortunately, considering a house is typically the most expensive purchase the average person makes in their lifetime, they assume that the equity will surpass the total outlay. Put simply, they expect the value will outgrow the cost. The truth of the matter is that your home, unless you bought it for cash or arbitraged some mortgage scenario in which your interest rate is well below the rate of appreciation on the property so that even through the eventual downturn of the real estate market (which is ridiculously hard to predict) it still maintains a positive value – which, at this second edition writing in 2023, mortgage rates have increased dramatically from around 3% when I first wrote this book to now more than double that in the 6.5% range, meaning that's next to impossible right now considering the average annual rate of appreciation of home prices ranges between 3 and 5 percent. Noting that appreciation depends on several factors, a critical one being, as they say in the real estate industry, "location, location, location". Even investment properties, unless you rent them out and the upkeep, property taxes and mortgage (if you have one) are *less* than your annual income from rent, are really a liability.

Rarely do people pay off their mortgage entirely, meaning cash flows *away* from the property, not into it. So, even as it appreciates in value, which may or may not happen over time, while that may diminish the expense, in most cases it never really eliminates it.

Sure, you could argue that you sold your house for substantially more than you paid for it. But did it really? Did you include the closing costs and any PMI (Private Mortgage Insurance, the bank's insurance against you defaulting on your loan), the cost of maintenance, renovation and upkeep over the years, utilities, property taxes, home owner association (HOA) fees and the like, that you paid over the years? Did you include the lost opportunity cost of mortgage interest that you paid out? Or other assets you could have purchased if you had no mortgage payments to begin with?

You see, in reality, if you don't make money out of your home or the land it's on (like a farm or vineyard) on an ongoing basis, it's more often an expense, not an asset.

Assets put money in your wallet. Liabilities take money out.

It's not your fault you weren't taught these things in school. No one is. That's a big fault of even college education these days, real finance isn't taught to everyone. But don't get me started on that.

One thing that I will point out is that I can pretty much guarantee that you suffer from a malady called **exponential growth bias**. But don't feel bad, even the smartest among us often share that problem. Exponential growth bias is the pervasive tendency to *underestimate* compound growth processes, or the future value of a variable growing at a constant rate.

I know. That's a mouthful. What it means is we have a really hard time understanding how compounding methods grow value over time. Especially as it relates to money either flowing into, or out of, our bank accounts.

Here's a perfect example: let's say I give you a penny, and every day for just one month — the next 30 days — through the magic of compounding, that money is going to double every day. Meaning, tomorrow you have two cents. The next day, four cents, and the day after that, eight cents, and so on, for 30 days. At the end of that month how much money will you have? Take a guess. Here's a hint: at the end of the second week (14 days in), you'll have $81.92.

So, what was your guess? A thousand dollars? Ten thousand? A million dollars?

Try $5,368,709.12. Yep, over five and a third million bucks. After doubling your money just 30 times.

Tell the truth. Your guess wasn't even close to that, was it? Don't feel like a dummy, I'm rather good at math and my guess wasn't close either. The problem with that lack of understanding is that households that suffer from exponential growth bias, especially in combination with **present bias** (which is the tendency of people to give higher value to payoffs that are closer to the present time when considering the trade-offs between two future events), borrow more, save less, favor shorter maturities for their investments, and in general, are in dire need of a financial advisor.

Imagine that was credit card debt if that helps you better see the importance of understanding how compounding works.

You see, what you don't know *can and will* hurt you when it comes to managing your money, especially over time. Once time is lost, you can never get it back, so in more ways than one, we need to take advantage of the time value of money.

There are many strategies to use compounding money over time to build wealth. Some are complicated. Some are not. One of those strategies is using dividend building cash value permanent life insurance to leverage later in life.

That strategy is known by several names such as 'Infinite Banking' or 'Bank on Yourself', and more recently pitched as a "7702" or "702j" plans (subsection 7702 of the IRS code discusses life insurance contracts and their tax implications) but whatever name it goes by, it's a strategy that the wealthy have used for over 100 years to shelter cash from the tax man and has been used time and time again by names you'd recognize to either start or grow their business (their assets). For example:

- Famous retailer, J. C. Penney borrowed thousands from multiple life insurance policies he owned following the 1929 stock market crash to help meet the company payroll. Had he not had that ready access to that capital, the company would have been forced to close its doors forever.
- Walt Disney borrowed from his life insurance policy in 1953 to help fund Disneyland, his first theme park, when no banker would lend him the money.
- Ray Kroc, borrowed money from two of his insurance policies in 1956, to overcome constant cash-flow problems in his fledging franchise restaurant business, McDonalds.
- Doris Christopher, founder of the kitchen tool company called The Pampered Chef, launched the company with a life insurance policy loan. Seven years later, in 2002, she

sold her company to Warren Buffett for a reported $9 million.

- The late Senator John McCain secured initial campaign financing for his 2008 presidential bid by using his life insurance policy as collateral.

So-called "permanent" or cash value life insurance (versus term insurance, which is like renting insurance) slowly builds up cash value that policy owners can use in difficult times as a ready source of money to cover personal or business expenses for emergencies and even to cover insurance costs. The most familiar type is Whole Life insurance.

Why didn't you know about that? Like I said, it's not your fault they don't teach you this stuff in school.

That said, that particular strategy uses something called **"paid-up additions"** to dividend paying Whole Life insurance policies. What are paid-up additions or PUA for short? In insurance parlance, a paid-up addition is a rider (an option to a Whole Life insurance contract). The simplest explanation is that a PUA is an immediate purchase of life insurance (your death benefit) in full. A PUA adds cash value to the policy equal to the paid-up price. There are no premiums, so you are essentially paying for more death benefit, in full, today. PUAs can be paid for out-of-pocket or can be purchased with dividends paid by the insurance company.

One of the main uses for PUAs is simply to add cash value to the policy, which then compounds over time. For many people who use this strategy, the benefit is higher cash value that is safe, liquid and tax advantaged (read that tax-free in most cases). And while it is not the Millennial Money Tree method, it could be called the root it was cultivated from.

Here's an interesting, and game changing, development since I first published this book in late 2020.

Section 7702, the IRS code that governs certain aspects of Whole Life insurance policies, in part, dictates the minimum guaranteed interest rate insurance carriers need to use for all new insurance contracts. When Section 7702 was enacted in 1984, it required insurance carriers to provide a minimum guaranteed interest rate of 4%. In other words, premiums paid, net of reasonable expenses, had to result in a death benefit return (i.e., the eventual cash value) at the insured's life expectancy of at least 4% compounded annually.

While it may not have been difficult for insurance carriers to invest premium dollars to meet that 4% guarantee in the 1980s (when the Moody's Aaa Corporate Bond yield was greater than 12%), interest rates dropped dramatically by 2021, down to the 2 to 3% range. This near-record low interest rate environment, the insurance industry lobbied, necessitated a reduction of the minimum guaranteed interest rate that Section 7702 requires, from 4% to 2%. The IRS not only agreed but buried deep within thousands of pages of the Consolidated Appropriations Act of 2021 was a change to Section 7702 of the IRS Code that allowed insurance companies to change that 'guaranteed' number *at will* in the future – effectively eliminating any guarantee.

Now that interest rates have increased again, could Section 7702 change back? It could, but knowing how things work between the insurance industry and our government, I doubt it ever will.

Chapter Eight

The roots of the Millennial Money Tree

At its roots, the strategy that makes up the Millennial Money Tree is education that the life insurance industry should have taught to the average working stiff during the last 200 years. Instead, the insurance industry had nearly fully concentrated on the death benefit qualities of a life insurance contract and neglected to adequately promote the financing capabilities that life insurance presents for policy owners until just a few decades ago. Likely for fear that it would be used too much in practice which might reduce the number of repeat buyers and increase the ratio of death claims that would be eventually paid out. Especially in comparison to Term Life insurance.

Paradoxically, regulators *require* life insurance companies to put your paid-in premium to work in various financial investments in order to pay the death claims.

This book will show you how your need for access to capital, during your lifetime, is as great as or greater than your need for insurance protection. Solve for this need through this strategy and you will end up with more life insurance than most companies will ever offer to issue on you at a ripe old age, never have to worry about qualifying for life insurance for the rest of your life, never worry about your policy lapsing during hard times and unlike term insurance, in less time than you think, access to far more money than you put into the policy, tax free.

Most everyone is familiar with the fact that you can borrow from a cash value Whole Life policy, but because of how slow that money grows, there is limited access to money to finance major items needed during a lifetime. Hence, a big reason some people use paid-up additions in those policies. Yet, the need for financing for the typical person in their lifetime is extensive. Aside from the now non-existent guaranteed interest rate, the underlying contract of a Whole Life, dividend paying, life insurance policy has not fundamentally changed in over 100 years. That contract is central to the entire "infinite banking system".

What the infinite banking or 'Bank on Yourself' strategies really do is simply add scale to that equation. The strategy taught in this book will show you how that scale can grow exponentially, far beyond the limited value of its predecessor, using methods that were first developed in 1997.

The whole idea of infinite banking is to recapture the interest that one would ordinarily pay to banks and finance companies for the major items that we purchase in our lifetime, such as automobiles, major appliances, education, homes, investment opportunities, business equipment, etc. Basically, financing *yourself* — through the prudent use of the cash value of your insurance policy whenever the need arises.

The fact that these basic principles have been around for your entire lifetime and then some, and no one taught them to you should make you take pause. I'll tell you firsthand that had I known them at age 25 when I bought my first business, my life would have been much simpler and much more profitable. At a personal level, the practice of either the infinite banking concept or the Millennial Money Tree strategy will help you develop a lifetime of disciplined saving and where possible, judicious avoidance of government regulated retirement accounts with their authoritarian rules and restrictive limitations. Someone, somewhere, should have recognized them and taught them long ago before R. Nelson Nash's book, *Becoming Your Own Banker* was published in 2000, but they never were, mostly because of the mentality that predominates the entire financial world that it's far too complicated for the common man.

I can assure you it is not.

This book is written for the nonexpert, not for financial advisors or insurance practitioners, but all life insurance agents should be thoroughly knowledgeable of its content and practice. Alas, that is not the case. *Very* few of them have more than a rudimentary understanding of this method, let alone how to prepare it in such a way that it doesn't do more harm than good. The good news is that it's not particularly hard to find someone who is an expert at the practice of arranging and implementing the Millennial Money Tree for you.

The Millennial Money Tree strategy is not technically an investment of any kind. Unless you call it an "investment" in your future. It is the use of a specific type of contract with an insurance company that they will credit your account with certain amounts when certain things happen.

It is not about rates of return in common practice. As time goes by, interest rates go up and down, but the process of financing goes on no matter what else is happening. It has no seasonality per se.

Some might say there is no such thing as "having too much money in the bank". I disagree. Banks are the safest place to *lose* money. While wealth must reside somewhere, there are better places to put it than in a bank. The amount of money you can make elsewhere, with zero risk of loss over what the FDIC insures bank deposits against, is opportunity lost if that money sits doing little more than encourage both the government and the banker to find ways to whittle it down. This is the disadvantage that most folks ignore in their thought process, and therefore, limits their financial effectiveness.

A word of caution is in order however — in this book you will be looking at tables from illustrations (projections) of life insurance policies that show how this strategy works as compared with how most folks go about solving their financial affairs in a normal way. The illustrations in this book were developed in 2023 and represent financial numbers in effect at that time. Rates may be different when you read this but in comparison with other methods of financing the things of life, the difference in results will remain the same.

Importantly, this is not a strategy to "get rich quick".

On the contrary, this strategy needs long term planning. It is a critical requirement. In fact, the longer the better, hence, my reference to planting your tree right now. Yesterday was better. So, if you're at retirement age or past it, it's never going to work as well for you as a 20, 30 or 40 year old even if you live to a ripe old age, but even twenty years can work wonders with the right inputs.

The Millennial Money Tree strategy is also not a tax-qualified method in any form. The US Internal Revenue Income Tax Code, as we know it today, has only been around since 1913, whereas Life insurance has been around for more than 200 years and is not regulated by any tax code. Boiled down to its essence, a life insurance contract is nothing more than an agreement between like-minded people to solve a financial problem. This strategy is no different, however, it does require careful avoidance of tax code restrictions that only an expert will know about, so this is not a do-it-yourself strategy, a duly licensed life insurance professional skilled in the art will be a required (and helpful) partner.

Hopefully, this book will also give you a whole new perspective on the idea of "retirement saving". Others prefer to use the words, "passive income". That is money coming in that you can count on and you don't have to do anything to earn it at that time. Study the illustrations carefully and you will see that the infinite banking concept is not the only vehicle to produce such income.

The Millennial Money Tree strategy may be a major paradigm shift for most folks. Saving is generally considered to be materially different from investing – conserving money you've set aside by protecting it against risk in exchange for a much more modest and predictable reward, versus putting your money at risk of loss for an uncertain, but hopefully higher gain. Understanding that the "secret sauce" of the Millennial Money Tree strategy that captures most, and in many cases *all,* of the market gain with zero risk of loss, provides tax advantaged savings and tax free distributions, and allows you so many other advantages over traditional retirement *investment* products, is actually no secret at all and has been used by an ever growing number of people who have watched their savings grow leaps and bounds and never lost a dime since 1997, sometimes makes people's head explode.

It may require more than one reading for a full understanding of its methods and benefits, but the basic concept is not complicated. It is not smoke and mirrors, or a long equation with the words "And then a miracle happens" written somewhere in the middle. Nor does it require blue sky trust that the U.S. economy or even the world must sail along happily for you to make money. It is simply different from the way the majority thinks and behaves in practice, but again, once you start the process, little is required for it to do its job for you. In fact, while it's not the ultimate in simplicity, from a wealth building standpoint, it may be the next best thing.

Chapter Nine

Now's the time

In the wake of various federal government program cuts shortly after Donald Trump's election and the potential for more entitlement and retirement program cuts in the future, The NHP Foundation, a non-profit provider of service-enriched affordable housing, conducted a survey of 1,000 non-retired Americans aged 50 and over to determine the status of their retirement plans, savings, and their level of probable reliance on the availability of federal entitlement programs such as Social Security at retirement.

According to The NHP Foundation, in 2018, about 10,000 of the estimated 78 million Baby Boomers were hitting retirement age each day. However, according to their survey findings, 73% of Baby Boomers expected to delay retirement for some period of time. In addition, 31% said that they have not prepared *any* retirement budget or savings, and 62% of those who have a retirement budget say that they expect Social Security Income to contribute to *at least half* of their monthly income.

A majority of the survey's respondents – 65% – said that they have not budgeted for any unforeseen health-related expenses either. Among respondents with no retirement budget that expect Social Security disbursements to account for at least half of their income, the majority is even higher at 72%.

Find any more recent surveys online and you'll note that those numbers have not noticeably changed.

Why are they so far behind? The simple answer is the most obvious one. They didn't plan ahead and waited too long if they started saving at all.

Do you want to be like them?

I doubt your answer was yes. No one today says to themselves "Hey, I plan to live 100% off my Social Security benefits in my old age". Especially considering that Social Security may not even exist by the time you retire.

So, what do you need to do, right now?

First, get your head on straight. Retirement for you might seem like an unimaginable future date so far away that you have plenty of time to consider your options. And if you're in your twenties or even your early thirties, you're right.

However, you also have the advantage of that time value of money we spoke of that can make your Money Tree so fruitful even before you retire that you can potentially change your family tree's destiny.

Whatever your age, here's the thing that you need to do right now. Yep, right now. Do it now. Say that fifty times.

Do it now.

Do it now.

Do it now.

Sit down and write yourself a budget. That means that whether you use an app or a piece of notebook paper, you nail down exactly what comes into your pocket (from where, how much, how often) and what goes out (to where, how much, how often) and why.

Your "why" is a big part of getting your mind right about saving money. Obligations are one thing, luxuries are another. I'm not suggesting that you live like a Spartan in order to scrimp and save (unless you like living that way) but there are things that you'll find that you could do without and apply that money (expenses) to an asset.

Making a budget isn't fun, I get that, but you can't knock down your expenses until you figure out where you're overspending and enforce some limits. It's not rocket science, especially with all the free or super low-cost apps available that take next to no time for you to set up and keep track of expenses almost by themselves, there's no longer an excuse not to have one.

To make a very simple budget, start by tracking every cent of your spending for at least 30 days (preferably 90 days since some things might be paid quarterly or even annually – Office 365 for example) to figure out where all your money is going. Then, divide what and where you spend into different categories and set monthly limits for each category. You could do this by taking a broad approach, limiting spending on essential needs to 50% of your income, reserving 30% for wants, and saving 20%. You could also make a detailed budget specifying how much you'll spend on dining out, groceries, rent, utilities, cell phones, clothes, and every other item you buy or pay for on a monthly basis.

Whichever method you ultimately use, the two steps that are critical are tracking spending to see where your money is going and then setting realistic limits on spending while reserving enough money to save.

After you've written down all the things that you absolutely must spend money on, prioritize it again. Slash it down to the bare essentials, a roof over your head, clothes on your back, food, transportation and a cell phone. Everything else is either a liability or a luxury. Get rid of the former and question your need for the latter. Pare down. Which brings us to our next step.

Next, find some money to save. This can be accomplished in two ways: eliminating your financial past (debt) and living a more realistic financial present (lifestyle). We have to start there, because if we don't, there will be no chance of a financially secure future. I know you're thinking "I'm already doing that". And so, anything I say now will fall on deaf ears.

It's the same reason 401(k) meetings at work (if you have them) are so frustrating. A well-meaning financial professional stands in the front of the room and tells everyone to save more for their future. You pipe up that you can't afford to do that and then they say, "You can't afford not to". Thanks for nothing.

Now is as good a time as any to let you in on a secret: You'll be able to pull this whole thing off because you will have saved money that you will have learned to live without.

Here's the hardest part: I need you to start thinking like a squirrel preparing for a long cold winter.

In order to have enough nuts for the long winter ahead, you can't immediately consume every nut you come across. And as long as your demand for nuts doesn't somehow magically increase when you need to consume your stored nuts, your demand for nuts will match your supply of nuts. Hopefully that makes sense. In other words, you're going to create a supply of cash that will meet your demand for cash in later years.

Here's the main thing - your commitment has to be strong enough that you *know* you'll starve otherwise, because in a way, you will starve. Not having enough money to live on after you retire can make an empty refrigerator.

Reducing your day to day (lifestyle) expenses even a little bit will allow you to eventually get out of debt. It may take you two years or it may take you twenty to be completely debt free, but with each debt you eliminate, you add the money you were applying to that debt to the amount that you've already committed to your savings, regardless of how small that starting number is.

During that timeframe you should also use any tax refunds, bonuses, or any other extra income to pay off debt. Assuming you don't become a debt reducing fanatic and it takes you a year or more to get to a point where you can actually start to save a reasonable amount, the goal is the same, plant the seeds of your Millennial Money Tree as soon as possible because the compounding effect on every dollar you save will amaze you. If you've already got a savings amount number in mind based on your current budget, great. If you don't have any debt, you're way ahead of the game already, but maybe one or two of these ideas will improve that number. If you think you don't have anything to save, consider this:

- Quit smoking and you could save big time. Not to mention the long-term effect on your health costs down the road but right now, and not only in reduced Life insurance premium cost. Given that the average cost of a pack of cigarettes as I update this in 2023 is $9.00, which means that for pack-a-day smokers, the weekly savings is $63.00 and annually that amounts to $3,285. If you're 35 years old, saving $2,248.40 annually for 30 years at an average growth rate of just 6% is $239,071.96 by age 65. Tack on another ten years if you're 25 and that number grows to $468,000.18.

- If you've tried to quit smoking with no success, the case for e-cigarettes from a cost perspective is notable. You can use high-end devices and still save over 50% compared to the price of cigarettes, and if you're vaping as cheaply as possible, the savings increase to over 80% or even more than that. And from a health perspective, according to studies done in the United Kingdom, e-cigarettes are substantially safer than smoking too, so switching might be a great decision for both your health and your wallet.

- Let's say you typically overspend somewhere on something else that you know is less than healthy, like just $5 a day on fast food or alcohol or, like I mentioned before, just one or two less cups of Starbucks coffee (not that coffee is unhealthy, just that Starbucks isn't the most cost effective way to get a caffeine boost). Saving $5 a day just on weekdays is $25 or $1,300 a year in savings. Applying the same 6% times 30-years equation, that's $108,942.18. Adding another 10 years more than doubles it to $213,261.99.

- The average (somewhat frugal) American spends more than $11.14 twice a week for lunch. That's not much, right? You can spend that at McDonalds or at your local kitschy grille in a single sitting. Packing your own lunch would save $22.28 per week or $1,069.44 per year (assuming a two-week vacation annually). Once again, over 30 years at 6% adds up to $89,620.87 and at 40 years it's $175,439.15.

Now let's combine just those just the last two $1,300.00 + $1,069.44 = $2,369.44. Over 30 years at just a 6% average gain per year is $186,893.55, at 40 years it's a whopping $365,857.29.

Get the idea? I know you're not going to give up _all_ your guilty pleasures, but my point is that when you know where every dollar is going, you're far more likely to change your habits to save some more.

We'll look for other ways to find some money in Chapter 18, but saving a little just here and there and applying an intentional and disciplined savings plan can add up to a lot of money over time. The problem is that most people lack the latter – discipline. Most people just can't stick with it, unless it happens without them having to think about it. Bad habits are hard to break, but it can be done.

Having said all that, frugality as a 'strategy' for increasing your investable dollars only goes so far. It makes no sense if you save

$25 a week giving up expensive coffee if you then spend that savings going out to dinner during the week. No one wants to live like a Spartan and never engage in anything fun because they're worried about spending a couple bucks. Making more money always has a greater effect on overall wealth over time than frugality. And while that may sound obvious, some people don't really think about adding additional passive revenue streams when they think about making more money.

We'll talk about how to make more money later but in the meantime, you can aim at saving a couple bucks here and there, or you can be more strategic (read that as smarter) and set it up so you're *forced* to save because it will be automatic.

Trust me. I get it. Sitting down and creating a budget is something akin to psychological torture. Thankfully, there are some really easy to set up budgeting apps out there, like Personal Capital, YNAB (You Need A Budget) and PocketGuard. PocketGuard also offers a feature called "In My Pocket" that calculates how much disposable income you have after accounting for bills and savings goals.

Used in combination with free "money manager" apps like NerdWallet, choosing basic allocation of your money, or in other words, where to put every dollar so it does the most good, can be a snap. These kinds of apps help you track and manage both your savings and debt while gaining insights to help you make better financial decisions.

Having an app on your phone makes it so much easier to keep track of where your money goes because there's no forgetting to stuff the receipt in your wallet or purse and remember to post it on your computer later. This way you'll get it the habit of logging where every dollar is spent.

Do that for 90 days and I can guarantee you that it'll become second nature. You'll not only have a working knowledge of how your money comes and goes on a monthly basis, but you'll be able to project it out over the year with a very high degree of accuracy.

If you don't already have a budget app set up on your phone, go do that right now. Yes…right now. Not kidding. Do it now or it won't get done. Put the book down. I'll wait.

Done? Good.

A word of warning about saving. You'll read advice from so-called "experts" that you should be saving for different things in different ways. Meaning, aside from saving for your retirement, you should be saving for other things including a down payment for a house (if becoming a homeowner is one of your goals), healthcare costs, a college fund for your kids, big purchases (like vacations or new furniture) or even a new/used car fund so you can pay cash rather than foot the bill of a car loan for years. Everyone seems to have some opinion about where and how money you're saving for different things should be kept. Most of those ideas haven't made it to the 21st century yet.

While I agree that healthcare costs should be separated into a Health Savings Account (an HSA), mostly for reasons of tax efficiency, everything else can be bunched up into 'saving for the future' and outside of the fact that none of the above should come out of your 'emergency fund' (barring a car wreck where you need to replace your car immediately and your car insurance doesn't reimburse you fast enough) there is no good reason that these things cannot be saved for in one place…***if***, and only if, that one place is guaranteed not to lose a dime of your hard earned savings and you can get a decent return on the money you put there.

Let's remember that the whole point of saving money is that you want it there when you need it, so putting that money at risk of loss is maybe not the brightest idea, so that limits your choices. That being the case, why not put it all where it's going to get the most bang for your buck without any risk of loss. Not to mention it makes things ultra-simple by not having to track a half dozen different accounts.

Yes. I know. To some, that may sound counterintuitive. And certainly, contrary to the common wisdom of "Don't put all your eggs in one basket".

Adhering to that axiom is essential in common practice when you have every dime you're saving at risk of loss in some fashion, clearly, you don't want to bet on the wrong horse with all your cash. Diversification of your investments in your asset allocation is a critical factor for anyone whose money is at risk of loss. In layman's terms "asset allocation" is the meticulous implementation of an investment strategy that attempts to balance your risk versus potential reward by (whenever necessary) adjusting the percentage of each asset in your investment portfolio over time, according to your risk tolerance, your ultimate goals and your investment timeframe.

If you speculate in the market (and don't be ignorant, even investing in a five-star mutual fund is making a guess as to which way the market will go) you're going to be wrong some of the time.

Effective asset allocation ensures that when you are wrong (and chances are you'll be wrong a lot) you won't lose your shirt.

If that sounds like a lot of work, or something you'd need to significantly educate yourself more about to do it effectively, you're absolutely right. Or you can pay a professional some percentage of your total asset value to do it for you, but you'll still have to meet with that professional whenever the need arises and review and agree to the changes he or she recommends. And we already know that even small fees are like termites eating away at the foundation of your long-term plan. Getting that asset allocation right is critical, because getting it wrong could mean you could lose everything – your home, your savings – and potentially end up looking for work when you should be enjoying your Golden Years.

Your call.

But what if there's no gamble involved, what if your money is absolutely guaranteed not to be lost either by economic events or fees? Maybe then, one basket, at least for the majority of your savings for future use is, in fact, the wisest thing you can do.

Consider that many "experts" in this case, who don't want you putting all your savings in one place, assume you're saving for your retirement in a 401(k) and withdrawing from a 401(k) prematurely creates significant tax penalties. Even taking a loan from a 401(k) means you'd be trapped in your job until you pay back the loan, or if you can't pay it back, you'd have to pay taxes on the unpaid balance plus that same 10% penalty (if you're not at least 59 1/2 years old) that you would pay if you withdrew the money.

With the Millennial Money Tree method, you can save for everything you'll need in the future that you might finance elsewhere, save much faster than any other savings vehicle, take loans whenever you need them, never pay a tax penalty and, done right (which I'll show you), not hurt your retirement fund one bit.

In other words, unless the experts you're listening to know and understand the Millennial Money Tree strategy and are giving their advice from the point of view that they know you are using it, ignore them. They don't have a clue.

Now before we even begin the next step let's talk about what your long-term goals are.

Yeah, I know, die rich and happy at a ripe old age. Sounds great, right? Trouble is, most people never achieve that.

How is this book going to help you in that regard?

Well, I certainly can't guarantee you'll be happy when you die. Although a stress-free life when it comes to your finances can certainly be a positive leap in that direction. Nor can I predict *when* you'll die. But the strategy presented in this book will guarantee that if you die younger than expected, your family will be far more financially secure than if you do nothing, or even worse, do the wrong thing.

Chapter Ten

A word...or two...about debt

Don't. Just *don't*.

Getting into debt is one of the best ways to derail your retirement savings.

But I get it. The U.S. Department of Education reports that 43.4 million borrowers had outstanding federal student loans as of the third quarter of 2023, representing $1.63 trillion in debt. And that number has stayed pretty constant since 2019. Twenty percent of all U.S. households have at least one person with a student loan today, up from 10% since 1992, meaning the number has doubled in that time frame. If the average loan size is about $33,000, that would take a $11,550 bite out of retirement savings, according to the calculations done by Morningstar.

However, those already saddled with student debt can do something right now that will make a difference – that being to save for retirement *before* trying to pay down your debt faster.

Wait…what?

If being in debt can derail retirement plans, then why wouldn't you want to pay off your student debt right away?

Of course, you *want* to pay your student loan bills first — and on time. And you should pay what's due, when it's due. But, if you do the math correctly, it may not make sense to put any extra money toward paying down your student loan early. Any other debt with high interest rates should be paid off as soon as possible, but student loans often don't fall into that category – or can be refinanced so they don't.

In reality, because they have generally lower interest rates, there are very few situations in which paying off a student loan *ahead* of schedule, with funds that would have otherwise been utilized in any well managed retirement savings plan, would lead to a higher net wealth at retirement. There's that opportunity cost decision again.

It's simple math really. The interest on your student loan is less than your potential return in a good retirement savings fund (even if it's simply socking money into a robo-advisor like Betterment, but especially using the strategy you'll learn in this book) so that positive difference will make a positive impact over time. The alternative is waiting until your student debt is paid off – which may or may not happen on time – and as you can imagine, any delay in saving even the smallest of amounts will make a difference long term.

I do agree with the premise that everyone should have at least one credit card – for emergencies. Or because you need one to rent a car or provide for a stay at a hotel (rather than having a sizable chunk of otherwise available cash in your bank account put on hold by using your debit card). Or, if you're one of those frequent flier miles/rewards junkies that use their credit card for everything under the sun in order to get some freebies on this or that, that's fine. Just make sure you can pay your credit card bill *in full* every single month.

No exceptions.

EVERY MONTH.

If you can't be disciplined enough to do that. Toss them all.

You'd be surprised how much less money you spend indiscriminately when you use cash. Seeing it disappear from your hand makes a huge psychological impact. Use that to your advantage, rather than impulsively reaching for your debit/credit card.

Sure, it's much easier to use a budget app and keep track of where every dollar goes if you use your debit card wherever possible, but that's assuming you actually use your budget app. Do it!

Living from paycheck to paycheck despite having a decent income is an especially troubling issue among Millennials. According to a 2018 survey by LendingTree, 44% of Millennials earning between $100,000 to $149,000 live paycheck to paycheck. Surprisingly, just 33.5% of those earning $50,000 to $75,000 said they lived that way.

The problem might be that, in general, some Millennials are not used to earning such big paychecks yet and give in to too many buying urges. It's also highly likely that they have the impression that they have to maintain a certain lifestyle – keeping up with the

Joneses if you will – now that they make six figures. If that's you, ***stop it***. Get serious about your future and quit wasting money.

Something else that I've noticed far too often today is that people are retiring when they are still carrying around significant debt. They still owe money on their house and sometimes some other weighty debt too. In doing so, some portion of their limited retirement income needs to go to pay debts before they even get around to funding their day-to-day living expenses. This makes an already problematic equation almost impossible to solve.

For example, if you still have a house payment of $1,000 a month when you retire, at the commonly used 4% withdrawal rate to spend down your savings, it would take an additional $300,000 in savings (for every year that you still owe on the house) just to pay the $12,000 in payments annually.

Make it your goal when you buy (or refinance) a home that it be completely paid off *before* you retire. In fact, using the strategies in this book, there's no reason why you can't be debt free long before you retire. Make *that* your goal.

Chapter Eleven

Speaking of income

For most people, when they think about retirement, they think about saving for it and then spending it.

Saving and spending.

When I think about retirement, the first word that comes to mind is 'income'. Here's what comes to my mind first:

- Allocating a portion of your current **income** to fund your post career lifetime **income**.
- Minimizing taxes on **income**.
- Maximizing Social Security **income**.
- Reducing, or better yet, eliminating **income** volatility.
- Generating predictable guaranteed **income** to cover essential expenses.

- Generating passive **income** to ensure your standard of living and cover unexpected retirement expenses.

These all seem like common sense to me, and they should to you too because if you hit all these even half right, you'll be golden in your golden years. The spending goes without saying, but there is no saving without an income, so to be truly secure you need one both now *and* in the future.

This is where the paradigm shift for you should be starting to sink in. Most people think of retirement as when they stop working their normal job and, hopefully, can live comfortably, doing whatever it is they want to do after their career ends, living off the fruits of their labor of the decades before.

Great. Get a boat. Go fishing.

The problem is that your boat needs both fuel and maintenance from time to time. So does your cash flow stream in retirement. Unless you're a financially independent, multi-millionaire when you retire, chances are high that you'll either run out of money or have to significantly reduce your lifestyle to a predictably uncomfortable level in order to simply survive.

No one wants to outlive their money.

So how do you prevent that?

Like Occam's Razor, the simplest answer is usually the right one. In this case, figure out how much money you'll need in retirement and then formulate a plan to far exceed that number. The alternative is to create one or more streams of income in retirement that don't require your direct involvement.

Given the right amount of time and the right strategies, both are doable. Without significantly upsetting your current work/life balance or derailing your plan to do a lot of fishing in retirement. The trick is having the discipline to actually implement your plans. The earlier the better. This book will help you put a lot of that implementation on autopilot, so you won't have to worry about it on a daily (or in some cases, yearly) basis.

So, let's just assume that your idea of "retirement" is the same as most people in that you want to be free of the *requirement* to work, but not necessarily the desire to work. Meaning that, especially if you loved what you did in your career, then you may not want to give up doing it completely. Or, you may want to do something totally different but not be fettered with having to work for someone else. In either case, you'd set your own hours and whether and how much (or if) you'd be paid is up to you, not someone else.

First, just to clarify, the Internal Revenue Service categorizes income into three broad types:

Active income – Active (or non-passive) income is defined as income received from performing a service. This includes salaries, wages, tips, commissions and income from businesses in which there is material participation. For example, any individual who works for a monthly paycheck receives active income.

Passive income – The IRS defines passive income as coming only from two sources: rental activity or "trade or business activities in which you do not materially participate".

Portfolio income – Portfolio income is revenue from investments, dividends, interest and capital gains. Royalties received from property held for investment are also considered portfolio income.

Each is taxed differently so it's important to know the difference to keep your tax base low.

For taxation purposes, income received from business activities is considered "active" if it meets the IRS's definition of *material participation*. The material participation rule was established by the IRS to stop individuals who don't actively participate in the business from profiting from tax losses.

The key tests are:

- The taxpayer works 500 or more hours in the business during the year.
- The taxpayer does the majority of the work in the business.
- The taxpayer works more than 100 hours in the business during the year and no other staff works more hours than the taxpayer.

For example, Jim and Joan have a partnership arrangement in a Shopify store online. Joan does the day-to-day operational work in the business (finding and posting products to sell, advertising on social media, responding to buyers, etc.); so, the IRS considers her income as "active". Jim helped Joan set up the store and occasionally helps her with some online marketing activities. Joan pays him for that help, but he works less than 100 hours a year in the business; for that reason, the IRS considers his income from the business "passive".

Obviously, there are disadvantages to participating in active income. The most obvious of which is that are only so many hours in the day that an individual can work, which limits the amount of income you can make. For example, a freelance writer who bills clients per unique article can only produce a limited amount of content per day.

Portfolio income, which relates to dividends, interest, and/or capital gains resulting from the sale of stock held for longer than twelve months (even if it's only one year plus one day), is currently taxed at no more than 20%. That income is also not subject to Social Security and Medicare taxes.

If you're going to put a portion of your savings at risk in the market despite all my admonitions against it, a good and simple way to increase your portfolio income in a way that may increase your holdings even in down years in the market is by buying stocks that pay an above average dividend. Companies may raise their dividend payments as revenue and profits increase, but many still pay dividends even when they have down years. There are even some companies that haven't missed paying out a dividend to their shareholders in over 100 years.

Dividend payments can be paid directly to the shareholder. For example, a company may pay a cash dividend of $3 per share annually, therefore, if the investor has a holding of 200 shares, he or she would receive a cash dividend payment of $600 ($3 x 200 shares). Or, the dividends can be used to purchase additional (fractional) shares in the company. In the previous example, if the price of one share of the company was $12, then the $3 dividend could go to purchase an additional .25 shares.

There's a catch with dividends though, that should make your ears perk up whenever you hear (or read) that word. Clever marketing and slick salespeople may leave out the tax rules on dividends so that it would seem that you don't pay any tax if you reinvest the dividend as soon as you receive it and never actually see the cash value. Is that true? In your dreams maybe.

Ever notice that when you're doing your taxes online through TurboTax, TaxAct or whatever app you use that the question always comes up "Did you receive any dividends?" There's obviously a reason for that. The IRS looks at any dividends you receive just like you're receiving cash, so it doesn't matter how you take the dividend – in stock, reinvested, cash, whatever. Once the dividend is distributed to you, you are taxed on it in the year you receive it. Period. It doesn't matter what you do with it. The only exception is if the dividend is paid on a stock held in a qualified plan (like a 401k or standard IRA), then the tax is deferred, and you'll likely end up paying *more* later.

You will have to do plenty of research to find good stocks (and buy them when they are a real bargain) and invest a significant amount of money to receive large dividend checks. However, if you consistently invest money into dividend stocks you can amass a nice residual income down the road, but the value of the underlying stock is going to go up and down with the market, so you'll have to completely ignore that.

Passive income often gets quite different tax treatment from the active (ordinary) income that people have. In particular, passive losses are typically deductible only against passive income, and you're not able to claim excess passive losses immediately, instead, you must carry them forward. It's important to understand the tax rules that affect passive income in order to wisely assess any investments into passive activities.

Income from equipment leasing or rental real estate is normally treated as passive income, with only limited exceptions. Any other business in nearly any industry, including sole proprietorships, partnerships, limited liability companies, and S corporations, can produce passive income as well, but only if the taxpayer in question doesn't meet the standards for material participation shown in those three bullet points previously. With the added test limitation of having had previous material participation in no more than four of the past ten tax years.

For personal services businesses, the limit is material participation in three previous tax years at any time. Examples of a personal services business might be bookkeeping services or appraisal services.

There are any number of ways to create passive income for yourself and create multiple streams of income that you don't have to actively participate in every day to earn and grow. We'll go into some of those in more detail in a later chapter, but for now let's concentrate on understanding why preparation is a critical component of your plan.

Chapter Twelve

Preparing for the unpredictable

Life has a way of mucking up even the best laid plans. ***Logan's Law of Unintended Consequences*** states that for every positive outcome, there is an equal and *negative*, not necessarily immediately observable, completely unforeseen, and unpredicted outcome.

Combine that with Murphy's Law and you get the picture. Prepare for the unexpected. Sometime, somewhere, something will happen that could potentially crash and burn your plans for your future. Most people have health insurance that will cover unexpected medical issues so excessive hospital bills hopefully won't disrupt your long-term plans, but what are some examples of things that no one really prepares for?

Divorce – You might be surprised to learn that 44% of women in the U.S. go below the poverty line for at least some period of time after divorce. About 20% never recover financially.

And men aren't any better off. The commonly held belief that when you get divorced, you lose half your wealth is actually wishful thinking.

On the average, here in the U.S. you can expect to lose 77% of your total net wealth as a result of divorce.

Read that again. Let it sink in.

Seventy-seven percent is the average, meaning while some people lose less, an equal portion lose more. I'm one of the latter. I know firsthand. Not being prepared for that seriously sucks.

The problem with divorce these days is that it's 'no fault' in almost every State, meaning only one party has to decide to divorce (for whatever reason) and the other party is basically forced to defend themselves in a lawsuit. While an amicable divorce may not cost more than a couple thousand dollars in legal fees, it's not uncommon for divorces where there are custody battles to ring up more than $100,000 in legal fees on each side.

Where does that money come from?

You guessed it. Usually out of your savings first.

So how do you protect yourself from that kind of disaster?

Protecting yourself against losing everything in divorce is a cloudy subject at best. My advice is certainly not to hide money from your spouse in some offshore bank account. Accounting forensics being so advanced these days that any attempt to hide money (anywhere) will backfire on you.

If you're already married, as lame as it sounds, my best advice is not to get divorced. Married people live longer and more cost effectively. They are healthier and wealthier than their single or divorced counterparts. Their kids do better in school, and on and on. If you're already married, work on making it work. You'll be better off. So will your family. If you don't get along anymore, separate, but stay out of the courtroom if at all possible.

If you're *considering* marriage, put an ironclad prenuptial agreement in place long *before* the ceremony.

I hear it all the time. "We don't need a prenuptial agreement; we'll never get divorced".

Yes, you do. Seriously. Shit happens. People change. You're an adult. Be pragmatic.

Don't let it happen to you because you were too "in love" to understand the reality of statistics. One in three first marriages fail (32%), usually within the first 8 years. Two out of three second marriages fail (67%) and if you're marrying for the third or more time, just be aware that the odds are nearly three out of four (72%) that you will divorce sometime in the future.

Even if you have nothing worth dirt today, tomorrow you might win the lottery or create the next Facebook or Amazon. The reality is that you want to go into any marriage fully aware of your betrothed's financial situation anyway and forming a prenuptial agreement requires an open robe look at your spouse-to-be's financial health.

If you own a business or have a substantial net worth before you tie the knot, a prenuptial agreement should be a no-brainer for you anyway. Don't even *consider* not having one.

Disability – When you ask most people what their biggest asset is, they often respond by saying their house. That's wrong. Your greatest asset is your ability to earn an income. Anything that interferes with that, whether temporarily or permanently, stands to potentially eradicate any chance of you retiring in the style and manner that you may have so diligently planned for.

Having been in the insurance industry for nearly two decades, I am constantly reminded of the fact that you are 65% more likely to become disabled to the point that you cannot work than you are to die outright. Yet, less than one third of Americans have any form of disability or 'income replacement' insurance.

Consider this. You have a family that is dependent on at least some portion of your income. You have a mortgage, a car payment, life insurance premiums, health insurance premiums and savings and monthly bills that fill the rest of your budget.

What happens if tomorrow, you can't work? You haven't died but some crippling malady or accident has taken you completely out of the game to the point that you can't even do one or more of the activities of daily living that health professionals use as the litmus test to determine levels of disability such as bathing, grooming, dressing, feeding yourself, work, homemaking, and leisure activities.

Does your company keep paying you even if you don't show up because they liked you so much? Does your bank forgive your mortgage balance because you were such a good customer for all these years? Does your insurance company continue to insure you if you don't pay your premiums? Does your finance company let you keep your car if you don't pay them?

Of course, the answer to all these questions is no, so if you can't work, where does your ability to pay for everything you and your family need to survive come from?

Wake up and smell the reality.

If you don't have a backup plan, you're screwed. Social Security will only pay you $914 per month for full disability, and that will take months before you'll get your first check.

The good news is that we'll cover your life insurance premiums and to a large degree, your retirement savings with our Money Tree strategy but you will still need to look into insuring yourself with an income replacement/disability policy so that at least some portion of your current income will be replaced if you should ever become disabled.

For private disability insurance, it depends on the carrier and the percentage listed in the policy. The benefit percentage usually ranges from 50% to 85%, depending on the type of policy you get, subject to a specified maximum benefit. Company sponsored disability programs are usually even less.

So, if you're highly paid, and you spend most of your monthly paycheck on things other than saving for the future, be prepared to take a *huge* step down in lifestyle.

Being able to replace or at least largely supplement your paycheck or other primary source of revenue in the event of a disability is yet another reason why having the multiple streams of passive income that we talked about in a previous chapter is a part of a good Money Tree plan.

Now, let me throw another monkey wrench in the works.

Let's say your aging parent or parents now require full time care and that falls on you. Ever price out what an in-home even part-time nurse costs? Or worse yet, one of your children gets a crippling disease that depletes your bank account. Are you prepared for that kind of disaster? In later chapters, we'll address both of those head on and how you can live through them without going broke.

Lawsuits – If you're a business owner you probably have some sort of insurance coverage for unexpected liability, but if you're the average working stiff, an unexpected lawsuit can be a crippling lightning strike to your retirement planning.

What kind of lawsuit am I talking about? Well, beyond divorce being a legal issue, let's say your dog bites some bratty kid that's teases it all the time, or someone slips and falls on your icy walkway and breaks their arm, or your toilet overflows in your second floor apartment and floods downstairs destroying your neighbor's priceless Persian rug, or a business partner sues you for breach of contract.

What I'm referring to is either a personal liability lawsuit or generally, any lawsuit, even if there's no criminal conduct involved, that, in all likelihood, could result in a plaintiff doing either of:

a) Outspending you into the poorhouse with ongoing legal fees to defend the case, or;

b) Winning a large judgment against you that you can't afford to pay, possibly in the millions of dollars.

Either way, your retirement savings plan is screwed if you haven't taken precautions against it.

Do all lawsuits fall into this category of retirement destroying monsters? No. But on a purely financial level if you lose an ordinary civil case and the plaintiff is awarded some extraordinarily large judgment that would bankrupt you — guess what? It will bankrupt you. The good news is that millions of people have filed for bankruptcy and come out of it okay…in the long run. However, the operative words in that previous sentence are "long run". If you have decades to rebuild, that's one thing but if it comes just before your planned retirement, the lack of adequate recovery time could be devastating.

And, just so you know, when I'm talking about lawsuits, I'm also talking about those that *you* might bring against others. I'm too often reminded that some people don't think through the consequences of filing a lawsuit against their employer. Sure, sometimes it might seem like it's the best idea at the time, but it may have long term impact that you haven't thought through. Remember Logan's Law.

Case in point: I know someone who had a well-paying job in a particularly well-paying industry, who chose to sue their employer in federal court in a case about an issue that was far from cut and dried. The case was eventually settled out of court, but the myriads of public documents related to the lawsuit, now nearly a dozen years later, still appear on Google on the first page of results if you Google this person's name.

While this individual got a hefty one-time payday (two years after filing the original lawsuit), now he is unequivocally ostracized from his desired profession, had a tough time finding reasonably close paying employment anywhere for years and his family took a significant, still continuing, drop in lifestyle as a result.

Needless to say, his plans for retiring on the back of that lawsuit not only didn't happen, but, even though for all practical purposes he prevailed in the case, it's adverse and unpredicted impact ruined any chance for him to execute his previous retirement plan.

Is that uncommon? Not as much as you'd think. Face it, no one wants to hire someone who has already shown that they could have a proclivity to cause significant angst and monetary loss to an employer.

If you happen to be in a line of business that is prone to lawsuits, like doctors, then insurance against such things is generally required these days, but that doesn't mean that in all cases your insurance will cover all the expenses nor the damage to your reputation that lawsuits tend to carry with them, regardless of the fact that they may have been frivolous to begin with.

I remember reading in some medical journal at a doctor's office that cardiologists are the physicians most frequently named in medical malpractice actions, and that cardiologists in the United States have a roughly 1 in 5 chance of being sued in any given year. I'm guessing their malpractice insurance premiums cost more than some of their office's administrative staff makes in a month.

Which brings us to how insurance plays a part in protecting you from lawsuits.

First, here's my ***VERY STRONG*** disclaimer: I am not an attorney and nothing in this book should be construed as legal advice. Consult an attorney before you implement any strategy that you read in this book related to lawsuits.

There. Do yourself a favor and consult with an attorney licensed in your state to make sure you do everything you can to protect yourself. Don't sue me if I'm wrong about this or that in your State. Read on.

Make sure you have adequate insurance.

For the general public, the two most important insurance policies to review are your car insurance and your homeowner's insurance (renter's insurance if you don't own a house) and in many cases, a 'catch-all' failsafe known as umbrella insurance. For each policy, make sure you thoroughly understand what your policy limits are, what your policy covers, and which exclusions apply.

Car insurance

Most people understand that your car's liability insurance covers you in the event you inadvertently cause someone injuries, death, and/or some other non-health related loss (i.e., property damage, loss of wages, etc.). Car insurance is mandatory in every state but, of course, every insurance policy has its limits. These limits are on the amount that the insurance company will pay for a specific loss event. Insurance is always a tradeoff. Higher premiums mean less risk, and vice versa. It's on you to determine your requirements and your level of risk and then select the most appropriate insurance policy for your needs. It is not always an easy decision, especially if you're on a strict budget.

In addition to confirming that you have suitable policy limits, be sure that you fully understand the exclusions in your policy, if any. Exclusions are the provisions in the policy that eliminate insurance coverage for certain kinds of losses. Meaning that the insurance company will *not* pay a claim under those circumstances. Every policy has its own (sometimes unique) exclusions, but two of the important exclusions to understand in an automobile policy are excluded drivers and business use.

Let's start with the business use exclusion. If you use your car for work (like delivering pizzas or groceries, or as an Uber or Lift driver transporting people), make sure your automobile policy does *not* exclude business use. Unless you selected a specific rider for that when you bought the insurance, it probably excludes business use by default. If it does and you get in an accident while you're "working", don't expect the insurance company to pay. Depending on your insurance carrier, you probably may need to purchase additional coverage to insure yourself for potential business-related accidents.

The second exclusion is excluded drivers. I am constantly amazed to see how many otherwise cautious and diligent people do not realize until only *after* an automobile accident has occurred that their own children were excluded drivers under their policy and they have then exposed themselves to a potentially life changing lawsuit.

Read your policy thoroughly and if you don't completely understand it, contact your insurance agent to find out if anyone is excluded under your policy. If anyone *is* excluded, they must ***never*** drive your car. EVER. Not even just the two miles to the grocery store to pick up some eggs that you forgot to get while you were there. Those eggs could ruin your retirement plans.

Home insurance

With regard to homeowner's insurance, beyond covering the structure and contents of your home, in almost every case, your homeowner's insurance includes the additional benefit of providing you with liability coverage for a wide array of potential claims.

However, as with any other insurance policy, make sure you have satisfactory policy limits and that you completely understand the exclusions to the policy. If you operate a business out of your home (like an internet based business or day care or even lawnmower repair) make sure you are either covered under your homeowner's policy (which is rare) or get a separate business/commercial insurance policy.

An umbrella policy

An umbrella insurance policy is usually an add-on to your existing coverage or may be a completely separate policy depending on the insurer. Umbrella policies are intended to protect you and all your assets from exceptionally large and potentially bankrupting liability claims or judgments. Personal umbrella coverage comes into play when your underlying liability limits (such as from a homeowners or auto insurance policy) have been reached.

Form a trust to hold your assets

A trust is a legal entity that holds assets for the benefit of beneficiaries. Beneficiaries might include specific family members or another entity, like your business or a limited liability company. Trusts are managed by a ***trustee***. This person has control over the trust's funds and property, and all the legal obligations that go along with it, and so, must govern it for the benefit, and in the best interest of, the beneficiaries according to the terms of the trust.

This is a well-known method of protection by the wealthy, but there's no reason that you can't use it too. Besides, you're going to want one later anyway.

There are several types of trusts that can be used to protect your assets from creditors (i.e., an asset protection trust, qualified personal residence trust, life insurance trust, etc.). Ordinarily, to protect your assets from a judgment, the trust must be irrevocable. What that means is that *you* cannot "cancel" it nor have any control over the assets that are included within it.

Typically, for a trust to truly shield your assets, a trustee (someone other than you) must have the discretion to make any and all disbursements. That could be your attorney or a trusted family member. When creating the trust, you would specify the terms and parameters in the trust document, and the trustee then governs the trust according to those terms.

It sounds hard to do for a reason. This is not something that you order up on LegalZoom and simply fill out and file. Forming a trust is complicated. Don't even think about it without consulting an attorney licensed in your state to evaluate your situation and determine the best options for you.

Form a corporation or LLC

If you own all or part of a business, whether as a sole proprietor or in a general partnership with someone else, you might be exposed to *unlimited personal liability* for the business's debts. If you are in a general partnership, you could also be held liable for the poor business decisions of your partners. Potentially, in certain situations, you could be held liable for criminal acts committed by your partners, including fraud that you were unaware of. For these reasons, a general partnership can be very risky — thereby exposing you to a great deal of personal liability.

To protect yourself from most personal liability, form a corporation (Inc), limited liability company (LLC), or limited partnership (LP) for your business. Creating one of those, in most cases, will reduce your personal exposure to your business investments.

Again, before you do anything, especially if you've never done it before, research your state's laws and even if you don't hire him or her, get some advice from an attorney who specializes in entity formation and taxation. What you can learn in a half an hour discussion with someone with that expertise might end up protecting your bottom line down the road.

Contribute to retirement accounts.

While this book aims to dissuade you from stashing the majority of your hard-earned dollars in most of the examples of retirement plans shown on the following page, I would be doing you a disservice by not mentioning that *some* retirement accounts have certain protections that prevent creditors from snatching the money they contain. So, if you're in an industry where lawsuits are a concern, these types of plans could work to your advantage. This is particularly true of plans that are regulated by the Employee Retirement Income Security Act (ERISA), which includes the vast majority of employer administered plans. These are commonly known as **qualified plans**. Some common examples are:

- 401(k) plans
- 403(b) plans
- Thrift Savings Plans (TSPs)
- Simplified Employee Pensions (SEPs)
- Traditional IRAs
- Profit Sharing plans
- Savings Incentive Match Plans for Employees (SIMPLE) IRAs
- Salary Reduction Simplified Employee Pensions (SARSEPs)

When you're enrolled in a *qualified* plan, you benefit from an upfront tax deduction (or reduction) when you put money in, but the trade-off is that you will have to pay taxes on the whole amount whenever you begin taking the money out. Your tax payments are delayed, aka deferred, *not* eliminated.

Remember that the government also imposes Required Minimum Distributions (RMDs) at age 73, meaning that you *must* start withdrawing your money by that date or you get penalized. You can begin withdrawing at age 59 ½ without any penalty. Before that, any withdrawal from the account would potentially incur a 10% penalty. There is one exception called the "Rule of 55". If you turn 55 during the year that you lose or leave your job, you can begin taking distributions from your 401(k) without paying the early withdrawal penalty. However, you must still pay taxes on your withdrawals. Not only does the Rule of 55 work with a 401(k), but it also applies to 403(a) and 403(b) plans. Cash out before age 55 and you guarantee yourself that penalty.

ERISA governed, qualified plans enjoy limitless protection from creditors (excluding the IRS and child support obligations). For retirement plans not covered by ERISA there are also some protections, but not as all encompassing. For example, non-ERISA covered IRAs, have a maximum of $1 million dollars that can be protected from any bankruptcy proceedings.

Take advantage of real estate protection laws.

A provision called a ***Homestead exemption*** will protect the equity in your principal residence (but not any investment property) from attachment by any creditors. Homestead exemptions vary widely between states and have assorted provisions.

Depending on your state's law and your personal financial situation, if you find yourself potentially facing the losing side of a lawsuit, it might make sense for you to pay some additional principal on your mortgage rather than keeping it in your bank account. For example, if you have $50,000 of equity your house (down payment, mortgage payments, etc.) but your state has a $100,000 homestead exemption, it may make sense for you to invest any available funds in your home rather than a bank account, which might be seized by creditors.

Finally, check to see how your house is titled. Some states allow married couples to take title of their home as '*tenants by the entirety*'. Under this ownership structure, each spouse has an indivisible share of the property. That means that both of you must consent to any sale or conveyance of the property so if a creditor obtains a judgment against you, he may not be able to force you to sell the house without your spouse's permission. Noting, of course, that if both you *and* your spouse are sued, that protection would not be particularly helpful.

Unsurprisingly, there is no magic trick to guarantee that no one will ever seize your assets. Protecting your assets will require some time and planning on your part and it's not possible to predict every possible situation. Nevertheless, if you do your homework in advance, you can put yourself in the best possible position to protect your assets from any creditor hell-bent on decreasing your wealth.

Stock Market Crashes – It should come as no surprise that the number one disaster that hurts people in retirement is a sudden and dramatic market downturn. It's critical to understand that the next major market drop will not have the identical characteristics of previous events so, for even experts in the industry, trying to predict them is futile.

For example, despite all their fancy software that is supposed to simulate every possible potential outcome (no matter how improbable), we still saw professional investors – the experts of the experts – be so blindsided that many lost 30 to 50% in their "bullet-proof" portfolios. We saw the 150+ year old, historically solid, investment firm Lehman Brothers, collapse in days like a house of cards and the investment arm of American International Group (AIG), one of the top 100 largest public companies in the world, teeter on the brink of disaster.

Why?

Aside from a profound lack of proper corporate governance, collusion at the highest levels of oversight and ridiculously dangerous risk management practices, we constantly heard the investment community say things like "This wasn't on the map" or "This is so different, no one could have predicted it". When in reality, not only was it predictable (read ***The Big Short: Inside the Doomsday Machine,*** by Michael Lewis about the build-up of the housing bubble during the 2000s and how a few, who chose to actually look into it, massively profited during the free fall of 2008), it was mostly manufactured.

The next crash, and there will very likely be *more than one* in your lifetime, will most certainly be different than they were in the past – only the outcome will be same.

The fact is that even a single stock market crash can be so upending to your investments that it can put a big red X on retirement for you and you could easily find you're in a predicament where you're forced to go back to work.

Fundamentally, planning for retirement is a big math problem with lots of variables, and anyone who's done any advanced algebra in high school can identify with why people tend to avoid it. There are several ways that math works against you when a market crash occurs.

First, percentages work against you. If the market takes a 50% tumble, the climb to just get back to break even is steeper than most people realize. You've lost 50%, so you need a 50% recovery to get back to your original portfolio value, right?

Nope. You would need a 100% increase to get to where you were before the crash.

Look at it this way. If you have a $100,000 investment that loses 50% of its value, that drops you to $50,000. A 50% recovery would give you back just $25,000 ($50K x 50%), meaning your total is $75,000, not the $100,000 you had before the crash happened.

Which brings us to the next part of the problem.

Historically, markets decline much faster than they go up. One of the things that will stand out when you look at historic stock charts is how quickly the market crumbles. The impact the recent Corona virus scare had on the markets is a perfect example. It took just 36 days to incinerate 3+ years of market growth. Another example, in the mid-1990s, the market went on a healthy bull run, but it took a little more than five years for it to reach its peak in 2000. By contrast, it took just 30 months for it to lose 50% of its value.

A common saying in the financial industry is that "markets take the stairs up and the elevator down". In both 2008, 2020 and 2022, that saying could have been revised to "markets took the stairs up and the window down".

If you had a 401(k) in 2020 that held only the Dow index 'DIA' you would have lost nearly 35% of your portfolio's value in less than 5 weeks. Similarly, if your 401(k) in 2008 had held only the S&P index 'SPY' you would have lost 38% of your portfolio value in less than 2 months. In 2022, 401(k) plans suffered $2.1 trillion in losses. The average 401(k) plan had over $135,000 at the start of 2022. By New Year's Day 2023, those assets had shrunk on average to about $101,000. The unfortunate reality is that most people aren't that diversified. In actuality, the average investor lost between 48 and 68% of their net investments in the 2008 market dive. The stock market erased $6.9 trillion in shareholder wealth in 2008. Add to that number that U.S. homeowners lost a cumulative $3.3 trillion in home equity during 2008, according to a report from online real estate database company Zillow, and that's a combined $10.2 trillion dollars in market value that simply disappeared. Now consider that the 2022 stock market plunge, *by itself*, erased $10 trillion in U.S. wealth from blue chips stocks in the S&P 500. That's 39% of the U.S. GDP that year!

Those are numbers that I can't even comprehend. To give you some perspective, Google "What does on trillion dollars look like?" Then when you see it, imagine it ten times larger. It's mind boggling.

Stocks on the Nasdaq lost over 20% in just 30 trading days. A drop of that magnitude has happened only 11 times in history and nine of those were during recessions.

Imagine having a 20 to 50% loss just a year before your planned retirement. Could you afford to lose more than half of your retirement fund? Why even take that risk if you don't have to?

To avoid that kind of disaster, some investors, who fancy themselves as market prognosticators, employ strategies that involve some degree of 'market timing'. One common market timing strategy is "Sell in May and Go Away". This well-known trading strategy is where an investor sells his stock holdings in May and waits to get back into the equity market in early November, thus avoiding the archetypically more volatile May-October period.

The origin of the axiom is likely the old English saying, "Sell in May and go away, and come back on St. Leger's Day". This phrase refers to the custom of Victorian aristocrats, merchants and bankers who liked to leave the city of London and go to the country to escape the heat during the summer months. St. Leger's Day refers to the St. Leger's Stakes, a thoroughbred horse race in mid-September and the last leg of the British Triple Crown.

American investment traders who are likely to spend more time on vacation than trading in the market between Memorial Day and Labor Day mimic this trend and the numbers seem to support this bit of folk wisdom.

Since 1950, the Dow Jones Industrial Average has had an average return of only 0.3% during the May-October period, compared with an average gain of 7.5% during the November-April period. Although the actual reasons for this seasonal trading pattern aren't known, reduced trading volumes owing to vacations in the summer months and higher investment flows in the winter months are often referred to as contributing causes for the divergence in performance between the May-October and the November-April periods, respectively.

But will it work for you? Maybe, but there are obvious drawbacks to implementing this strategy in practice, such as additional transaction costs and considerable tax implications as a result of the rotation in and out of equities on a less than multi-year basis. Another drawback is that actual results may vary greatly from the theoretical ones.

The reality of trying to time the market is that you're highly unlikely to miss all the worst days, and more likely to miss the really good days.

Other financial pundits advocate a "buy and hold" strategy, encouraging people to ride out the markets. They say, "Time IN the market is better than TIMING the market". And in general, they're right. One reason is that, human nature being what it is, people tend to sell at the worst time, fearing the markets will drop further and then are slow to get back in until they confirm the market is back on the rise. Too often, doing so means you'd often miss out on the market's best days, which could send your portfolio value soaring.

However, the buy and hold strategy has its downside too. A good example is why the 2000s are going into the history books as the "lost decade" of investing. Why? The reason is that for every dollar invested into the S&P 500 on January 1, 2000, you'd have had roughly only 90 cents left on December 31, 2009. Quite the opposite result of what all the financial experts and pundits preach about the long-term average gain of stocks being in the 8-10 percent range. I'd say a decade would generally fall into anyone's definition of 'long-term'.

But actually, *losing* money in stocks over a ten-year period? You can't make that stuff up. How does that happen?

Stocks went through one of the roughest decades in history through most of the 2000s. In terms of an asset class, they performed among the worst. In fact, over the same period, had you invested your hard-earned dollars in U.S. government bonds you would have essentially doubled your money, but who knew to do that?

Very few.

Why? Because we have too much faith in people who don't know or understand good alternatives.

Another good example of the failure of a "buy and hold" strategy is that some "blue chip" stocks take much longer to recover, if they ever do at all.

Look at Cisco Systems Inc. (CSCO is the stock symbol), a multi-national company and one of the largest employers in Silicon Valley, Cisco develops, builds and sells computer networking hardware, tele-communications equipment and other high-technology services and products, and was a long-time darling of the investor set in the 1990s. Cisco's stock was hovering just under $80 dollars a share in March of 2000. Tons of people had bought in as it rose from $5 just three years before. Unfortunately, when the tech bubble burst, Cisco's share price had dropped to $13.62 by April 2001 and down even further to under $10 in 2002. The "buy and hold" strategy would say to hold that stock and let it recover, the problem is that if you bought Cisco during its run up in early 2000, then you're *still* waiting (as I write this, now 23 years later) for that recovery.

This is a big reason why so many people have lost trust in investing in the stock market in general and are looking for other *safer* places to invest their money. Can you blame them? If you'd been told that investing in the stock market would give you average annual returns of nearly 10% and diversification would help you prevent volatility and then you actually lost money in the market over the course of a full ten years, you'd think about just sticking it in the bank and earning the less than two percent they offer now too.

Of course, that doesn't even cover inflation rates, which is why I mentioned before that a bank is really one of the safest places to *lose* money.

The reality is that the 'lost decade' outcome described on the previous pages could have been prevented by rebalancing your portfolio at very specific times over those ten years, by taking some money out of equities and putting it into bonds, but even that assumes that you'd have kept close watch on the results over time and know exactly *how* to rebalance it to prevent such stagnation, or that you'd have been working with some financial professional to do so. Either way would have required some diligent attention on your part, knowledge of what to do and when to do it, and some extra cost in fees and transaction expenses.

To make matters worse, the big dogs of the financial services industry are warning that those "balanced" portfolios, like the 60/40 and 40/60 shown on the J.P. Morgan chart, that financial advisors have relied on for decades as the best way to avoid big losses and still make headway toward your financial goals, may not do so well in the future.

Consider this example from an Investopedia post in late 2019 entitled: Why Morgan Stanley Says the 60/40 Portfolio Is Doomed

> As U.S. stocks set new record highs, Morgan Stanley warns that returns on a traditional balanced portfolio with 60% stocks and 40% bonds could approach 100-year lows and drop by half versus the last 20 years. "The return outlook over the next decade is sobering--investors face a lower and flatter frontier compared to prior decades," Morgan Stanley wrote in a note to clients, as quoted by Business Insider.

> "Investors will need to accept much higher volatility to eke out small incremental units of return," the note added. Morgan Stanley forecasts a 2.8% average annual return over the next 10 years for a 60/40 portfolio. The average has been nearly 8.0% since 1881 and about 6% over the last 20 years, after double digit annual returns reaching as high as 16% from the early 1980s to the early 2000s.

That means that either equities are going to have much lower incremental increases or more likely, bigger swings of ups and downs (the latter being even more important) than the last decade, meaning your risk of loss if your financial advisor isn't psychic is even greater.

Then there are market downturns that are known as Black Swans. A **Black Swan** in the stock market is a completely unpredictable set of circumstances or events that have a *dramatic* negative impact on the market overall. The Black Monday flash crash in October of 1987 was a Black Swan event. More recently, the impact that the Corona (CoVid-19) virus had on the stock market in March of 2020 was another perfect example of what one could call a Black Swan.

The Corona virus pandemic was a global event that impacted the market so dramatically that it ended the record-breaking 10+ year bull run and put the Dow, the NASDAQ, and the S&P 500 officially into bear market/correction territory. In the 30 days of February 12th to March 12th 2020, the Dow dropped more than 28%, from over 29,500 to 21,200, and in the single week ending on Friday the 13th of 2020 the Dow had two of its worst days since 2008 dropping more than 2,000 points on Monday of that week, rallying back some and then dropping another 2,352 points on

Thursday the 12th. Then, adding more confusion by having its biggest rally since 2008 on, of all days, Friday the 13th, with an almost 2,000 point gain!

In the weeks that followed the markets traded like a seesaw, up in the morning, down in the afternoon, up some overnight, down more the next morning, clawing back some by the closing bell. By March 23rd the Dow had dropped to pennies short of 18,592, 38% off its high the previous month, three days later it was back up to 22,552, then down again. The S&P had similar volatility. The idea that a flu-like disease could that have that much impact on a strong economic market in the U.S. was unprecedented and literally, no one saw it coming.

To say that kind of up and down market had people pushing their panic buttons in an understatement. And when the dust settled, for many, the damage was already done.

The Dow Jones Industrial Average was down by another 635 points by the closing bell on March 31, 2020, a quarterly loss of more than 24% for the blue-chip index and its worst first-quarter performance in history. The S&P 500 recorded its worst first quarter since 1938, down by more than 20%, and the tech-heavy NASDAQ closed down 31% from its high in mid-February of 2020, its worst first quarter performance since it was established in 1971.

In the last week of March 2020, a staggering 3.28 million Americans filed for unemployment, the most on record for a single week, and consumer confidence took a nosedive. The following week, that number more than doubled to 6.6 million in a single week, yet, that same week stocks had their best single week in 45 years with the Dow up 12.67%, the S&P up 12.1% and the

NASDAQ up 10.59% for that week. Unemployment offices across the country were overwhelmed.

Highly paid corporate executives whose skillsets had heretofore afforded them the confidence that their talents or experience would *always* provide them with a comfortable living, found themselves standing in line at the unemployment office because their job/industry was "non-essential".

When it began, some economic modelers predicted that the original government estimate of 20 million unemployed was low, and with good reason. By the first week of the shutdown, more than two thirds of the more than one million restaurants across the United States had closed completely or were only doing take-out business, meaning an estimated 12 million jobs were lost in the that industry alone.

Initially viewed as "doom-and-gloom-sayers", they were right. By mid-May 2020 over 36 million people had applied for unemployment benefits, and another 3+ million that were ineligible for unemployment benefits had joined the ranks of the unemployed. In all, just shy of 30% of America's workforce of 157 million had lost their jobs in the months that followed - almost five and a half times the 8.7 million jobs lost during the 2008 recession – with some States experiencing unemployment rates that rivaled the Great Depression.

All this despite a series of emergency actions by the Federal Reserve to bolster the economy and backstop losses for businesses and individuals, as well as a massive $2 *trillion* fiscal stimulus package meant to prop up small businesses, help families make ends meet and support big corporations (especially those in sectors of industry who saw their incoming revenues decimated as people sheltered in place) in the fight against the large-scale economic damage inflicted by the outbreak.

Anyone who had their retirement savings leveraged in the equities markets got completely blindsided. REITs collapsed along with the stock market. Panic set in.

Equally terrifying, according to the Economic Policy Institute, around 13 million people who lost their jobs also lost their health and life insurance since it was tied to their employment. Others who lost their jobs but had a personal Term Life policy lost that as well when they had to make the hard choice of prioritizing bills like the critical cost of a non-work related health insurance policy, their rent, mortgage, car payments, cell phone bills or even food over life insurance premiums, so they lapsed quickly.

At one point, several States had a "shelter-in-place" order so you couldn't even go out to look for alternative employment!

Of course, if you're not getting a paycheck, you can't have any money deducted from one to go into a 401(k) or an IRA.

However, since our oh-so-generous Congress recognized that the CoVid-19 ignited all-stop financial crisis was serious enough to put some emergency-like measures in place in what was named the Coronavirus Aid, Relief, and Economic Security (CARES) Act, like foregoing the pre-59 ½ age limit 10% tax penalty for tapping into your 401(k) – if you had one – and *only if* you could prove a hardship. Unfortunately, that would have set your retirement back by however many years it took to save that money.

I'll wager very few of those 30 plus million receiving unemployment benefits knew that any and all State unemployment benefits, as well as the additional $600 per week that was provided by the federal government under the CARES Act (through July 31, 2020) was *taxable* as ordinary income on their 2020 tax return. The government "cares" just enough to charge a tax penalty to those who underpaid their taxes during the year.

Nobody warned that something like this could happen. It was unprecedented. Emergency funds evaporated in weeks, not months.

Can something like that happen again?

Of course it can. Will the next downturn be as bad or worse?

Who knows? I sure don't and neither do any of the "experts".

My question to you is, why take that risk *at all* when the Millennial Money Tree strategy can allow you to take advantage of any and all upswings in the market, not put any of your cash at risk of loss in downturns, ensure that your life insurance stays in force even when you can't afford to pay a few (or several) premiums, give you access to cash *whenever* you need it (emergency or not) without any tax penalties, and have the peace of mind that it's all done almost literally on an autopilot that guarantees growth?

Chapter Thirteen

A little history

The US stock market has been around for over 100 years.

Hold on a sec, I know what you're thinking right about now. You're questioning what good can come from knowing what happened last century when you're *way* more interested in knowing what's going to happen in the next 20 to 40 years. "Why do I need to know all this crap?" Right? I get it. This stuff is simply overwhelming to some people, but I promise that if you'll bear with me, I'll skip the minutiae and carve out the really good stuff so you'll never be in a position of repeating the bad parts of stock market history because you didn't know enough about it. Deal? Okay, let's dig in.

Historically, going back 90+ years to 1928, there have only been 31 down years in the market, nearly a third of those (nine) occurring during the Great Depression between 1929 and 1941. In the last 60 years (1965-2024) there have only been 15 years that the

S&P 500 was in negative territory, and of the other 45 that were in positive territory, only 13 years had less than a double-digit gain. The average gain in those 45 positive years since 1965 was 15.95%. In '73 and '74 the S&P lost a combined 47.09%. In 2000 thru 2002 the S&P lost 46.55%, in 2008, the S&P lost 38.49%, and in the latest full year of losses 2022, the S&P lost 19.44%, but the Nasdaq also was down 33.6% in 2022.

What does that tell us?

That, historically, there have been more up years than down years and most of those up years were greater than a single digit gain. But when the stock market decides to tank, like we saw in the first beginning in 2000, then in 2008 and then again in 2022, it loses BIG. Obviously, while history is no predictor of the future, statistically, the odds are in your favor *if* you don't lose any money in the down years of the stock market and capture as much of those double-digit gains (when they occur) as you can.

That's exactly what the Millennial Money Tree strategy does — using a wealth building vehicle that captures some or all of the market's annual growth during upswings, but none of its losses during downturns – ensuring you automatically keep those gains and build on them year over year over year.

Anyone who's wealthy will tell you that it's not necessarily how much money you *make* that makes you rich over time, it's how much money you *keep*.

Warren Buffett, the business magnate, investor, philanthropist, and Chairman and CEO of Berkshire Hathaway, who (as of November 2024) is the eighth richest man in the world at nearly $147 billion in net worth, has a reputation for being frugal. His modest home in Nebraska is worth just .00023% of his total wealth and it's said that he never spends more than $3.17 on his daily breakfast from McDonald's.

Buffett isn't just good at making money, he's good at giving it away too, having already given away more than $51 billion to various causes. But that's by choice.

Buffet is said to have two rules when it comes to investing:

#1 Never lose money

#2 Never forget Rule #1

If you're investing in the market, for most of us that's next to impossible. While common wisdom says that the best place to grow your wealth for retirement is by investing in stocks, and even with the fact that the average return on the S&P 500 over the last 50 years was 8.14%, because it also included three of the worst market downturns in history in that timeframe, less fees and transaction costs, the *actual* net returns for the average investor are only around three to four percent.

That barely covers inflation.

According to InflationData.com, the average annual rate of inflation between 1913 and 2013 was 3.22%, but noting that inflation can skyrocket in a single year like in 2022.

Let's use that 3.22 figure as a starting point. In just twelve months' time, the price increases of the items you purchase on a regular basis may be next to imperceptible to you. But now let's fast forward into the future. Using this average inflation rate of 3.22%, your income would have to double close to every 22 years in order to keep pace with the purchasing power of the goods and services that you buy today.

Or putting it a different way, if you're 25 years old today, something that costs $10 today will cost about $35.50 when you turn 65, meaning if you stuck a one hundred dollar bill in a book and found it 40 years later, it would be worth about $29 in goods and services in today's dollars. Or in reverse, a dollar in 1918 has a mere 4.2 *cents* of purchasing power today.

You get the picture.

If you retire at age 65, the odds of you living in retirement up to 20 or more years are better than average now, by the time *you* retire those odds might be substantially more. However, if you aren't generating any income from employment, your savings will not only have to provide an income stream but will have to keep increasing over time just to keep up with inflation. Meaning whatever you *think* you'll need to comfortably retire based on today's dollars – triple it – then add some more to be safe.

Unfortunately, America's transition from a pension system to a largely self-funded retirement system built around 401(k)s and IRAs has led us to a retirement savings crisis.

Auto-contributions help some, but the average family has $95,776 saved for retirement, a figure that is hugely skewed by the disproportionately higher sums accumulated by wealthier families and Baby Boomers — the median is just $5,000.

The reality is that overall, we save far less now than previous generations. The chart below is from the Federal Reserve Economic Data showing personal savings rates going back to 1960 and, aside from the brief, but enormous spikes when the government was sending everyone big checks during the Covid shutdown, it shows just how far down the scale we've come. From over 10% in the '60s, trending up past 17% in 1976 and now down to 3.4% since 2023.

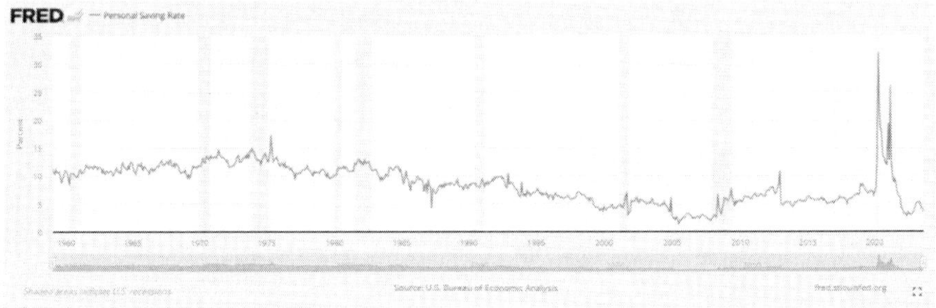

The painful truth is that most of us won't have enough to continue in the lifestyle to which we've become accustomed, when or *if* we retire. And yet, we're still too often guided to the market like sheep to slaughter by financial advisors and pundits alike who continually pontificate that there's no better way to grow a substantial sum over time.

Use of the stock market *is* still the best way to grow your wealth over time; however, the operative phrase in that sentence is "use of" not "participating in". I'll explain the difference later in the book but suffice it to say that the individual trader is being taken to the cleaners with every stock trade they make. It is not inaccurate to note that until the late 1990s, with the advent of electronic trading, you had somewhat of a level playing field. That's not true now.

With the turn of the century came the increasing prevalence of electronic High Frequency Trading (aka HFT). As I mentioned earlier in this book, HFT companies use high-speed computers that are often linked to the "market-maker" (the exchange that your brokerage company uses to make your trades) that use algorithms to make hundreds of thousands of trades, back and forth, earning profits on micro-changes in stock prices.

If you trade stocks online, you've probably noticed that from time to time, regardless of how fast your computer is, in the time between when you click the "buy" button and you see what the trade results are, the stock price has gone up or down by some amount – sometimes a few cents, but sometimes a few dollars. What you may not know is that in the second or so it took to complete the trade after you clicked your mouse button, High Frequency Traders can make thousands and thousands of trades exploiting the price direction of the equity you just bought or sold.

What happens is that those HFT computers can see thousands of traders just like you buying and selling stocks before the trade actually happens – and in the milliseconds it takes for your brokerage to send your trade to the market to complete the trade, HFTs can make millions in profit on those micro-amounts you see in the difference in trade costs by trading mind-boggling numbers of stock in that timeframe.

Electronic trading first emerged in the '90s alongside the exchange floors where brokers and traders shouted out orders back and forth. By 2010 it had killed off nearly all the "pit" floors, a notable exception being at the New York Stock Exchange, which is now really just promotional scenery for companies listed there. The real business of the NYSE takes place at a 400,000 square foot data center in suburban Mahwah, New Jersey. That's more than 9 acres of row after row of computer servers. Now you have a better understanding of why these facilities are often called server "farms". When many Wall Street banks were forced to close their proprietary trading desks after the 2008 crisis, independent firms filled the gaps.

Little known to the investing public, these companies, nicknamed "prop shops" (the "prop" being short for proprietary) made billionaires out of their owners. Speed was essential. Traders paid exchanges to "co-locate" computers right beside "trade matching engines", the computerized equivalent of an exchange floor. That way they could receive incoming market signals first and be able to automatically adjust their orders accordingly, beating investors' orders outside the building.

How important is speed to these companies? One company paid hundreds of millions of dollars to reshape the landscape in the Appalachian Mountains while laying a direct link of fiber optic cable from the Chicago stock exchange to its headquarters in New York in an effort to shave less than 1.5 milliseconds off its transmission time between the two sites. Some HFTs today are already making trades in microseconds (one millionth of a second). Soon these companies will be making trades in nanoseconds – that's one billionth of a second.

A June 2017 report by J.P. Morgan detailed that high-frequency trading accounted for 52% of the May 2017 average daily trading volume of about 6.73 billion shares. During the peak levels of high-frequency trading in 2009, about 61% of 9.8 billion of average daily shares traded were executed by high-frequency traders.

Information about an accurate volume of these types of trades is much harder to come today likely because these companies are afraid of regulation going against them, so they are far less willing to make their business practices public knowledge and so far, the SEC is ignoring any advantage they have over the average investor.

The more volatile the market, the more money they make.

One of the big promises from the first consumer online stock trading company E*Trade was that trading on a computer leveled the playing field between the individual trader and the big brokerage houses, but now, it's not likely you can compete with robots making algorithmic based trades at the speed of light even if your trade went first – which it doesn't.

Can you still make money in the stock market? Of course you can, just know that the system is rigged to help the big guys and not you, so when things go south, guess who will be left holding the bag?

Think I'm exaggerating?

Get on YouTube and watch the 2010 documentary "Inside Job". Narrated by Matt Damon, it details how the 2008 global financial meltdown, which caused millions of job losses and foreclosures and plunged the United States into a deep economic recession, could have been avoided but greed, collusion and the blind trust of the uninformed investor made it far too easy for the Fat Cats of the financial industry to literally conspire to defraud ordinary investors like you, and then walk away without any penalty.

And of course, that again begs the question: Why would you want to risk *any* of your money if you don't have to?

Chapter Fourteen

A tortoise on steroids

Everyone knows the story of the Tortoise and the Hare, and its moral that slow and steady wins the race.

Expanding on that theme, at the core of the Millennial Money Tree strategy is a get rich *slow* vehicle. Unless you're a hard-core subscriber to the ideology of the FIRE (Financial Independence Retire Early) movement, in most cases we're talking about a 20-year time-frame minimum. If you're in your twenties, love what you do and don't plan on leaving your career until age 70, we're talking more than 40 years.

I get it. That's definitely turtle slow.

That's snail slow. Molasses in January slow. Glacier slow.

But the paradox is that this race is best won by ensuring that you have the longest amount of time to run it. A mega-marathon, not a sprint.

For some of you, that's more than your lifetime away. And we all know that life has a way of interfering with long-term plans. That's why, unless you have military strength discipline, whatever vehicle you use to save for retirement *has* to be simple, automatic, flexible and not be tied to your job or some person you take advice from.

The beauty of this vehicle is that it's multi-purpose. It provides all the critical components of a good retirement plan in one incredibly flexible package, including: a) a method to continually build wealth without a need to monitor the market; b) protection against loss of the gains you make; c) life insurance coverage; d) tax advantages and e) living benefits, all rolled into one.

The foundation of the Millennial Money Tree plan is something called an **Indexed Universal Life Insurance policy** or **IUL** for short. There are other things you'll likely want to build onto that foundation, but an IUL, of and by itself, set up correctly, can be your best single vehicle to a secure financial future, bar none.

What the heck is an IUL?

Everybody has heard of Term Life insurance. It's usually the cheapest way to cover any life risk and protect your family's future in the event of your death. It pays out a specific amount that you choose based on how much you pay in monthly premium, generally based on your age (your life expectancy and your health – young and in great health is always cheapest because the risk to the insurance carrier is the lowest). Premiums never go up or down and your death benefit never changes. But a Term Life policy expires after a certain time period, and if you outlive it, you've paid in a lot of money and received nothing in return.

Not to mention, *now* you are decades older, your life expectancy is much less (more risk to the insurer) and a new Term policy will cost you an arm and a leg. That is *if* you qualify on the health side at all.

Statistically, less than three percent of all Term Life polices ever pay a death claim, and those that do are generally from an accidental death. Most people outlive them, or they terminate when people move from job to job. Meaning most people pay into these policies for years and never get a dime in back from the carrier. No wonder insurance companies love to sell them.

There *are* some companies that offer something called Return of Premium on select Term Life policies, and it's exactly what it sounds like – you get all (or most) of your money back when the term expires – but there's no interest paid on that money over the decades you paid in, so there's no return on your investment. Plus, that option always increases your monthly premium cost by as much as 10x, and once again, when the term expires, again, you're left without life insurance coverage.

In some cases, depending on the insurance carrier you chose, you can convert a Term Life policy into a permanent (Whole Life) policy before the term expires. However, the face value (the amount of death benefit the policy will pay) is generally an amount far reduced from the original death benefit of the Term Life policy, your premium will increase substantially and any cash value attached to the policy (Whole Life policies have cash value that grows over time) will grow so slowly that when you die, you may have paid in more than what your beneficiaries would get back.

Not good.

On the flipside of that scenario, what if you could own a policy where you could adjust the amount of life insurance premiums and/or the face value (the death benefit) and increase its cash value when you needed (or wanted) to, without having to 'requalify' — would you go for it?

What if the cash value of that policy tracked alongside a diversified **ETF** (Exchange Traded Fund) and captured all or most of the market upside but without the inherent downside risk of directly investing in the equities market?

What if you could get access to some or all of your death benefit *before* you died? If you were diagnosed with a critical or terminal illness for example.

What if you got disabled and couldn't pay your monthly premiums, and so the insurance company paid them for you? What if this policy had a guarantee that it would never lapse?

What if you could be your own finance company? Or at least quit paying piles of money in interest payments to banks, loan companies and/or credit cards over prolonged periods of time. What if you could be your own bank and have a safe place to put your money that would increase over time instead of paying monthly fees? Of course, nobody is suggesting you close all your bank accounts, or give up any existing services you like. It's merely that some individuals (or businesses) that keep large amounts of cash in checking or savings over long periods may want to know about an alternative.

What if you could borrow money from this policy's 'account' for whatever reason, at any time, without any government-imposed penalties, *tax free*?

Sound interesting?

All of this is possible with an Indexed Universal Life insurance policy.

Indexed Universal Life (IUL) policies are a type of insurance policy in which the components of the life insurance policy (death benefit, savings element and premium) can be altered throughout the contract. IULs also provide market-linked gains without market-based risk because it's not an investment in the stock market. With an IUL's principal-protection guarantee, gains from the previous year are locked in and the principal cash value remains the same if there is no market gain. Simply put, you make money when the market is positive but even if the stock market crashes, there are no losses.

In addition, with an IUL, there are no taxes due during the accumulation phase when the policy's cash value builds up. Then, whenever you want (pre or post-retirement), you can take tax-free distributions of the cash value up to the amount paid in or tax-free loans over the amount paid in. IULs also allow the exchange of one policy for another without triggering income taxes. And when you pass away, the tax-free death benefit protects your loved ones against any financial uncertainty.

This combination of flexibility and investment growth with ***zero risk of loss***, combined with a selection of living benefit options and tax advantages make IULs a near perfect vehicle to grow your wealth. In fact, a properly designed Indexed Universal Life Insurance policy offers guaranteed, risk free growth and tax advantages that no other *single* product, insurance, or investment, can provide.

The chassis of an IUL is the 'UL' part, Universal Life (aka Flexible Premium Life) insurance. In 1979, Life Insurance Company of California (later E.E Hutton Life and now First Capital Life) combined the two elements of Whole Life and Term Life into a single contract originally called Total Life and later called Complete Life. A few small companies followed the lead of Hutton in 1980, and 1981 saw the entrance of major companies into the Universal Life market. By 1984, nearly all major insurers had introduced at least one Universal Life product, and many offered more than one version and Universal Life became an established product.

Under the terms of a UL policy, as premium payments come in, the cash value is credited each month with interest, and the policy is debited each month by a cost of insurance charge (COI – generally based on the life expectancy of the policyholder), as well as any other policy charges and fees drawn from the cash value, even if no premium payment is made that month. Interest credited to the account is determined by the insurer but has a contractual minimum rate (often between two and four percent).

Universal Life policies come in lots of varieties, from fixed-rate types to variable versions where you can select from various equity accounts to invest in. Neither of those just mentioned work best in the Millennial Money Tree formula because fixed rates build cash too slowly and variable ULs have market risk of loss just like any other security-based investment.

When a UL's earnings rate is attached to a financial index such as a stock, bond or other interest rate index, the policy is an "Indexed Universal Life" contract. These types of policies offer the advantage of guaranteed level premiums throughout the insured's lifetime at substantially lower premium cost than an equivalent Whole Life policy at first, but cost of insurance is always increasing as the policyholder's life expectancy decreases with age.

The first indexed life insurance policy was introduced by Transamerica in 1997. Sales volume of the product was less than a half million that year, whereas the total 2023 sales in the indexed life insurance market, as a whole, came in at over $3.7 billion. And that was down .2 billion from the record the previous year but there was an increase in the number of policies sold by 20%. IUL policy face amount increased 11% in 2024 and the number of policies sold increased 13%, with five of the top ten having double-digit sales increases in 2024. Sales in 2025 are projected to be slightly higher, with IULs maintaining a 25+ percent share of the overall insurance market. The only insurance product with a greater share is Whole Life, but chances are IULs will overtake Whole Life within the next decade if growth trends keep up.

And yet, despite this tremendous growth, it's still an insurance product that you've likely never heard of. Or, if you have, know very little about, even if you work with a financial planner on a regular basis.

Indexed Universal Life grants the owner the flexibility to apportion cash value amounts to either a fixed account or various equity 'index' accounts. A stock ***index***, or stock market index, is a measurement of a section of the stock market. It is computed from the prices of selected stocks (typically on a weighted average) from a specific group, industry or type of security. It is also a tool used by investors and financial managers to describe the market, and to compare the return on specific investments.

These policies offer a variety of well-known indexes such as the S&P 500 or the Nasdaq 100. IUL policies are more volatile than fixed ULs (but only in terms of going *upward* in value from year to year), but less risky than Variable Universal Life policies because no money is actually invested in equity positions. As such, Indexed UL offerings are regulated by the state insurance departments for each individual state. They do not require the presentation of a prospectus because it is not a securities product, but an '**illustration**', a detailed description including historic performance of the choices of funds available and various tables showing projected performance under various scenarios (guaranteed and non-guaranteed), is required.

IUL policies offer tax-deferred cash accumulation for retirement while maintaining a level or increasing death benefit. People who want the protection that permanent life insurance affords but hope to take advantage of the possibility of significant cash accumulation through an equity index often use IULs as retirement/estate-planning vehicles, or for key person insurance for business owners, and for plans where premium financing comes into play.

If you've never heard of one, don't be surprised. Wall Street isn't about to promote anything that doesn't involve having its fingers in the pie, and from a life insurance agent or financial advisor's point of view, IULs are considered advanced life insurance products that are more difficult to adequately understand and explain. Additionally, IULs often have more complex underwriting requirements which often delay commission payments, and many carriers don't pay very high commissions for the amount of work involved by the agent, when compared to other types of policies that can be offered, so many insurance agents and financial advisors simply avoid talking about them.

An IUL works like this.

When a premium is paid, a portion pays for annual renewable term insurance based on the life of the insured (the COI part of the UL chassis of the policy). Any fees are paid, and the rest is added to the cash value. The total amount of cash value is then credited with interest based on increases in an equity index the policyholder has chosen (but it is not directly invested in the stock market). Most carriers allow the policyholder to select from multiple indexes for diversification.

IULs typically offer a guaranteed minimum fixed interest rate and a choice of indexes. Policyholders can decide the percentage allocated to the fixed and/or one or more indexed accounts.

The value of the selected index is recorded at the beginning of a specific timeframe and compared to the value at the end of that timeframe. These points in time are the basis for the amount credited to each index, and therefore the policy itself. If the index increases during the timeframe, the interest is added to the cash value. Typically, these "***point to point***" crediting strategies occur on a monthly, annual or multi-annual basis.

For example, if the chosen index gained 7% from the first of March of the current year to the end of February of the following year, then, in an annual point-to-point strategy, the current cash value is multiplied by 7%. The resulting interest is *added* to the cash value. Some policies calculate the index gains as the sum of the changes for the period. Other policies may take an average of the daily gains for a month or year.

Here's the great part. If the index goes down instead of up, typically no interest is credited to the cash account, but there is no penalty either – the account value would stay the same even if the market crashes dramatically.

There is zero risk of loss with an IUL.

In fact, there are several IUL providers that offer a small gain (between .5 and 2 percent) even when the index goes down.

The gains from the index are credited back to the policy based on a percentage rate, referred to as the ***participation rate***. The participation rate of a particular IUL product/policy is set by the insurance company. It can be anywhere from 25% to more than 100%.

For example, if the point to point (timeframe) gain is 6%, and the participation rate for that IUL policy is 75% and the current cash value total is $10,000, then $450 is added to the cash value (6% x 75% x $10,000 = $450).

The maximum and minimum that is credited in any timeframe is also set by the insurance company. The maximum amount is called the '***cap***'. The minimum is called the '***floor***'.

The cap, the floor, the participation rate and the historic performance of the index you choose are critical components of the IUL that should fully understand *before* you choose one.

I know what you're thinking.

"*Man, this is getting complicated*".

I get it. But bear with me and I'll simplify this for you as we go forward. Remember, we're going to have an expert at your disposal to recommend the best deal for what you want to accomplish, so you don't have to be a financial genius to determine what's best for you and your family.

If you're more of a visual person like me, jump ahead real quick to the chart shown on page 302. That'll give you a good idea about the comparative value we're talking about here. Go take a peek and ask yourself which would you rather have if the next 20 years are similar to the last 20?

And remember, 100% of the money you take out of your 401(k) is taxable, so the actual value is far less than what's shown on that chart. By contrast, any money taken from an IUL can be tax free, plus, once it's set up, you never have to agonize over what the market is doing because you'll never lose money. Put it on autopilot and watch your account grow over time, worry free.

So, here's how the cap and floor, in combination with the participation rate affect the interest rate credited to your account.

First, let's look at the participation rate again. Some carriers may offer IUL '*crediting strategies*' (insurance parlance for how they pay you) that have participation rates well over 100%. IUL policies typically credit the index interest to cash accumulations once a year. The highest participation rate I've seen is 205%, offered by an Ameritas IUL for a specific fund they offer (Note: This second edition was written in 2023 so things might be different now, nor is this an endorsement of Ameritas or its IULs).

That sounds great, right? That means they apply more than double your current cash value to the associated interest rate that the particular fund or strategy you've chosen has. Who wouldn't want that, right?

Hold your horses. Remember, there are multiple parts to the equation. In general, those IULs that offer a more than 100% participation rate will have a much lower cap (remember that's the maximum interest rate they'll pay in any given crediting timeframe) than those that have a 100% participation rate (or less) or the fund that they offer the much higher participation rate for, in general, hasn't done as well as other funds that other companies offer.

Unfortunately, too often, what looks great, turns out to be more of a marketing ploy than a really good system to build your wealth.

Let's take some examples from real life, but without the company names and compare one IUL from company A that has a 170% participation rate and a cap of 7.45% vs company B's IUL that offers a 90% participation rate and a 16% cap.

Confused yet? I know, right? It makes your brain want to explode unless you're a finance wizard. It helps to see some numbers instead of trying to do complex equations in your head.

Let's say the market does very well one year and goes up by 20%. And for this example, we'll assume that you've already had an IUL for a few years and have some cash value already available. In this example, we'll assume that the cash value in your IUL started the year at $10,000, (including all the internal fees and expenses that go along with them) the following table shows what your year end result would be with company A versus company B:

IUL	A: % Increase in Index	B: Index Cap Rate	C: Participation Rate	D: Interest Credited (Smaller of A and B) x C	New Total Value
IUL A	20%	7.45%	170%	12.66%	$11,266
IUL B	20%	16%	90%	14.40%	**$11,440**

Obviously, in some scenarios, having the larger participation doesn't necessarily mean your point to point gain (amount credited per the timeframe) will be higher.

In a less volatile year the numbers look different:

IUL	A: % Increase in Index	B: Index Cap Rate	C: Participation Rate	D: Interest Credited (Smaller of A and B) x C	New Total Value
IUL A	5%	7.45%	170%	8.5%	**$10,850**
IUL B	5%	16%	90%	4.5%	$10,450

So, there are advantages and disadvantages to both sides.

This is a key reason you don't want to try to find the best fit for your situation by simply researching IULs on the web. Implementing the Millennial Money Tree strategy is not a Do-It-Yourself. It behooves you to consult an expert in this strategy to ensure you find the perfect vehicle for the race you want to run and get it set up correctly. The latter can make as much difference as what insurer you chose.

The good news is that I'll make it easy for you to find one.

You should note too, that no one has ever lost a dime in any Millennial Money Tree strategy due to the failure of the underwriting insurance company, nor as a result of any political, financial or economic calamity. Nor can changes in tax laws or Social Security have any impact on your Money Tree Strategy plan. However, if you're the ultra-cautious type and worry about the potential of the insurance company you're doing business with (that's likely been doing business for over 100 years) suddenly becoming insolvent, and it being such a pariah that no other company takes it over, then diversify — split up your savings into multiple top rated companies.

Chapter Fifteen

What about Mutual Funds?

So clearly there's a good argument for using an IUL for retirement savings rather than a 401(k) plan or IRA, but how do they compare to other forms of savings, like a good, well managed, low cost, high growth, Mutual Fund?

In his book **Money - Master the Game** (a book I highly recommend that you read next), Tony Robbins asks his readers to imagine this scenario: Someone comes to you with an investment opportunity. He wants you to put up 100% of the capital and take 100% of the risk, and if the investment makes money, he wants you to pay him 60% (or more) of the upside in fees, and if it loses money, you take the hit for the losses but he still gets paid out of what's left. Then he asks, "Are you in?"

Naturally, he knows your immediate response is going to be "No way". But he goes on to explain that if you're invested in a typical mutual fund, those are the terms to which you've already agreed. And he's right.

Robbins asked (the now late) Jack Bogle, founder and (at the time) retired chief executive of The Vanguard Group, the largest provider of mutual funds in the world, with over $5.1 trillion in assets under management, how 92 million Americans were convinced to buy into such a scheme. His answer?

"Marketing".

Bogle pointed out that most people don't do the math. They only look at the advertised results and think "I need to get into that".

Few people understand that over time typical fees paid to the active managing firm of whatever mutual fund you're in can eat up to 60 to 75 percent of the profit over a lifetime of savings. Nor do they realize that mutual fund promotional material uses "time-weighted" returns. The time-weighted return method simply combines the returns over short periods of time, a month for example, called "sub-periods" and by compounding them together, results in the overall period return which *rarely* reflect actual real-world investor gross returns, let alone net returns.

The share of retirement account assets managed by mutual funds in the United States in 2017 for direct contribution plans (like 401(k) plans) was a historically high 59%, and for IRAs the number was pretty steady for the last decade at 47%. Chances are, if you have one or both, you're invested in a mutual fund.

In other words, the consumer market is huge.

In the United States alone, in 2018, according to the Investment Company Institute's annual Factbook of trends and activities in the investment company industry, the number of individuals who owned mutual funds that year was 101.9 million, meaning 45.4% of American households owned one or more mutual funds. Today there are 10,000+ mutual funds and ETFs to choose from, managing assets worth nearly 19 trillion dollars. That's an awful lot of choices for even expert investors. How do you know which one to pick?

If you own one, whether it's part of your 401(k) or you bought it on your own, you probably bought that particular fund because it had some stellar five star rating from Morningstar and/or their promotional material showed that the fund 'outperformed' the market year after year. I hate to tell you but that's exactly what they wanted you to do.

If you don't know, Morningstar, Inc. is a global investment research and investment management firm headquartered in Chicago. Founded in 1982, Morningstar provides ratings of various investments using a zero to five-star rating system – five being the highest rating. Unfortunately, a 2017 Wall Street Journal article "The Morningstar Mirage," showed that a high percentage of top-rated (five-star) mutual funds don't sustain those top ratings over time, but that achieving that five-star rating attracts a boat load of cash from investors into those funds. As a result, it claimed, many investors have suffered financially from choosing top-rated funds.

Of course, Morningstar executives disputed the investigative piece but the performance deterioration of mutual funds that are (or were) top-rated by Morningstar has been known as far back as 1999 from a study by Matthew Morey and Christopher Blake called "Morningstar Ratings and Mutual Fund Performance" and again by Morey in 2003 in "Kiss of Death: A 5-Star Morningstar

Mutual Fund Rating?" And the fact that investor cash flows follow the top-rated funds was documented in a white paper published in The Journal of Financial and Quantitative Analysis, by Diane Del Guercio and Paula Tkac entitled "Star Power: The Effect of Morningstar Ratings on Mutual Fund Flow" in 2008. Several studies have been published since these papers confirming, updating and expanding their findings.

Add to that, over the five years from 2012 to 2017, starting smack in the middle of the longest bull in history when the S&P seemed to be breaking records every few weeks, 76.49% of active managers of large-cap mutual funds, 81.74% of mid-cap mutual fund managers, and 92.90% of small-cap managers failed to match the benchmark of the S&P composite index. Meaning they didn't "outperform the market".

That's according to the SPIVA® U.S. Mid-Year 2018 Summary published in October of 2018. SPIVA is an acronym for **S**&**P** **I**ndexes **V**s. **A**ctive mutual fund management. Similarly, over the 15-year investment timeframe ending in 2019 which included an overall drop in the S&P of 50%, 92.43% of large-cap fund managers, 95.13% of mid-cap managers, and 97.70% of small-cap mutual fund managers failed to outperform the S&P index.

When I wrote the first edition of this book in 2020, the Mid-Year report didn't look much different. Through June of 2020, 87.2% of ALL domestic stock fund managers had underperformed the S&P since June of 2005. While that's a slight improvement, the first half of 2020 was a rollercoaster of equity volatility. The S&P reached all-time highs in February and then, with the onset of

Corona, dived downward in March. Millions of active traders bailed and were whipsawed by the market's gains and losses.

The same thing happened in 2022 with a huge drop in April, then again in August. Over a 24-year horizon back to 2000, more than 70% of actively managed funds failed to outperform their comparison index in 38 out of the 39 categories of equity and fixed income funds that SPIVA measures performance in.

SPIVA started in the US in 2002 and is now international in its review of fund performance. As the name suggests, they wanted to compare simple index performance against active managers whose job it is, based on their expertise, to pick stocks for their funds to invest in. SPIVA has access to a database of mutual fund data and they then compare funds of a particular type against an appropriate benchmark index. For example, large-cap US funds are compared against the S&P 500, mid-cap funds against the S&P MidCap 400, and so on. Then every six months they compute the data and ask how did the average fund do? How many of them beat their respective benchmark market index? How many of them "underperformed" (a more courteous term than "sucked")?

Unfortunately for mutual fund shareholders, typically the answer is that the very decisive majority of active funds sucked.

Meaning you would have been smarter than 90 plus percent of active expert mutual fund managers if you simply bought the S&P index and did nothing else.

Sound like a lot of statistical baloney? I thought so too at first, until I did a deep dive into SPIVA data and the researchers on the Dalbar QAIB team agree. From an October 2017 press release, they said:

"[The] *basics of mutual funds make it impossible for any more than 1% of investors to ever outperform an applicable index and causes the average investor to lag that index by several percentage points. Anyone who chooses to believe* [that a large percentage of mutual fund investors outperform the market] *should understand the myriads of performance limiting factors that guarantees that over 99% of investors have and will underperform indices:*

- *Non-uniform acquisition and withdrawal dates, performance is measured over specific time periods, but investors transact on every business day*
- *Sales charges (loads, 12-1 fees, redemption fees, etc.) are not included in the calculation of benchmark returns*
- *Operating expenses that pay for the management, operations and distribution of investments are not factored in*
- *Portfolio trading costs that are incurred every time a fund buys or sells a security are absent from equities or indices that trade "free"*
- *Asset allocations into low performing asset classes such as cash and other defensive investments*
- *Dividends and capital gains taken in cash are excluded since indices assume that all distributions are reinvested*

- *Leakage from loans, margin interest, fees or other deductions never occur in an index*
- *Opportunity cost of being out of the market during periods of appreciation is never experienced by an index which is assumed to always be fully "invested"*
- *Investor trading activity ebbs and flows unlike an index that reflects a buy and hold posture*
- *Psychological factors such as loss aversion, herding and excessive optimism do not influence the benchmarks*
- *The irrational belief that higher prices (expenses) will yield better investments is derived from consumerism where the expectation is that prices in some way reflect value*

The theory that most investors actually earn benchmark level returns is in contradiction to the fact that the balances in their individual accounts show underperformance".

Wow. Talk about getting spanked, eh? Even so, let's look at a real-world example. Unless you're in the high end of the financial industry, you may not know that over a decade ago Warren Buffett made an interesting wager. In his February 2017 letter to Berkshire Hathaway shareholders, in a section entitled "The Bet (or how your money finds its way to Wall Street)", Buffett outlined a unique wager he had made on a website called Longbets.org. Specifically, Buffett offered to bet that over a ten-year period from January 1, 2008, to December 31, 2017, the S&P 500 index would outperform a portfolio of hedge funds when performance is measured on a basis net of fees, costs, and all expenses, so at the time he wrote his letter to the shareholders, the timeframe of the bet wasn't quite finished.

In his letter, Buffett explained:

"Long Bets was seeded by Amazon's Jeff Bezos and operates as a non-profit organization that administers just what you'd guess: long-term bets. To participate, "proposers" post a proposition at Longbets.org that will be proved right or wrong at a distant date. They then wait for a contrary-minded party to take the other side of the bet. When a "doubter" steps forward, each side names a charity that will be the beneficiary if its side wins; parks its wager with Long Bets; and posts a short essay defending its position on the Long Bets website. When the bet is concluded, Long Bets pays off the winning charity.

Subsequently, I publicly offered to wager $500,000 that no investment pro could select a set of at least five hedge funds – wildly-popular and high-fee investing vehicles – that would over an extended period match the performance of an unmanaged S&P-500 index fund charging only token fees. I suggested a ten-year bet and named a low-cost Vanguard S&P fund as my contender. I then sat back and waited expectantly for a parade of fund managers – who could include their own fund as one of the five – to come forth and defend their occupation. After all, these managers urged others to bet billions on their abilities. Why should they fear putting a little of their own money on the line?

What followed was the sound of silence. Though there are thousands of professional investment managers who have amassed staggering fortunes by touting their stock-selecting prowess, only one man – Ted Seides – stepped up to my challenge. Ted was a co-manager of Protégé Partners, an asset manager that had raised money from limited partners to form a fund-of-funds – in other words, a fund that invests in multiple hedge funds.

For Protégé Partners' side of our ten-year bet, Ted picked five funds-of-funds whose results were to be averaged and compared against my Vanguard S&P index fund. The five he selected had invested their money in more than 100 hedge funds, which meant that the overall performance of the funds-of-funds would not be distorted by the good or poor results of a single manager.

Each fund-of-funds, of course, operated with a layer of fees that sat above the fees charged by the hedge funds in which it had invested. In this doubling-up arrangement, the larger fees were levied by the underlying hedge funds; each of the fund-of-funds imposed an additional fee for its presumed skills in selecting hedge-fund managers".

He then went on to publish the results of the wager to that date. In summarizing the data, he wrote:

Bear in mind that every one of the 100-plus managers of the underlying hedge funds [that Seides had chosen] *had a huge financial incentive to do his or her best. Moreover, the five funds-of-funds managers that Ted selected were similarly incentivized to select the best hedge-fund managers possible because the five were entitled to performance fees based on the results of the underlying funds.*

I'm certain that in almost all cases the managers at both levels were honest and intelligent people. But the results for their investors were dismal – really dismal. And, alas, the huge fixed fees charged by all of the funds and funds-of-funds involved – fees that were totally unwarranted by performance – were such that their managers were showered with compensation over the nine years that have passed. As Gordon Gekko might have put it: "Fees never sleep".

For those of you too young to understand that reference, Gordon Gekko is the fictional corporate raider and villain in the 1987 movie "Wall Street" and its 2010 sequel "Wall Street: Money Never Sleeps".

How "dismal" were the results? Buffett's pick, the S&P 500 index, gained 125.8% over those ten years. The five hedge funds picked by Protégé Partners head Ted Seides, had an average gain of about 36%.

In other words, the S&P index averaged about a 3.5 times better result than the "experts" using their expertise.

Later, in 2018, Buffett wrote about his winning the bet:

"Let me emphasize that there was nothing aberrational about stock-market behavior over the ten-year stretch. If a poll of investment 'experts' had been asked late in 2007 for a forecast of long-term common-stock returns, their guesses would have likely averaged close to the 8.5% actually delivered by the

S&P 500. Making money in that environment should have been easy. Indeed, Wall Street 'helpers' earned staggering sums. While this group prospered, however, many of their investors experienced a lost decade. Performance comes, performance goes. Fees never falter".

Beyond the cost of hidden fees in mutual funds, there are also other significant differences.

First, IUL cash values grow tax-deferred like any qualified plan (IRA, 401(k), 403(b)). Mutual funds don't — unless they are held *inside* a qualified plan. Meaning, with an IUL, your cash value benefits from triple compounding:

a) You earn interest on your premium investment;

b) You earn interest on your interest;

c) And you earn interest on the money you would otherwise have paid in taxes (and fees) on that interest.

Second, you control your taxes, not the fund manager. IULs grow tax-deferred and amounts over the already taxed paid in value are *never* taxed if distributions are taken in the form of policy loans (which can be paid back from your death benefit when you die).

Next, mutual funds often make taxable distributions to fund owners, even when their fund value has gone down. Since an IUL grows tax-deferred, it does not require any annual tax reporting when it increases in value, nor does it lose any money in a market downturn.

In some cases, a sharp increase in value, for example, mutual funds may cause taxation of your Social Security benefits. Again, the growth within the IUL is tax-deferred and since it is taken as tax-free income via loans, you, as the policy owner, are in control of your reportable income vs. the mutual fund manager, thus enabling you to reduce or even eliminate the taxation of your Social Security benefits.

Additionally, the record-keeping requirements for owning mutual funds are far more complicated. Having detailed records (redemptions, purchases, dates, values, commissions, etc.) is often an individual's only defense in the event of an IRS audit. When you own an IUL, the insurance company keeps your records. Copies of annual statements are mailed to the owner, and details of distributions (if any) are totaled and reported at year-end.

Owning mutual funds, dependent on the asset value, can also sometimes cause Medicaid disqualification. Nor do they inherently provide lifetime income. An IUL can provide their owners with a stream of income for their entire lifetime, regardless of how long they live. Plus, insurance is often classified so that it is not considered assets for Medicaid disqualification of nursing home costs. In contrast, mutual funds are almost always counted in the tally of Medicaid assets.

All IUL policies allow an owner's easy access to cash from their policy, often waiving any surrender penalties when such individuals suffer a serious illness, need at-home care, or become confined to a nursing home. Mutual funds do not provide a similar waiver and contingent deferred sales charges still apply to a mutual fund account whose owner needs to sell some shares to fund the costs of such a stay.

Indexed Universal Life insurance provides tax free death benefits to the beneficiaries of the IUL owners. Mutual funds provide no such guarantees or death benefits of any kind and assets in a mutual fund may be hit with estate taxes, further reducing the value to heirs.

IULs allow the tax-free exchange of one policy for another. A mutual fund owner cannot move funds from one mutual fund company to another without selling shares at the former (thus triggering a taxable event), and repurchasing new shares at the latter, often subject to sales charges at both.

Mutual funds don't provide cost-free asset rebalancing whereas IULs do. Rebalancing one's portfolio within a family of mutual funds always requires the sale and purchase of shares, often generating both taxes and commissions.

Lastly, mutual funds are at the mercy of the market 100% of the time.

Noting some other advice from the sage of Omaha, on making money from the stock market:

"[It] *does not require great intelligence, a degree in economics or a familiarity with Wall Street jargon,*" he wrote. "*What investors need instead is an ability to both disregard mob fears or enthusiasms and to focus on a few simple fundamentals. A willingness to look unimaginative for a sustained period – or even to look foolish – is also essential*".

In short, your investment plan should be boring and automatic. And the big question yet again is why put *anything* at risk if you don't have to?

Most so-called financial experts will answer "There's always a risk when you invest in the stock market".

My answer is: Consider the source. Why not take advantage of the gains without participating in the losses?

Chapter Sixteen

Death and Taxes

At age 83, Benjamin Franklin wrote a letter to French scientist Jean-Baptiste Leroy in 1789 that in it said, *"Our new Constitution is now established, and has an appearance that promises permanency; but in this world nothing can be said to be certain, except death and taxes"*.

Of course, he's right on the first part, and finding exclusionary methods on the second part is getting harder and harder.

Way back when, Social Security benefits were tax-free, but that all ended in 1983 with the signing of the Social Security amendments to keep the program from going broke. Now, up to 85% of benefits are taxed for those with incomes above certain levels. Higher-income taxpayers also pay a Medicare premium surtax; the higher the income, the higher the surtax.

Today, the first tax bracket typically allows the government to tax 50% of a retiree's Social Security income, and the second bracket moves up to the 85% level. Which means that for someone with a $1,000-per-month Social Security income, that either $500 or $850 could be subject to taxation along with any of the retiree's other income sources.

You're probably going to see similar changes come within the next decade. While Congress always talks as if such changes will only affect the wealthy, far too many people who consider themselves as middle class pay a bigger than fair share of these penalties. You'd be wise to prepare in advance to be one of them.

The problem stems from the fact that Social Security is primarily funded through a dedicated payroll tax which means that money contributed by the current American workforce is then later distributed to retirees who are eligible for the benefits (i.e., people who, themselves, paid into the program for decades). In other words, benefits are largely funded on a pay-as-you-go basis, with the contributions made by today's workers and businesses going to pay the benefits of currently retired individuals who worked and paid contributions in the past. There is no private account component to the U.S. Social Security system that safeguards and grows your contributions. They're paid out as soon as they come in.

Like a giant Ponzi scheme. And it's about to collapse.

According to the Social Security Administration's Agency Financial Report for Fiscal Year 2019, retirement benefits paid out each month had already exceeded the tax revenues and interest that fund the program. Social Security's annual deficit in 2023 was

$41.4 billion. That's a boatload of cash that has to come from somewhere.

The puzzle is that the number of benefit recipients is rising rapidly and the number of workers paying into the system is declining. For instance, the number of workers paying into the program was 16.5 per retiree in 1950; by 1960 that number was only 5.1; it has since declined to 2.8 in 2013 (the last date I was able to confirm from the Social Security Administration website www.ssa.gov) and is projected to decline to 2.1 by 2035. At the present rate of depletion, the Social Security Disability Insurance Trust Fund will be exhausted by 2035, with just enough money to cover 89% of benefits that year, according to the 2019 OASDI trustees' report. Other sources say only 77%.

Now consider that during the "Baby Boom" years, the highest birth rates were in 1957 through 1964, equaling 70% of that generation's population. That equates to an average of 11,200 Americans who turned 65 every day in 2024, and will again in 2025, and 2026. This record number of people reaching retirement age is known as "Peak 65" or the "silver tsunami". And while the number goes down slightly after 2026, it will still be 10,000+ every day until 2029.

It's a fact that Social Security is already paying out more in benefits than it receives in revenues. The actuarial deficit (meaning the difference – negative amount – between Social Security's obligations and the income rate of the Social Security Trust Funds at the present time) was 2.78% in 2019 when I first wrote about it. The program's projected annual deficits are expected to increase over the next several decades, reaching 5.08% of taxable payroll in 2080 and 4.64% in 2098.

That still sounds small but here's exactly what the OASDI says in their annual report published in June 2024:

"The OASDI actuarial deficit is 3.50 percent of taxable payroll for the 75-year projection period through 2098, which is smaller than the value of 3.61 percent of taxable payroll for the 75-year projection period through 2097 in last year's report. The open-group unfunded obligation for OASDI is 3.32 percent of taxable payroll over the 75-year projection period through 2098, which is smaller than the value of 3.42 percent of payroll over the 75-year projection period through 2097 in last year's report. Expressed in present-value dollars discounted to January 1, 2024, the open-group **unfunded obligation for OASDI is $22.6 trillion over the 75-year projection period through 2098. This value is $0.2 trillion more than the measured level in last year's report** of $22.4 trillion over the 75-year projection period through 2097, discounted to January 1, 2023."

And it goes on to say:

"The **OASI Trust Fund reserves are projected to become depleted in 2033**, at which time OASI income would be sufficient to pay 79 percent of OASI scheduled benefits."

That's not that far away anymore. Even worse, by 2050, nearly 20 million Americans are expected to be over the age of 85. And it's not just Boomers. A 2024 AARP survey found that 20% of *all* adults ages 50+ have no retirement savings. Who's going to support them if Social Security implodes?

Yep, you will, through some other yet-to-be enacted form of taxation.

You should know that this isn't the first time that Social Security's future has been threatened by its spending outpacing its incoming revenue. It also happened in 1982, hence the changes made in 1983 that I mentioned previously.

Back then Congress made, what were considered at the time, sweeping changes to put Social Security back (at least temporarily) on solid financial ground. Aside from subjecting some Social Security payments to federal income taxes when a retiree's income rises above specific levels for the first time in history, they increased payroll taxes and raised the "full" retirement age.

And the coming changes are unlikely to have any public input or debate. No one in Washington DC seems to understand that the longer they wait, the more severe those changes will need to be, so be prepared to have them presented to you down the road as a fait accompli.

On top of that, the cost of living adjustments (**COLA**) in Social Security payments for current retirees have been small to non-existent over the past few years. So, people have been forced to lower their expectations as to how much they'll be able to rely on Social Security to supplement their retirement income.

While I was writing the first edition of this book in 2020, the cost-of-living increase of 2.8% received in 2019, was the highest in seven years. That increased the average Social Security recipient's monthly benefit by about $39 – maybe enough for one fill-up at the gas station at the time if they had a small car. In 2020 it was back down to 1.6% but amid record high inflation in 2022, Retirees received an 8.7% increase to their benefits in 2023, the highest increase in 40 years. For 2025, that dropped back down to 2.5%.

However, what good are these cost-of-living increases if you'll almost always pay more for Medicare each year and likely pay more taxes on those benefits IF they do find a way to keep Social Security solvent. Currently, depending on your "provisional income" (a math problem we won't go into) up to 85% of your Social Security benefits are subject to federal income taxes.

While we're on the subject, you might be surprised to learn that you have no legal right to *any* Social Security benefit. They could actually shut it down if they can't agree on a way to fix it.

Naturally, most people think they are "entitled" to receive Social Security benefits since they've paid into the OASDI program for so long. But the mistake is in the second part of that last sentence. There is no Old-Age, Survivors and Disability "Insurance program" in the traditional (or legal) sense.

Our government perpetuates the belief that you are entitled to Social Security by referring to money taken out of your paycheck as "contributions" but Social Security is a tax like any other tax. In fact, just two years after the Social Security Act was signed into law, the U.S. Supreme Court case Helvering v. Davis, ruled that Social Security was NOT a contributory insurance program, saying, *"The proceeds of both the employee and employer taxes are to be paid into the Treasury like any other internal revenue generally, and are not earmarked in any way".*

Meaning, there is no real "trust fund" or "lock box" or any other separate account by any other name where that money is held. It's simply a line item on the General Accounting Office's ledger. It all goes into the U.S. Treasury's general account which can be used for *anything*. And unfortunately, our elected officials decided decades ago that it would be 'wise' to quietly spend all the surplus revenues in the system without any public debate.

Later, in 1960, in Fleming v. Nestor, Pp.363 U.S. 608-611, the Supreme Court ruled that *"A person covered by the Social Security Act has not such a right in old-age benefit payments as would make every defeasance of "accrued" interests violative of the Due Process Clause of the Fifth Amendment"*. Which means that you have no legally binding contractual rights to your Social Security benefits, and that those benefits can be cut or even totally eliminated at any time.

In other words, Social Security is not an insurance program at all. It is, and will always be, just a tax you'll pay based on your income. And any future Social Security benefits will always be subject to the caprice of whomever the 535 politicians in Congress may be.

If Social Security is still around after 2034, which, at this writing just a decade away, is still a big "IF", then you'll be entitled to its benefits. For now, without going into all the arithmetic that determines the rate, let's just assume that any Social Security benefits you receive in the future will be taxed at least at a 50% tax rate.

A poll by Newsweek found that recent inflation took a huge toll on the American public in terms of burning through their savings to pay for ordinary expenses. Fifteen percent said they only had between $1,000 to $5,000, 10% had savings of $5,000 to $10,000, 13% boasted $10,000 to $20,000 of cash in their bank accounts while only a meager 20% said they had more than $20,000. Those numbers challenge other studies, but right or wrong it's clear double digit gains in everyday prices caused a lot of people to break open their piggy banks.

Worse yet, according to investment account giant Charles Schwab, most Americans are planning for at least a 23-year retirement, which means that all the predictors tell us that the typical household will need $969,680 or more to pay the bills during that period.

Some of that will come from Social Security (maybe).

Today the average recipient will collect $1,862 per month in 2025, $22,344 annually (just $7,284 over the 2024 poverty threshold of $15,060 for individuals 65 and over, according to the US Dept. of Health and Human Services) in Social Security benefits. Multiply that by 23 years of retirement and you get $513,912. Do you see any problem with that?

That result points to the high probability that some 42% of Americans will have a potential $455,738 shortfall – per person – based on their current savings level of $0 to under $10,000. Imagine if there is only one breadwinner in the household, meaning only one person gets any Social Security benefits. Obviously, that doesn't bode well for anyone down the road, especially Millennials. Who's going to support them when they run out of money? If it's a new government program, count on your taxes to go *way* up.

Just to give you an idea of what might happen, on the following page is a historic look at the tax rates for both the highest and lowest income taxpayers (through 2018) going back to when the IRS first started. Compare the percentage changes after WWII from the high end to the low end, then consider the current national debt and the situation Social Security is in. Unless your plan is to be poor, it's pretty easy to see that your taxes have a good chance of going up in the future rather than down.

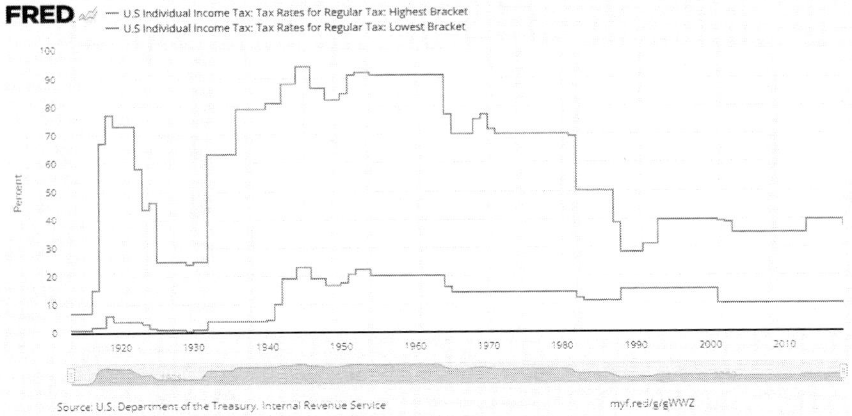

Any investments you have get taxed in different ways. Sales of **stocks, bonds and mutual funds** that have been held for more than a year are taxed at what are known as "***long-term capital gains***" rates. These rates can be quite favorable in some cases. For example, as of this writing, a single person won't pay any capital gains tax if their total taxable income for taxes paid in 2024 is $47.025 or less. The same is true for married taxpayers regardless of whether they file jointly or separately.

Single filers will be subject to a 15% on capital gains if their income is between $47.025 and $518,000 for 2024, and beyond that annual income total, the rate jumps to 20%.

However, married folks (filing either jointly or separately) don't get that big of a gap. Their top end for the 15% rate is only $291,850 (for 2024) and beyond that number they pay the 20% rate.

Additionally, those capital gains may also be subject to something called the Net Investment Income Tax (**NIIT**), which is an additional levy of 3.8% if the taxpayer's income is above certain 'threshold' amounts. The income thresholds depend on the filer's status (individual, married filing jointly, etc.) and aren't all that high, i.e., $200,000 for singles, $250,000 for married filing jointly and only $125,000 for married filing separately. Sometimes I think the folks who make the tax rules at the IRS purposefully favor people who aren't married simply because there tend to be fewer of them as income increases.

Short-term capital gains from sales of investments that were held for under a year are taxed at your ordinary income tax rate. And while the tax brackets for the 2025 tax year, set by the 2017 Tax Cuts and Jobs Act, aren't changing, the cutoffs for each band of taxation will shift slightly higher.

The tax rates will remain at 10, 12, 22, 24, 32, 35 and 37 percent, respectively. However, if your income didn't go up too much, you'll get a break because it will take more income to reach each higher band of taxation. For instance, a single taxpayer who earns $100,000 in 2025 will have a top marginal tax rate of 22% (in 2024 it was 24%), whereas someone who earns just over $3,351 more ($103,351), will have a marginal tax rate of 24%. The top marginal rate of 37% in 2025 will apply to individuals with incomes above $626,350 or $751,600 for a couple, an increase of about 2.8% from 2024.

If you purchased any ***annuities*** that provide a stream of income in retirement, the portion of the payment that represents your principal is tax-free; the rest is taxable. For example, if you purchased an annuity with $100,000 and in 10 years it is worth $185,000, you would only pay tax on the $85,000 of interest earned. The insurance company that sold you the annuity is required to tell you what is taxable and what is not.

Different rules apply if you bought the annuity with pretax funds (such as from a traditional IRA). In that case, 100% of your annuity payment will be taxed as ordinary income. In addition, be aware that you'll have to pay any taxes that you owe on the annuity at your ordinary income-tax rate, not the preferable capital gains rate despite the fact that you may not have had access to that money for decades while it accumulated value.

Dividends are the profits gained from stocks.

There are two types of dividends, taxed at different rates. Qualified dividends, which are typically the most common type of dividends that investors receive, are taxed at long-term capital gains rates. And non-qualified dividends are taxed at your ordinary income tax rate, which is generally higher than the capital gains rate.

It sounds confusing, but to be considered as "qualified," dividends you receive have to be held for at least 60 days during a 120-day period which begins 60 days before the "ex-dividend" date. The ex-dividend date is the day after a company distributes dividend payments to its shareholders.

Note that if the dividends originate from a tax-deferred account funded with pretax dollars (like a 401(k) or IRA) and the dividends are reinvested, then they aren't subject to taxes at that time. But when you start making withdrawals, they will be taxed at your ordinary income tax rate.

Income you receive that is ***interest payments*** from things like Certificates of Deposit, simple savings accounts and money market accounts will be taxed at your ordinary income tax rate.

The interest on ***municipal bonds*** is not taxed at the federal level, but capital gains from the sale of these bonds can be taxed. Interest from bonds that are issued in an investor's home state is commonly exempt from state income taxes as well.

Keep in mind that although municipal bonds are tax-free, interest earned will be factored into calculating Social Security taxation.

A huge majority of ***pensions*** are funded with pretax dollars, so that means the full amount of your pension income would be taxable. Distributions from either private or government pensions are usually taxable at your ordinary income rate, assuming you made no after-tax contributions to the plan.

The tax rate you'll pay on a ***traditional IRA and 401(k) and 403(b)*** withdrawals would be at your ordinary federal income tax rate. And unless you live in one of seven states with no income taxes at all, you can expect your home state to ding you in retirement as well.

Savers love these kinds of tax-deferred retirement accounts because they don't pay taxes on their contributions. Their contributions reduce their taxable incomes, saving them money on their tax bills in the current year. And, of course, their savings, dividends and investment gains continue to grow on a tax-deferred basis, but what they tend to forget is that they do have to pay taxes down the line when they retire and start taking withdrawals, and those taxes apply to both their contributions *and* their gains. Plus, at some point, you must withdraw money from the accounts. The IRS forces you to take Required Minimum Distributions (RMDs) beginning no later than age 73 for holders of traditional IRAs and 401(k)s. The minimum RMD percentage is determined by various factors including the age of the account holder and the account balance, and the percentage that the IRS requires you to withdraw each year goes up as you get older. And keep in mind that *any* withdrawal from these types of accounts is taxed as ordinary income, *not* as capital gains, and depending on where you live, your state may want taxes from that withdrawal as well.

Unlike their 401(k) and traditional IRA cousins — which are funded with pretax dollars — ***Roth IRAs*** come with a long-term tax advantage. You pay the taxes on your contributions to a Roth up front, so your Roth withdrawals are tax-free once you retire.

Fair warning though, you must have held your account for at least five years before you can take any tax-free withdrawals. Even though you can withdraw the amount you *contributed* at any time tax-free, like with a traditional IRA, you must be at least age 59½ to be able to withdraw the gains or you'll face the same 10% early withdrawal penalty.

In contrast, life insurance proceeds paid to a beneficiary because of the insured person's death are not taxable. And, under IRS rules, there is no tax liability to fret about as your money builds up and your cash value grows because the earnings inside the policy are tax deferred. Once the account has built up enough cash, and you want to start taking money out, insurance policies will allow you to take tax-free distributions. That means a much bigger chunk is spendable cash for you.

Now, imagine a secure retirement without ***any*** tax liability.

Zero. Zilch. Nada. So, you don't have to worry about *any* of the mind-numbing information you just read in the last few pages.

You can access the cash for any reason by taking tax-free loans or even partial surrenders that are also tax-free as long as your IUL is structured properly and doesn't become something called a Modified Endowment Contract (which I'll explain in a minute). This system of withdrawing the cash creates a completely IRS approved, tax-free method of supplementing your retirement plan while still having the tax-free death benefit for your surviving loved ones.

It took a while for the insurance industry to figure out how to do this right.

Tax-free growth is one of the principal advantages of cash value life insurance, and in the mid 1970's social instability and cultural change were making traditional Whole Life insurance irrelevant to the needs of large segments of the consumer market. By the early 1980's, consumers were facing a triple whammy of double-digit inflation, double digit unemployment and double-digit interest rates. Consequently, many competitive life insurance carriers looking for ways to attract new business took wholesale advantage of the tax-free growth element by offering single-premium and Universal Life products that featured substantial cash value accumulation.

The appeal of an insurance plan that was as cost effective as Term Life, but at the same time offered (at the time) double digit growth of cash value and tax protection of that internal growth had enormous appeal, and as result, market share grew massively – especially among the wealthy. Imagine paying a single premium of $250,000 to fund a $250,000 face value policy and then enjoying immediate double digit tax deferred growth of the cash value of that policy AND tax free benefits to your beneficiaries. Policy owners could then withdraw both the interest and principal as a tax-free loan, and as long as the policy did not lapse before the owner's death, there was no tax consequence. Of course, this strategy effectively allowed the policy to function as a large scale tax shelter and that didn't go unnoticed.

Using insurance as a tax shelter was certainly not a new idea. The wealthy had been using cash value generating Whole Life policies as a perfectly legal method for stashing cash out of the grasp of the tax man since before the turn of the 20th century but when it looked like it might become more mainstream, the government interceded.

Congress decided that life insurance shouldn't be used in that manner and in response, Section 7702 of the United States

Internal Revenue Code was written as part of the Deficit Reduction Act of 1983. Shortly thereafter, they passed the Technical and Miscellaneous Revenue Act of 1988 (TAMRA).

For the first time Section 7702 defined what is considered life insurance for federal tax purposes and imposes limitations on premiums and compensation related to death benefits. It applies to all life insurance contracts issued after 1985. TAMRA created what's called a **Modified Endowment Contract, or MEC**. A MEC is a tax qualification of a life insurance policy whose cumulative premiums exceed federal tax law limits.

Specifically, a life insurance policy is considered an MEC by the IRS if it meets three criteria:

- First, the policy is entered into on or after June 20, 1988. Life insurance policies entered into prior to that date are not subject to the payment of premiums over the money allowed under federal laws. However, the renewal of an older life insurance policy after this date is considered new and must be assessed with what's called the "7-pay test".
- Second, it has to conform to the statutory definition of a life insurance policy under Section 7702.
- Third, the policy must pass the TAMRA "7-pay test". Policies become a MEC when the 7-pay test determines that the total amount of premiums paid into a life insurance policy, within the first seven years, is *more* than what was required to have the policy considered "paid up" in those same seven years.

That's a lot of government and insurance double-speak to explain that the taxation structure and IRS policy classification change after a life insurance is classified as a MEC. And not in a good way.

Unlike traditional life insurance policies, taxes on gains are considered regular income for MEC withdrawals under what is referred to as last-in, first-out (LIFO) accounting. For that reason alone, we want to avoid the classification of a Modified Endowment Contract. And, for withdrawals before the age of 59 1/2, a premature withdrawal penalty of 10% generally applies which, all together, translates into significantly more taxation.

MEC limitations expire after seven years, so long as no material changes to the policy occur. But once a policy has been classified as a MEC, that classification is irrevocable and it cannot regain its former tax advantages under any circumstances, so naturally, we want to avoid your IUL policy ever becoming a MEC.

Next, for all intents and purposes, we must also consider inflation as a "stealth" tax. As I write this near the end of 2024, according to Bloomberg, since the Federal Reserve started raising interest rates in 2022 to curb the highest inflation rate in a generation, the middle class has lost more than $2 trillion in wealth - due entirely to inflationary expense. The government doesn't collect it from us directly, but the inflation rate is adjusted from time to time by the Federal Reserve when it raises or lowers interest rates.

High interest rates are bad too. Loans are more expensive and harder to come by and people found out the hard way in the 1980s that while getting a 10% return on CDs sounds great, when the inflation rate was 13.5%, they were actually seeing a 3.5% *decrease* in the value of their money.

Unfortunately, the alternative is deflation, which is actually worse. Consider that if your money was worth more tomorrow than it is today, few people would be spending. That would bring the economy to a standstill, people would lose jobs left and right because companies couldn't afford to keep them and with no income, you can't buy anything, no matter how far the prices fall. Obviously not good. This is why the Federal Reserve will adjust our monetary policy sporadically, but usually only enough that no one complains too loudly, hoping none of the public at large will notice slight changes. However, even if the Fed keeps inflation rates relatively low, it steadily eats away at the value of our nest eggs over time.

The biggest problem with having *any* money in a taxable account when you retire is that you really can't predict how much money you'll eventually have. Since no one can confidently predict what the tax rates will be in the future, the percentage the government will take from you becomes a moving target. And it's certainly hard to plan for the future when you don't know how much money you'll actually be able to keep.

Prepare for that.

Chapter Seventeen

Planning your plan

In study after study, the top lessons that current retirees would pass along to today's pre-retirees are: start saving earlier, save more, and plan on retiring later.

In a recent poll by The American College of Financial Services, a panel of Retirement Income Certified Professionals was asked what 'one thing' they wished their clients understood better about planning for the cost of retirement. The respondents said consumers typically underestimate the amount of savings they should have stashed away in their 401k or other retirement accounts — by a wide margin.

The poll found that advisors strongly agree that knowledge is lacking in several other areas, as well. For example, those surveyed believed clients need to acknowledge the importance of comprehensive retirement *income* planning, "including scope, the need to start planning early and the importance of continuing to plan *through* retirement".

According to advisors who responded to the poll, creating a detailed strategy should be a priority for consumers, not an afterthought. Clients largely overlook retirement risks too, such as "longevity risk, long-term care risk, health expense risk and inflation risk". Advisors said it is an *essential component* to success for retirement savers to identify potential unexpected expenses and design methods of dealing with each before it occurs.

Correspondingly, the latest results of the Wells Fargo/Gallup Investor and Retirement Optimism Index survey, of adults with $10,000 or more invested in stocks, bonds or mutual funds, either within or outside of a retirement savings account, shows that most non-retired U.S. investors have not carefully calculated how much money they will need in retirement or whether their retirement accounts will cover their annual expenses. Only one in five say they have done each of these calculations, two in five admit that they have not given much thought to either, and one-third say they have only roughly estimated what their retirement expenses and revenue might be.

Let's say you're 35 today and want to retire in 30 years at age 65. Assume you want to be retired for 30 years and replace at least half of your income in retirement from just your savings. Most retirement apps will say you need to invest 15% of your income a year and that's a good benchmark for anyone. However, if you plan to work just five years longer — and retire at 70 — most apps will say you'll only need to save about 7.5% a year. Both of these calculations assume an 80/20 equity to bond investment mix (the standard for investment based retirement savings plans).

So, what does that tell you?

It should tell you that simply the fact that you're reading this book puts you way ahead of the crowd, but it's the design, implementation, discipline and execution that will make your retirement savings plan a success, not just the vehicle you use. The old axiom of "Those who fail to plan, plan to fail" most certainly applies to saving for retirement.

In terms of getting some idea of what it's going take (numerically) for you to retire there is a good "When can I retire?" calculator online at;

networthify.com/calculator/earlyretirement?income

There you can plug in numbers about your after tax income, savings rate, average investment return, etc., and it will show you how many years it will take to reach a point where you can withdraw 4% (or your own percentage) annually and expect to cover your expenses. However, even that calculator is flawed, since it assumes your income will never go up over time and it has no input for inflation or assumptions of increases in your own expenses. Finding how to reach the right number is easy if you know what it is.

There is also a simple interactive calculator that uses sliding scales with assumptions for increases over time at:

bankrate.com/retirement/retirement-plan-calculator/

The first thing you have to do when you plan for your retirement is figure out what it is that you really want. Do you really want a life of leisure starting at some early age or are you the kind of person that loves their work so much that they'd feel lost without something to do every day that's related to your business? Remember, things will change over the coming decades and your preferences for how you'd like to live your golden years may change too. The old adage "Expect the best but prepare for the worst" applies here.

Not to mention that your life expectancy may be much greater than the 84-86 average today. And as people start living longer the biggest challenge may not be simply saving money. It may well be figuring out how to stay in the workforce well into one's 70s and perhaps 80s.

You should also consider the possibility that by the time you die, your children may be in their 40s, 50s or 60s. Wealth passed on may not be as useful at that point as when they were younger. That's a reason that tax free "inheritances" might be planned to be shared earlier, or instead, being given to grandchildren or even great-grandchildren, as a leg up for their future.

I'll say this about planning to leave a legacy: there is little value in passing on your wealth if you don't pass on your wisdom along with it. The real truth is that wealth does not create wisdom, however, wisdom has the ability to both create and maintain wealth.

Everyone has heard stories of lottery winners, or young highly paid athletes that burned through their wealth in what would seem to be the blink of an eye. The old maxim that money doesn't bring happiness is true, money brings opportunity, and capitalizing on that opportunity the right way can certainly make not just your life easier, but, done right, the lives of generations that follow you.

Money (especially when coupled with the knowledge of how to use it wisely) passed along to the right person at the right time could change your whole family tree. So, sit down a minute and do some self-reflecting and then put your thinking cap on.

When you think about how and where to put your money to save for the future, these 5 things should be critical components of your plan:

- Capital preservation. Remember, it's not what you make, it's what you keep. *Don't lose money!*
- A rate of return sufficient to *far* exceed the rate of inflation.
- Expectations based on *realistic* objectives. The market does not compound at 7% or more, the Millennial Money Tree strategy does.
- Higher rates of return should not require an exponential increase in the underlying risk. Why risk anything if you don't have to?
- You can regain lost money, but you can never replace lost time. Time is the most precious commodity that you cannot afford to lose.

One of the most important aspects of a good IUL is that it covers all five of those critical components with the right "design". And by that, I mean what mechanisms are included, what length of time horizon it has to build cash value, what kind of living benefits or riders are included, what (if any) distributions are planned and when, just to name a few. And while your financial advisor or insurance agent who will be helping you create that design will know better about what to include and what not to include (both of equal importance, and that part you need to leave to the experts), it's always wise to know what those moving parts are, what they do for you, how they impact your policy over time *and* whether they cost extra.

We'll go through all the parts of an IUL from more of a standpoint of building a foundation than one of practical application in this chapter. Later, I'll show you how various combinations work in application. But first, there's an important rule you need to know and understand that will help you make decisions about most any investment. That is the **Rule of 72**.

The "Rule of 72" is a mathematical formula that tells you how long an investment will take to double in value, given a fixed annual rate of interest or average investment return.

How it works is like this: Suppose you had the opportunity to invest $1000 in something that would guarantee an annual 10% return (for ease of math I'm using round numbers) or had an interest rate of 10%. How long would it take for your money to double to $2,000? Most people will say 10 years. Ten years of 10% is 100%, right?

Wrong. The answer is not 10 years; it's 7.2 years because over time you're earning interest on the interest you earned! That's called **compounding**, hence the term compound interest, and it is the magic behind the time value of money.

The equation is simple: Dividing 72 by your annual interest rate (or your rate of return) equals the number of years it takes for your investment to double.

For example: 72/6 (the interest rate) = 12 (the number of years before your investment doubles). Let's try it with a 7.5% interest rate.

72/7.5 = 9.6

Or just over nine and a half years for your investment to double in value.

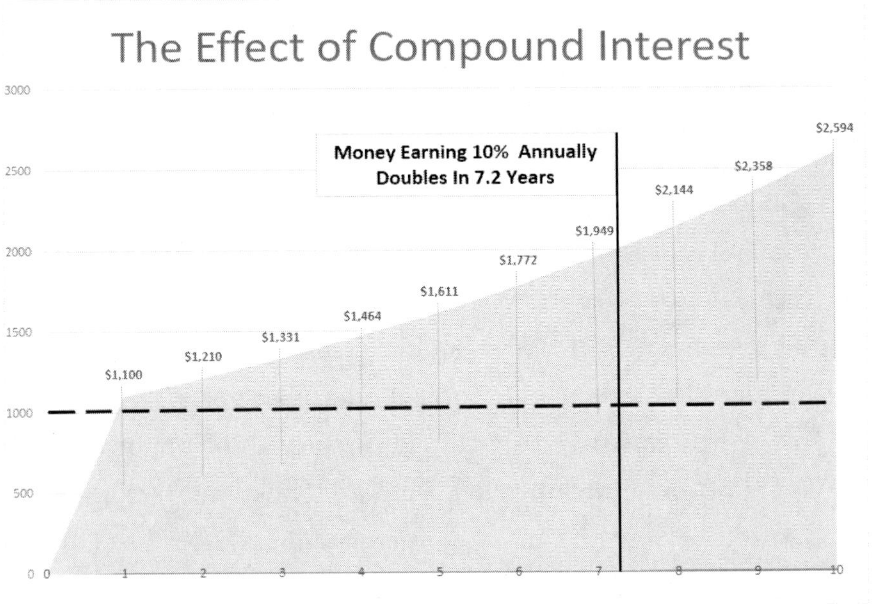

Pretty simple, right?

And in reverse, divide 72 by the number of years you want your investment to double to find the investment return you'll need to make that happen. i.e.: 72/9.6 = 7.5 (percent).

However, compound interest is a double-edged sword in that it's how credit card companies make money too. The interest on your debt piles up quickly and eats up most of your payment if you only pay the minimum payment each month, meaning they make far more than you originally financed.

We've already agreed that you should pay off any credit card you have every month and never carry over a balance, but if you think that's a grey area, let me spell it out to you in black and white

– **paying interest on credit cards is one of the worst financial mistakes you can make**. The interest on any credit card will regularly exceed the long-term returns on anyone's investment portfolio. Credit cards should be paid off immediately and always. If it seems like I keep banging that idea on your head throughout this book, it's because I do.

Don't throw away money on credit card interest payments!

I also caution against applying for any credit card with a high amount of cash back or frequent flier miles or whatever the reward might be **if** it has a higher than average interest rate.

I get it. You're thinking the interest rate doesn't matter since you *intend* to pay off the balance every month and thus incur no interest charge. Here's the problem. For some people, credit cards are like alcohol to an alcoholic. Going cold turkey is tough and the occasional relapse can turn into a binge that will cost you dearly. So, until you're in a place where you are totally disciplined to *never* carry *any* credit card balance…***ever***…go for the cards with a good rewards package *and* lower interest rates.

A famous quote that's often attributed to Albert Einstein (in truth, no one knows who really said it first) says of compound interest "*He who understands it, **earns** it. He who doesn't, **pays** it*", the point being that compounding rewards the saver and penalizes the debtor.

You can find a very cool Rule of 72 'calculator' online at moneychimp.com/features/rule72.htm .

Just as important as how much you save is *when* you start.

Today is good, yesterday would have been better.

That said, I've always found that telling people how compound interest works on their behalf over time never really sinks in, but showing them an example of how timing can make a big difference, even using small amounts of money has a much better chance of making an impression that they'll take action on. With that in mind, here's a good example of how procrastination will hurt you:

Imagine that John and Mary were born the same day.

Mary's father is a prosperous and generous man. He promises Mary that he will pay for her college tuition on three conditions, 1) that she gets a job, any job, even as a waitress, year round while she's in school and 2) invests at least $37.50 a week ($150 per month) until she turns 26, in a tax-deferred account that he knows will earn an average of 7% annually in growth and dividends *and* 3) that she uses that money for her retirement fund and never, ever, touches it until she is 65 years old except in a dire emergency. Mary never puts another dime into that account after age 25.

John's father doesn't have that kind of money. John pays for his own schooling by working full time as a landscaper and works hard enough that he makes enough to pay for school, all his living expenses and then some. But John parties a lot and doesn't get serious about saving any money for retirement until he gets married, has kids and starts his own landscaping business at age 30 and his wife tells him it's time to get serious about their future. Then he starts investing in the same tax-deferred account that Mary invested in (making 7% average total gain annually) and he invests the same amount per month, $150, every month ($1,800 a year) until he is 65 years old.

At age sixty-five, who do you think has more money?

It's gotta be John, right? He invested way more money over time. Right?

	Mary		John	
18	$1,800.00	$1,926.00		
19	$1,800.00	$3,986.82		
20	$1,800.00	$6,191.90		
21	$1,800.00	$8,551.33		
22	$1,800.00	$11,075.92		
23	$1,800.00	$13,777.24		
24	$1,800.00	$16,667.64		
25	$1,800.00	$19,760.38		
26		$21,143.61		
27		$22,623.66		
28		$24,207.31		
29		$25,901.83		
30		$27,714.95	$1,800.00	$1,926.00
35		$38,871.66	$1,800.00	$13,777.24
40		$54,519.51	$1,800.00	$30,399.21
45		$76,466.43	$1,800.00	$53,712.39
50		$107,248.13	$1,800.00	$86,410.33
55		$150,421.05	$1,800.00	$132,270.88
60		$210,973.30	$1,800.00	$196,592.68
61		$225,741.44	$1,800.00	$212,280.17
62		$241,543.34	$1,800.00	$229,065.78
63		$258,451.37	$1,800.00	$247,026.38
64		$276,542.97	$1,800.00	$266,244.23
65		**$295,900.97**	$1,800.00	**$286,807.32**

As shown in these abbreviated tables, surprisingly, it's Mary.

By almost $10,000 dollars. Even though Mary didn't add any more money to the account after age 25 (just 8 years for a total of $14,400 invested) while John paid in the same amount annually for 35 years (a total of $63,000 invested – more than four times what

Mary invested), he still comes up short in comparison. That is the amazing magic of compounding over time.

The point of that example is that *now* is the best time to start saving. However small. Don't put it off. And even if you have to cut back or stop for some period later, the money that you put in now will work for you 24/7/365 while you sleep, even if you do little else.

But if you set up your Money Tree plan correctly, you can take money out whenever you need it and pay yourself back over time. We'll demonstrate how that works in another chapter, however, let's get back to setting up *your* overall financial plan.

A good first step, in creating any good financial plan involves what we'll call buckets. "Buckets" is also a term used in insurance lingo for the fund (or funds) that you allocate your money to in an IUL, and for this purpose the definition is nearly the same – where you are allocating your net income.

Of course, you've already created a budget that you're going to stick to like glue, but these buckets will merely describe some broader sections of that budget. There are three buckets:

Bucket #1 is your **Liquid Capital** – this is your day-to-day living expenses, meaning money you can't invest because the time it lingers in your pocket before you spend it is too short a timeframe. However, this also includes your emergency fund of a minimum of three months (preferably six months or more) of your regular day-to-day expenses (food, rent or mortgage, utilities, insurance, student loan or other debt payments, etc.), anything that absolutely has to be paid every month, needs to be included in that emergency fund. This bucket is made up of cash on hand, whether it's in your pocket, in a checking or savings account at the bank or credit union or stuffed under your mattress, this is money that you can get access to preferably 24/7 for emergencies, or at the very worst, within 48 hours (holidays being a hindrance sometimes). An emergency fund does *not* include using a credit card unless it is absolutely a last resort.

The one place you *never* want to keep money for your emergency fund is in any kind of investment or margin account. Even if you have access to some of the capital without selling any of the equities in play. You might be shaking your head now thinking: "If I leave that much cash in the bank, I'll earn practically nothing on it". And that's entirely accurate these days, but look at it this way, when you fund a savings account, your emergency cash stash is protected from any risk (provided you stick within FDIC limits of $250,000 or less, and let's face it, 99.99% of us will). This means that if you put $12,000 in the bank, you're guaranteed to have that same $12,000 (plus whatever modicum of interest is added on, less any monthly service fees) available to you exactly when you need it. Not a week later. Most banks have money market accounts that pay a decent interest rate and still give you immediate access to your money.

Plus, you'll have the peace of mind that you won't have to worry about any market activity or political turmoil or any of the myriads of other possibilities that might cause equity values to fall off a cliff without any warning. And you also won't have to bear the risk of potentially taking a serious investment loss because you needed money at the worst possible time.

Bucket #2 is your **At-Risk Capital** – this includes ANY investments you have made. Whether it's in a brokerage account, a 401(k) or an IRA. Or even precious metals and cryptocurrencies. And this includes non-liquid capital, like the equity in your house or rental properties. This is money that may increase in value, but it may substantially decrease in value as well. Even money that is invested in your own business is at-risk capital. Things happen, businesses go bankrupt every day. Any money you have invested anywhere that has the ability to decrease in value is at-risk capital. As you learn more about the Money Tree strategy, you'll want less and less in this bucket.

The ONE AND ONLY exception to that last sentence is currently Bitcoin. However, you must completely understand how Bitcoin cycles work to fully take advantage of the ups and downs of the king of cryptocurrencies. If you want to learn more about that, read this blog post: .millennialmoneytree.blog/investing-in-bitcoin-101.

Bucket #3 is your **Safe Money** bucket. This is money invested in things that *guarantee* growth with no loss of principal – ever! This bucket includes things like Treasuries, CDs, annuities, and cash value life insurance products (not Term Life or even traditional Universal Life).

Before you have any at-risk capital invested anywhere, you need to have at least a 3-month emergency fund. Once you have that, you can start your Millennial Money Tree strategy using an IUL and any excess beyond that can go into some at-risk investment but not before. Period.

Naturally, you'll want to make sure you understand all the IUL related jargon, so you'll know what's what.

Knowing the language of Indexed Universal Life will help you better understand your advisor's recommendations and what components are critical versus just 'nice to have' or, worse, a deal breaker.

You've learned a lot of it already, so I'm not going to insult your intelligence by including a whole glossary of terms in this book when you can very easily do that research on your own. Simply Google "glossary of insurance terms" and you'll find all the definitions you need, but I'll explain all the key terms of an IUL as we build it.

Obviously the first thing you're going to need to know is your budget for the premium for the IUL. How much can you afford to spend per month in premium and not take food off your table to do so? You can tap into your emergency fund to start an IUL only if you can replace that money within a month or two at the most. My advice is to make the initial premium hard to bear the first few years, and the payoff will be handsome. The reward for scrimping and saving early on is to be able to live carefree later.

We can approach this several ways:

Determine what kind of money you will need on an annual basis in retirement to be able to live out your life in the standard of living that you aspire to. Then back into that. Don't sweat it. Your advisor will show you how to figure out the design once you have the numbers, but here are some things to consider.

In "the good old days", a decade or so before the Corona virus downturn, conventional wisdom centered on a retirement strategy you may have heard before called "The 4 Percent Rule", which assumed you had a lump sum of cash in an investment fund, and that if you would only withdraw 4% from your investments the first year of retirement and adjust it upward annually based on inflation, you should never run out of money. The four percent rule was created using historical data based on stock and bond returns over the 50-year period from 1926 to 1976. Prior to the early 1990s, 5% was considered a safe amount for retirees to withdraw each year. However, in 1994, skeptical of whether this amount was sufficient, a financial advisor named William Bengen conducted a wide-ranging study of historical returns, with a heavy focus on severe market downturns that occurred in the 1930s and early 1970s. Bengen determined that even during volatile adverse markets, no historical circumstance existed in which a 4% annual withdrawal depleted a retirement portfolio in less than 33 years.

While its validity was confirmed by many financial researchers of the day, unfortunately, in the last two decades we've experienced some unprecedented "historical circumstances". Meaning that in a highly volatile stock market, combined with low interest rates, the 4% rule will put you at risk of running short on cash. While interest rates aren't what you'd call 'low' now (in Q4 of 2024) when you plan your IUL, the amount you take out will be based on what your cash (surrender) value is at the time you start to take your distributions. The economic environment might be vastly different then. And of course, you'll want to plan those distributions based on your life expectancy or in a way that you'll never run out of money, guaranteed by the insurance company.

Not to mention that this isn't 1994 anymore. You have a computer in your pocket that has access to applications that can easily determine what your actual "spend down" rate should be, no guessing involved, yet some pundits still talk as if the 4% "rule of thumb" is the default you should depend on. Others say it should be more like 2.5%. You'll need to be the final judge on that because you'll be able to change it at will.

On the flip side of the coin, while (again) there is no magic number that applies to everyone, many financial planners agree you will need about 70 to 80 percent of your current income to maintain your standard of living in retirement and that you should save enough to target that level of spending on an annual basis. The theory behind the lower percentage rule is logical because you may no longer have the expense of commuting to work (if you commuted to begin with), you also won't have payroll taxes withheld or incur other work-related expenses and are less likely to have ongoing debt like a mortgage payment.

However, there are conflicting studies that say it's either spot on or too high. Regardless, you should avoid a "one-size-fits-all" formula in developing your retirement plan and instead personalize your plan based on your individual goals and your preferred lifestyle in the golden years. And when you're planning on the number you think you'll need to hit, there are other factors to consider *beyond* just a percentage of your current income.

For instance, while your plans for retirement probably don't include having to deal with a serious malady, reality dictates that people face more health challenges as they get older. In fact, according to the annual Nationwide Retirement Institute® survey, one in three retirees say health issues are changing their retirement plans in ways they hadn't planned for.

When you experience health problems at whatever age, physical limitations may be compounded by financial struggles. Those problems often exacerbate as you get older. Today, too many seniors are not adequately prepared to cover the costs of healthcare because they incorrectly believed that Medicare provided more comprehensive coverage.

While that's as much an educational issue as a financial literacy one, in reality, according to a study conducted by Employee Benefit Research Institute, someone who uses a lot of prescription drugs might need as much as $370,000 to have just a 90% chance of affording proper care during retirement. And that's factoring in a supplemental Medigap plan (insurance that you buy from a private company to pay health care costs not covered by Medicare, such as co-payments, deductibles, and health care if you travel outside the U.S.) paying for some costs outside of Medicare coverage.

The bottom line? Know how you'll cover healthcare costs. This could include adding living benefit riders to your IUL (if they're not automatically included in the base policy) or buying ancillary or supplemental insurance like some companies such as Aflac offer that will pay for costs your health insurance doesn't cover. Not to mention that having a huge cash value policy that you can borrow from tax free should you need it, wouldn't hurt.

Along those same lines, you should also be prepared to need long-term care (LTC) for at least some period in your life, just in case.

Once you've reached the age of 65, there's about a 70% chance you'll need either assisted living or full-blown nursing-home care at some point. Nursing homes cost an arm and a leg by most people's standards, and Medicare and most health insurance policies don't pay anything unless you qualify for a skilled-nursing facility with specialized care — most people don't. If you don't want to spend every dime you've saved on nursing-home care, you need a plan to pay for care in a facility or long-term care at home.

I know what you're thinking.

"A nursing home?!? That's forever and a day away. I don't need to worry about that stuff right now, I have enough on my plate".

I get it. It does seem like you have plenty of time to act on that stuff later, but I'm going to continually beat you with the "Do it now" stick because in what will seem like the blink of an eye it'll be 10-20-30 years from now and you'll be kicking yourself for not planning ahead. If you don't start planning now, when exactly will you start?

Plans without action are dreams. Execution equals progress.

Ruminate on that, but let's get back to the subject.

Choices to cover LTC expenses could include buying long-term care insurance — which can become prohibitively expensive or come with coverage limits or having an LTC rider embedded in your IUL — or working with a good estate planning attorney to create a trust to protect your assets while allowing you to qualify for means-tested Medicaid, or some combination of the above.

Medicaid pays for nursing-home care, but you can't qualify if you have more than a few thousand dollars in net worth. However, there are certain perfectly legal ways to structure ownership of your wealth so you *can* get covered. Obviously, you'll need to act well before you need care if you hope to safeguard the maximum amount of assets through Medicaid planning, since Medicaid reviews five years of historic transactions to determine if you've made improper asset transfers in the years immediately before trying to qualify for coverage. Don't be dodgy. They will catch you and you'll end up paying a penalty or not qualifying at all.

Naturally, having a million plus dollars in reserve makes a significant difference in what your options are, but a large balance in and of itself doesn't guarantee a secure retirement. The real question is whether your nest egg will be able to generate enough income (combined with Social Security benefits, if they're still available when you retire) to maintain your standard of living in retirement.

There are plenty of retirement income calculators out there on the internet where you enter information such as your age, current income, how much you have saved already and how much you're saving annually for your retirement, and the calculator will estimate your chances of being able to retire on schedule with sufficient income. Here's a short list of ones that I've found that provide you with some realistic data:

One that I've found that does a respectable job in calculating most of the critical components is from T. Rowe Price. The URL is:

https://www.troweprice.com/usis/advice/tools/retirement-income-calculator

This one from Kiplinger will give you a very realistic number for what you should be saving each month from now until you retire (based on your current assets and other assumptions). That URL is:

https://www.kiplinger.com/retirement/retirement-planning/600895/retirement-savings-calculator

And this one from SmartAsset.com lets you change the inputs very easily to see what even minor changes would do long term. The URL is:

https://smartasset.com/retirement/retirement-calculator

If your probability of success is uncomfortably low, then you'll want to re-run the analysis to see how small changes like saving more, investing differently, and/or delaying retirement a year or two (or more) might improve your chances. Showing what you might take as a distribution from an IUL as "other income" will help you determine if you'd be on track with an IUL. Obviously, these tools are considerably basic, but they could give you a better understanding of the kind of ballpark annual investment you'll need in an IUL.

A few comments about retirement calculators and Social Security:

All the retirement calculators that I've seen include some factor for Social Security benefits. Almost everyone overestimates what Social Security will do for them because they think their benefits will be bigger than they eventually turn out to be. According to a

Nationwide Retirement Institute® Consumer Social Security PR Study, most future retirees expect they'll receive nearly a third more than the average monthly benefits received by current retirees.

Also keep in mind that no matter how much money you made during your working years, the absolute maximum monthly Social Security benefit for someone retiring at age 70 in 2025 is only $4,994 ($59,928 a year). More importantly, that maximum amount is only payable to those who had the annual maximum taxable earnings ($176,100 in 2025) for at least 35 working years. Chances are high that's not going to be what you receive even with many years of Cost of Living increases, the average benefit currently being under $22K per year and cuts to benefits in the future being almost inevitable.

On average, Social Security is said to replace about 40% of preretirement income, with the caveat that it varies widely by individual – mostly on the downside. The reality is too many people are way off when estimating their expected benefits. That Nationwide study reported that for one in ten retirees, their actual benefit was *half* of what they had expected it would be.

Overestimating how much you'll receive in Social Security creates unrealistic expectations and will spell disaster if you're not saving what you need to early on. If you make this mistake when you're older, you might retire too early and have to seriously cut back your cost of living.

If you're closer to retirement than to 2034, find out how much your Social Security benefits may well be at what age you plan to start using them, go to the Social Security Administration website: www.ssa.gov/myaccount .

You'll be able to calculate your projected benefits at 62, at 67 (full retirement age for you, currently) and at 70. Most advisors will tell you that if you're young, set your retirement savings goals as if you'll receive the lowest benefit.

If you're closer to 2034 than to your planned age for starting to take your Social Security benefits? Sorry, all bets are off. In my humble opinion, I think you should exclude Social Security benefits entirely from your retirement planning process. If it still exists, your benefits may be highly taxed or severely cut back from today's calculations, so assume that you'll get nothing from Social Security and you'll be far better off in the long run. Plan for the worst and then any benefits you *do* receive will be extra spending money.

I also recommend trying out this retirement calculator by Vox. Click on the 'Show advanced options' link and it poses the question of how our government will deal with the coming shortfall of Social Security. The URL is:
www.vox.com/2014/7/31/5882885/retirement-planning-saving-how-much-do-i-need

Then, once you have the magic number that you want to achieve at your retirement age, then you and your advisor can start experimenting with designs on how to get you there. Remember, not one size fits all – if your family has good genes and you expect to be healthy well into your 80s, you might consider continuing to pay into the plan longer than most. One of the beautiful aspects of a well-designed IUL is that the cash value continues to grow long after you stop paying into the policy.

In general, you'll want to start with a policy big enough to cover all of your current liabilities, from a life insurance point of view.

Depending on your age and health, that might be amazingly easy to do or might result in a super-funded face value to keep the IUL from becoming a MEC. There are plenty of ways to achieve a big dollar face amount with a (relatively) small dollar premium if your budget is tight. You don't have to cover all your liabilities right away if you can't afford to. A nickel isn't as good as a dollar, but nickels compounded over time could add up to far more than dollars invested later. Go back to page 232 and look at the John vs Mary comparative investment tables to refresh your memory.

Any amount to begin with is better than waiting because a) the time value of compounding money will work for you; b) you can always increase the amount you contribute annually later; and c) who knows what's going to happen between now and then that might make you uninsurable on the health side of the equation. Don't wait. It might cost you dearly.

When you're trying to determine what your monthly premium for your IUL should be, keep in mind that not all the premium paid into the policy is "investable". The premium payment is reduced by the "cost of insurance" (COI) and operating expenses of the insurance company. These charges vary between companies, and it is important to choose an insurance company that is efficient in these areas and treats you, the policyholder, fairly.

When it comes to the "universal" part of an IUL, flexibility is a tremendously advantageous component. This is what really differentiates Indexed Universal Life from its counterpart in the permanent life insurance world of participating dividend paying Whole Life insurance.

The latter, in a nutshell, is also known as a "fixed premium" plan because it does not allow any deviation from the scheduled fixed premium dollar amount during the policy payment period, whatever that may be. You could pay in more of course, but never less.

An IUL, on the other hand, is by definition, a *flexible premium* plan. This allows you, as the policy owner, the flexibility to skip a payment (or more) entirely if things get too tight financially, without fear of the policy immediately lapsing.

More importantly, that flexibility extends to more than just premium payments into areas such as policy design options. While it's very likely that the same company that you might buy an IUL from might also offer their own version of Whole Life, some insurance companies are simply more inventive when it comes to the ways that IUL policies can be designed and the riders that are available to support an optimal plan. In other words, flexibility is only a part of the policy design equation.

Plus, not only are you able to skip payments when needed, but you can catch up by making large contributions later. In contrast, if you were to skip contributing to your 401(k) or IRA in any given year, the IRS won't let you double up the next year. IULs on the other hand will allow you to skip any number of payments, so long as there is enough left in the account value to cover ongoing expenses and the interest on any existing policy loan. Then, when you have a good year in earnings, you can play catch-up and there are no limits to the amount that can be contributed annually to an IUL once it passes the seven-year mark. Prior to that, remember, the IRS puts limits on hyper-funding or it becomes a Modified Endowment Contract (MEC).

Performance also varies according to the age of the policy and the degree to which the amount paid in is above or below something called the "***7-pay premium***". Given this premium flexibility, insurers generally set the 7-pay premium equal to the amount of *annual* premium (remember the seven year timeline for MECs) needed to endow policy cash values in an amount equal to the policy face value (the death benefit) amount, and therefore make policy death benefits permanent, based on the insurer's actuarial expectations regarding the company's mortality experience and operating expenses, and based on the historical performance for the policy cash value's various underlying asset classes.

I know what you're thinking. Who understands that crap besides the insurance guys?

The layman's short version is that the 7-pay premium amount is equal to the premium required to cover expected cost of insurance charges and policy expenses. That's what the IRS looks at during the first seven years of an IUL policy. Premiums paid in excess of that target premium are generally intended to increase the policy cash value (i.e., the policy investment account). Consequently, premiums paid up to the insurance premium are subjected to COI charges to cover expenses unique to the insurance component of the policy, while amounts paid *above* the 7-pay premium usually incur no COI charges and very little expense charges, if any.

So, anyone interested in accumulating the most cash value possible in a given policy would want to pay in as much as possible *above* the scheduled premium while still qualifying to meet the definition of life insurance by the IRS. There will always be an upper limit to the premium size for those first seven years, assuming that you want to avoid having the policy be deemed a MEC for tax purposes.

And, the above might include some withdrawals along the way, like large purchases you want to finance yourself (college tuition for your kids, a new car from time to time or even a down payment on a new home or rental property or business).

Your advisor can also show you ways to plan for increases in your premium as your career develops and your income increases. Such a 'ladder effect' is an uncomplicated way to automatically increase the potential for maximum growth over time.

You can also set up an IUL so that it pays you a set amount of money as a distribution (either a loan or cash withdrawal) on an annual basis once you retire. These payments work similarly to an annuity in that they can be set up to pay out over a certain timeframe, say 20 years, or be set up to pay out your entire life. The amount depends on what your cash value is when you start the distributions, almost exactly the way annuities work. The only downside is if your IUL isn't designed correctly, or you're taking too much money out along the way and not putting it back in, you could run out of money.

That said, if you plan to use your IUL for a retirement income stream, the illustrations that you see before you sign on the dotted line will provide a good estimate of what the numbers will look like and how long your money will last but something you need to fully understand is that the illustrations use averages, meaning they are never quite accurate. The good news is that they are more likely to err on the conservative side and a well-designed IUL, funded according to your plan, will never run out of money if it's designed for lifelong income.

If you're a business owner, then an IUL can be looked at as either a boot-strapped startup or a well-capitalized venture. Both ways can be equally successful, but starting big or small, they both begin with a first premium payment.

One final thought on designing your IUL in terms of managing expectations, I've found that too many people think $1 million dollars by the time they retire is a good goal to aim for. Here's some bad news for you. It's not. You'll probably need more. Maybe a lot more.

While it's reasonable to assume that a long-term real return, after adjusting for inflation of say, 2%, on a diversified investment portfolio that, using that 4% annual distribution rule of thumb, $1 million would provide an annual income of $44,650 for 30 years. Unfortunately, that leaves no margin for emergencies, or increased living expenses beyond inflation, or a higher inflation rate. It also leaves a big fat zero after 30 years to pass on to your heirs.

If you're single when you turn 65 with $1 million, you might be okay for 30 years. But what if you're married? While the adage "two can live as cheaply as one" has some application when it comes to housing, it doesn't apply to food, clothing, health care or entertainment. Or transportation, if you travel by any mode other than your car.

We already saw what the cost of just food might be. In most cases, about one third of our cost of living is housing, so then it would be reasonable to conclude a couple would need an income of around $75,000 to enjoy the same lifestyle as a single person living on $45,000. If that's true, then a couple with a million dollars only has about sixteen years of retirement income. If they retire at age 65, that assures both of them enough money only until they reach the age of 81. If the average life expectancy is between 84 and 86, there's an exceedingly high probability at least one spouse will run out of money in their later years. Obviously, that doesn't spell success in financial planning.

Worse yet, how about a much more typical situation of a couple that has saved less than $1 million? On a retirement fund of $500,000, they would run out of money in about eight years.

If it hasn't sunk in yet, you need to start saving *right now*. Even if you don't have a detailed plan yet. And, ideally, you should be saving at *least* 10% of your income. If you can't save that much right now, don't throw up your hands and quit. Save what you can. It'll pay off later.

My point in showing you that example isn't meant to scare you into saving more, it's meant as incentive for you to plan better.

Simple things make a difference, like retiring later than 65, for example. If you're able to keep working past 65 or maybe even to age 70, it may be worth it. Even two or three more years of earnings can make a significant difference in your retirement lifestyle. That said, if you manage to create an ultra-high income for yourself while you're still young, you can always design your plan to retire early or change the plan once you get there.

Chapter Eighteen

Finding the money

When you think about some of the challenges you face in saving for retirement, behavioral psychology might not be first on your list of things to address. If you're like most people, the dilemma may have more to do with the fact that your paycheck already doesn't cover all the things you want it to.

However, as it turns out, what's going on in your head has a lot to do with why so many Americans aren't saving anything for retirement. If you're one of them, you may be falling prey to one or both common human cognitive errors known as "present bias" and "exponential growth bias".

Present bias is the all too common human tendency to place more value on *immediate* rewards than on those that will come in the (perceived) distant future. For example, a person with present-biased preferences might express eagerness to invest a tax refund she knows she will receive in six months into a retirement savings account, but then when the refund actually arrives she will decide not to do so, favoring some other immediate use of the money, even though nothing has changed except the passage of time.

Studies show that this individual will save less for retirement than another person who also favors investing the tax refund (in the same timeframe) but does not suffer from present bias and as a result doesn't change her mind as the refund date nears.

Sounds logical, right?

But that kind of bias may be imperceptible to you. To give you an idea of how subtle that bias may be, Hal Hershfield, an assistant professor of marketing at New York University's Stern School of Business, showed present bias in action with some interesting experiments.

Hershfield took pictures of older people with happy, sad, and neutral expressions and inserted them into a retirement-savings slider tool, and then showed them to a group of college students. The idea was to show users how their decisions affected both their future income and their well-being in old age. Some subjects used a tool with pictures of themselves that had been digitally aged like you might see in the phone app Oldify. That group set aside an average of 6.8% of their pay for retirement, versus 5.2% for those using a tool with current (non-aged) pictures of themselves. Later, his team ran the experiment using a national pool of online participants who uploaded their own head shots. And even with variations in photo quality and static expressions, the "aged face" tools prompted people to save 6.2% on average, versus 4.4% for the "current self" tools.

Apparently, seeing an older version of yourself brings the future closer to the present so you think slightly differently. Who'da thunk that?

If you know you struggle with present bias, at least now you can recognize the error and take steps to correct it. But even if you don't think you do, a good start would be to write down, and frequently revisit, a detailed retirement plan that includes specific goals about how you plan to spend your future income and exactly what you plan to do at that time. Don't hide it in a file cabinet either. Put it somewhere where you'll see it often. This will help you envision your future self and the lifestyle you want that person to have.

Exponential growth bias is a perceptual bias that relates to an individual's understanding (or more likely, lack thereof) of compound interest. This really has more to do with financial literacy than any subtle brain function, but it does, in fact, create some behavioral bias.

An individual who ignores compounding or simply doesn't understand how it works, will expect retirement account balances to grow linearly over time, while someone who incorporates it will expect that same retirement account to grow exponentially. The former individual may save less because he or she believes the expected return to saving to be less than it really is.

Ignore the pun, but one compounds on the other. If you suffer from both, the likelihood that you'll ever save enough to retire comfortably is slim to none.

So now we know that your psychological mindset is important, but when push comes to shove, your frame of mind isn't what makes your nest egg grow. Saving for retirement takes a conscious effort, a bit of know-how, and of course, some extra money. But what if you feel like you're already stretching your budget, where can you find an extra dollar or two, so that you can afford to purchase an IUL? The good news is that no matter how far away you are from that fateful date, there are plenty of simple ways to go about it.

As I mentioned in Chapter 11, creating additional revenue streams is a smart way to get ahead of your financial goals even if you do nothing else. There are hundreds of ways to create passive income for yourself both pre and post retirement. Some require only a monetary investment, some require just your time and effort for a limited period, others are businesses that you can simply buy outright.

For our purposes, we want to concentrate on only those that require very little or zero monetary investment because every extra dollar you have, that isn't going to work for you to generate three more, should be going into your Money Tree plan. Here's a list of half a dozen great ways to earn an extra buck or two that don't require you to invest hundreds (or thousands) of dollars up front:

1. Sell an eBook online

Self-publishing is a pretty conventional method these days. When you purchase an eBook on Amazon there's a fairly good chance you're buying a self-published book. Self-publishing is also ridiculously easy compared to the alternative. And it doesn't have to be a novel. One of the most popular eBooks ever written was a book about how to build sheds. Another was a cookbook. This book is self-published. So, chances are high that you know enough about one of your favorite subjects to create a book that others would be interested in reading. To self-publish a book, you'll first need to write it (or hire a ghost writer if you suck at writing), and edit it, create a cover, and then upload it to a program such as Amazon's Kindle Direct Publishing. Don't expect instant success though. Unless you hit on an unmet need by a huge market (like this book), there will need to be a lot of presale promotion and marketing before you count on turning an eBook into a passive income stream. But again, there are lots of folks that will do that for you.

2. Create an online Course

Instead of watching videos on any of the (now) many online course marketplaces you can become a producer by creating your own video course, and then allow others to purchase it. For anyone particularly knowledgeable in a specific subject matter, this is a marvelous opportunity even if you're not the best at public speaking. It's much faster than writing a book but you do need to learn how to create and edit video. Thankfully, there are plenty of apps that will help do just that. If you're still in college, this can also be a terrific way to turn traditional tutoring into a passive income stream.

3. Sell Stock Photos

Have you ever pondered on where websites, online and even some print magazines get their photography? These are customarily bought from stock photo providers, nearly 100% of which are online. If you enjoy photography, or if you're simply someone who constantly snaps a picture of cool stuff they see on their smart phone, you can submit your photos to stock photo sites and receive a commission each time someone purchases one of your pictures.

There are dozens of stock photo websites that you can choose to work with, including some of the biggest like Getty and Corbis, or even some that work directly through an app on your phone like FOAP. Once you're registered, you simply upload your photos (or videos) onto the websites and you'll earn money whenever someone uses any of them. Generally, it's a few cents to a few dollars (if your photos are popular) per use but over time it can add up to some real money.

4. Licensing Music

If you're musically inclined, like stock photos, you can license and earn royalties off of your original music when someone chooses to use it. Music is often licensed for use in YouTube Videos, commercials, and more. There are even opportunities for people who just write the lyrics for songs.

5. Create an App

If you own a smartphone or tablet then it's safe to assume you have several apps downloaded. But have you ever had an amazing idea for an app? If so, you could consider hiring a programmer to create your app for you. Then you could sell it on the App store and generate some residual income.

6. Design T-Shirts

If you're an artist, sites like Zazzle, Blue Cotton and Cafe Press allow users to custom design items like T-shirts. If your design becomes popular and generates sales, you'll be able to earn royalties.

Even Amazon has gotten into this business. Amazon has a service called "Merch by Amazon ", where you simply upload your T-shirt designs and Amazon takes care of the rest (making, packing and shipping it).

You will note that some of these require starting either a personal blog or website for marketing purposes. Just consider how much time you spend daydreaming about some great idea and then it dies on the vine. We're too often so wrapped up in our nine-to-five careers that our youthful creativity wanes to the point of non-existence at some point in our lives. In contrast, there are bloggers who net over $15,000 a month talking about things like food. Also, there have been multiple personal finance bloggers who have traded their websites for seven figure paydays.

Michael Shih is famous for taking his first Shopify store to more than six figures in six months just selling t-shirts on demand with next to nothing in upfront costs. In other words, it can be extremely profitable if you do things right.

Taking advantage of the internet to create, promote, and sell something is an exercise that every creative person should try at least once in their lifetime. The only real risk is some wasted time, a couple hundred dollars and a dented ego, but the upside could be life changing. You can start a website for as little as $2.95 a month and go from there. Some will even give you a free domain name for a year.

Let's switch gears and say that you're not the creative type, you don't have a clue about internet marketing and you aren't the best communicator either in writing or, gosh, just plain talking, but you do have some "passion" or hobby that you enjoy in your free time.

How can you turn that into a revenue stream?

Whether you enjoy cooking, or knitting, or woodworking, or fixing things in your garage or simply spending time with dogs, there are more and more ways to make money from these types of hobbies.

If there is something you enjoy doing, you can probably figure out a way to get paid for it. Google it and see what comes up. Here are a few good examples:

DogVacay and Rover — Now merged, the Rover network allows you to offer dog sitting in your own home or take someone's dog for a walk.

TaskRabbit and Thumbtack — These websites allow you to market home services like house cleaning, gardening, handy man services and simply run errands for people.

Etsy — Sell your handmade goods.

All but Etsy require some background checking but unless you're a felon, chances are you'll be approved pretty easily.

The idea is not that every waking minute of your life should be consumed with wondering if what you're doing is the most profitable course of action, but the more you think about how to financially benefit from things that you enjoy, the more ideas you'll probably get. If you're still in the dark about how to raise some extra money doing something beyond your regular job, simply Google "side hustles" or "passive income" and you'll find a myriad of ideas to choose from.

In addition, there are lots of places that money can come from besides straight out of your wallet or bank account that you may not have thought about. Here's a brief list of ideas to consider when you're looking for ways to fund an IUL, aside from creating another revenue stream.

The first, and most obvious choice, is canceling other life insurance policies that will be redundant when you have an IUL and using that premium money to help fund your IUL. Any Term Life policy you already have will become unnecessary, especially those that are work related and the premiums are deducted from your paycheck. That's money that can go toward creating cash value instead of renting the insurance. Any Whole Life policy may already have some cash value that you can deposit in a lump sum into your IUL and create instant cash value there that will grow much, much faster linked to market returns instead of some low fixed interest rate.

In addition, the Internal Revenue Service allows you to exchange an insurance policy that you own for a new life insurance policy insuring the same person (you, in this case) without paying tax on the investment gains earned (if it has cash value) on your original contract. This can be a substantial benefit for some folks. Because this kind of trade is governed by Section 1035 of the Internal Revenue Code, these are called "**1035 Exchanges**".

If you're married, this can also apply to policies your spouse owns. With an IUL, your spouse (and/or any other family member) can be added as an additional insured to your policy and the additional cost is sometimes ridiculously low.

However, never EVER cancel an existing life insurance policy before you have a new one issued and in hand! The last thing you want is to find out you're now uninsurable for some reason *after* you canceled a policy you already had in place.

With non-life related insurance policies that you pay for every month (health insurance, auto insurance or home or renters' insurance), remember, every dollar counts.

The auto insurer that had the best rate when you bought your coverage may not be the most competitive after you add a teenage driver, get married, move, buy a new car, or improve your credit score. It's a wise idea to re-shop your auto insurance every year or so, even if nothing has changed. In a study by the Texas Insurance Department, people saved an average of $125 per year just by calling other insurers to compare rates. Weigh any premium savings against long-term customer discounts you may be earning. Also, you'll usually get a big discount if you keep your auto and home coverage with the same company.

Raising your deductible from $250 to $500 or $1,000 can cut your premiums by 15% or more. It also makes you less likely to file small claims that could boost your premiums or lead to cancellation of your policy.

And don't forget to ask your home insurer about discounts for home improvements that reduce claim risks, such as installing storm shutters or impact-resistant glass. You could also snag a discount of up to 5% for a home generator.

If your family is in relatively good health, you can save a ton of money on health insurance premiums — and benefit from an HSA's triple tax benefit — by signing up for a high-deductible health insurance policy (which can dramatically lower your health insurance monthly premium). There are eligibility requirements, but your contributions are tax-deductible or pretax (and you may get an employer match), and the money can be used tax-free for medical expenses in any year.

If you don't have an HSA but your employer offers a Flexible Spending Account (FSA), you could contribute to that and that money then escapes the clutches of federal income and Social Security taxes. Like an HSA, FSA funds can be used tax-free for eligible medical expenses. The downside of an FSA is that you must use the cash in your account by either December 31 or March 15, depending on your employer, or you'll lose it. Funds in an HSA account rollover indefinitely.

The next most obvious place to find money is to reallocate payments currently going into qualified and/or non-qualified retirement plans you already have, or college funding vehicles like 529's, or investment accounts, etc. If you have a 401(k) with a matching component funded by your employer, *definitely keep paying into that*, up to the maximum amount of the match, that's 100% free money, but anything above and beyond that is at risk of loss *without* any guaranteed gain. It's better used in an IUL.

Another potentially viable way to free up money is by refinancing your current mortgage and lowering your monthly payments, if that's doable. Certainly, DO NOT elongate the term of the mortgage, even by one month, but if you can get a better interest rate with the balance you currently have in the same or lesser timeframe, by all means, do it and use those extra few bucks a month for your IUL.

Any potential method for reduction in current interest rates or monthly payments should be looked at in every feasible way to get rid of them. Such as taking equity out of your home to eliminate credit card debt or an auto loan, to free up those higher interest payments if you have any.

A word of warning: I am in no way suggesting that you borrow money from any source to start an IUL, even if the interest rates on the loan are ridiculously low. Refinancing current debt and using the money saved by doing so is one thing, adding to your existing debt or creating debt where none exists today is another. Never, ever, borrow money against your home for any sort of investment or insurance plan. If anyone ever suggests that you do that, don't walk away…run.

It all boils down to helping you set better financial priorities. Sure, you've made mistakes in the past. Everybody has made a blunder or two when it comes to finances. Now's the time to fix them.

It's the bottom line that counts now. Make sure every dollar you're spending is being used to its most potential. Take advantage of every opportunity you can while they are available to you, because you never know when that opportunity might disappear.

Do that, whenever possible and you'll be well on your way to making your Money Tree into a giant Redwood.

Chapter Nineteen

All the bells and whistles

There are several working parts to an IUL beyond how much you'll contribute to it every month. First and foremost is the life insurance policy that is the basis for the plan. How much the face value is depends on a number of factors. For any life insurance policy, the ***face value*** is the value of the ***death benefit***, and those terms are interchangeable. That differs from the amount of accumulated funds that are available to you at any given time, which is referred to as the ***cash value***.

Of course, how much your premium is, would be the determining factor in most insurance policies. The higher the premium paid, the higher the death benefit (face value). However, with an IUL, a well-designed plan can allow you to put in a larger amount of capital than normal and keep the death benefit small, thereby allowing more money to go to the cash value, which in turn, allows it to grow quicker.

Conversely, if you're working from a tight budget but still need to insure yourself and your family against certain liabilities, your advisor/agent can show you how to have a higher face value with a lower than ordinary premium to start. Naturally, this means it will take longer for your cash value to grow but dependent on what your needs are, that might be the best way to begin. Remember, you can always contribute more later.

When designing an IUL, two alternatives are available for determining whether the IUL meets the requirements to qualify as a life insurance contract for tax purposes. One way is the ***Guideline Premium Test (GPT)*** the other is the ***Cash Value Accumulation Test (CVAT)***. Your life insurance benefit will vary depending on which test is used.

Being able to pass the cash value accumulation test is incredibly important to both the policyholder and the insurer. If an insurance policy fails to pass, it is no longer considered an insurance product and is then taxed like an investment or a MEC. Insurance policies are able to grow in value on a tax-deferred basis, with both cash values and death benefits being exempt from income tax. Most other investments are taxed as ordinary income, meaning that failing to pass the test will lead to a higher tax rate and we don't want that.

The CVAT method is often used when the policyholder does not want to be limited to the amount of premiums that he or she will be able to pay into the policy and wants to maximize the death benefit that can be received. Alternatively, this method can be used when the policyholder plans to roll a hefty sum into the policy upfront but wants to limit the initial death benefit.

In addition to the CVAT, an insurer has the option of designing a policy so that it passes the guideline premium test, or GPT. The basic difference between these two tests is that CVAT limits the cash value relative to the death benefit, while GPT limits premiums paid relative to the death benefit. If an insurance policy fails either of these tests, then it is not considered a life insurance policy and all income tax benefits are eliminated.

The insurer must indicate which test is going to be used at the issue date, and once the policy is issued the insurer cannot decide to use the other test option instead. The choice of test can determine what the policy premiums, cash value, and benefits will be. Both tests can be performed using a level death benefit (meaning your death benefit stays the same over a prolonged period of time) or an increasing death benefit (meaning your death benefit starts to grow in value almost immediately, in sync with your cash value growth).

Depending on the design of the IUL, one way may work significantly better than the other. Always try both to be sure which is more efficient for long term value. Either way, I recommend using an increasing death benefit. In general, if you make only the expected premium contributions, this method will show better growth over time.

Another way that IULs differ from many other insurance policies is that you can limit the time that you intend to pay premiums. Many IULs are commonly set up so that you stop paying premiums into the plan at age 65 (or whatever age you expect to retire) and start taking distributions at that point. However, again, in a well-designed plan, when you stop paying into the IUL the cash value (and the death benefit) will continue to grow in value.

Now, it's up to you when you plan to retire and if you'll want or need distributions from your IUL as an income source for your retirement or as simply a fallback for financing large expenditures from time to time or if you'll use your IUL for other purposes, like leaving a legacy for your beneficiaries. You can do one or all of the above with an IUL.

We'll talk about diverse ways to use distributions beyond just creating your own personal pension in another chapter but for now, let's look at other options to consider in your design.

Most IULs will include options for ***living benefits*** like access to some or all of your death benefit when you're diagnosed with a ***terminal illness*** (something that is certain to reduce your life expectancy to a few years or less), a ***critical Illness*** (something that is life threatening and may or may not reduce your life expectancy dramatically, a heart attack for example) or a ***chronic illness*** (an illness or condition that cannot be cured and doesn't go away on its own; examples of a chronic condition would include diabetes, arthritis, and asthma).

Other optional riders are things like ***Long Term Care*** (LTC) benefits; or a ***disability*** rider that provides a fixed monthly benefit in the event of total disability; ***additional insureds*** (like your spouse or children); ***accidental death*** benefits (that pay more than the scheduled face value if you die in an accident rather than by natural causes); a ***children's benefit*** rider (this benefit provides level term insurance for each insured child if death occurs usually before they reach the age of 25, or they marry); an ***unemployment*** rider that provides a one-time lump sum benefit in the event of unemployment; most policies also offer a ***waiver of premium*** rider that will pay your premium (so your policy stays in force) if you're ever disabled. Some companies also offer a ***Lifetime Income Benefit Rider (LIBR)***, that once exercised, guarantees your income for life – that's money that you cannot outlive regardless of the account value of the policy.

Most IULs also offer a ***no-lapse period***. Standard universal life policies will normally expire (lapse) if the cash or account value dwindles to the point that it is insufficient to cover a policy's ongoing COI and expense costs. With the no-lapse feature or "secondary guarantee," the policies promise to stay in effect for the guaranteed period (usually the insured's life) if the premium is paid regularly and on time, even if the cash value has run out. I want to point out here, however, that the no-lapse feature is aimed at guaranteeing the death benefit. If your goal is to maximize your cash value over time (meaning design the policy correctly), the no-lapse feature (which has a cost attached to it) is not something you want to have embedded in your policy. Policy design is key. Know what the goal of your policy is.

Some IULs also offer a guarantee of insurability. This rider provides options for future face value increases, usually at predetermined dates, without any evidence of insurability, meaning no exams or underwriting requirements. Generally, these types of guarantees end at a fairly young age, say 40, but options are also available at the insured's college graduation, marriage, or the birth or adoption of a child. This is a great option to have if you're young and expect the need for more coverage in the future.

Chapter Twenty

Understanding the illustration

Once you've designed your IUL, your advisor or agent will create an "illustration" that estimates the future value of your policy based on the inputs provided, usually from software that the insurer provides. I tell all my clients that the only thing I can guarantee about any illustration I show them is that it's wrong. Nobody can predict the future, so keep in mind that any IUL illustration you see is a best guess based on past performance. Chances are high that what you'll see is a very conservative estimate, but it's still an estimate, not a given by any means.

Any cash insurance policy has moving parts: Inflows from premiums and interest credits both increase cash value; and "mortality charges and expenses" (the COI) both decrease it. An illustration must show you all that and typically has two key components:

1. ***The guaranteed illustration.*** This is the legally required disclosure of a worst-case scenario. It outlines policy performance based on the carrier's minimum filed credit rates for a particular policy and the maximum COI allowed by law based on the most recent standard mortality table for insurers.

2. ***The current (nonguaranteed) illustration.*** This is the insurer's best representation of policy performance based on credit rates and mortality charges currently in effect.

An illustration involves three key variables: the premium, cash surrender value and death benefits. The insurer's software will compute one variable based on selected assumptions for the other two. Illustrations must contain at least the guaranteed and current or nonguaranteed rates.

When looking at an illustration, you should understand the only *true* guarantee is that the policy's actual financial results will be different from those shown in either the guaranteed or nonguaranteed columns. On the next page is an example of what those guaranteed rates on a page from an illustration might look like.

In most cases, the guaranteed results will be based on an interest rate so low that the world's economy would have to crumble before the guarantee would take effect. And the nonguaranteed results, even though they show averages, may or may not be closer to the true results over time. As we all know, the only thing we can count on in the future is constant change.

That said, if you're the ultra-cautious type, any CPA can evaluate an illustration's validity using something called an "80 percent test".

Example IUL
Indexed Universal Life

Ledger

John Q Public
Male 36 Verified Standard Non-Tobacco
Riders: ABR, CMG, DBPR, ICSR, LIBR, OPR, SAR

Face Amount: $120,196
Death Benefit Option: A (Level)
Initial Premium: $130.00 Monthly (EFT)
State: North Carolina

This illustration of Example values assumes payments are made in the amounts shown and that the Guaranteed Illustrated Rate and maximum monthly deductions will continue in the future. The interest rate used in the calculation of guaranteed values is 2.50%. The annual floor is 0%.

Guaranteed Illustrated Rate

Policy Year	Age	Planned Annualized Premium	Accumulated Value	Cash Surrender Value	Net Death Benefit
1	36	$1,560.00	$858	$0	$120,196
2	37	1,560.00	1,730	0	120,196
3	38	1,560.00	2,613	452	120,196
4	39	1,560.00	3,507	1,719	120,196
5	40	1,560.00	4,411	2,803	120,196
6	41	1,560.00	5,324	3,967	120,196
7	42	1,560.00	6,241	5,141	120,196
8	43	1,560.00	7,161	6,326	120,196
9	44	1,560.00	8,081	7,517	120,196
10	45	1,560.00	8,997	8,711	120,196
		$15,600.00			
11	46	1,560.00	9,935	9,935	120,196
12	47	1,560.00	10,872	10,872	120,196
13	48	1,560.00	11,820	11,820	120,196
14	49	1,560.00	12,777	12,777	120,196
15	50	1,560.00	13,736	13,736	120,196
16	51	1,560.00	14,693	14,693	120,196
17	52	1,560.00	15,636	15,636	120,196
18	53	1,560.00	16,568	16,568	120,196
19	54	1,560.00	17,472	17,472	120,196
20	55	1,560.00	18,336	18,336	120,196
		$31,200.00			
21	56	1,560.00	19,164	19,164	120,196
22	57	1,560.00	19,945	19,945	120,196
23	58	1,560.00	20,691	20,691	120,196
24	59	1,560.00	21,393	21,393	120,196
25	60	1,560.00	22,035	22,035	120,196
26	61	1,560.00	22,599	22,599	120,196
27	62	1,560.00	23,060	23,060	120,196
28	63	1,560.00	23,403	23,403	120,196
29	64	1,560.00	23,614	23,614	120,196
30	65	1,560.00	23,682	23,682	120,196

The policy as shown using the Guaranteed Illustrated Rate will lapse in policy year 39 unless a higher premium is paid. This is based on the guaranteed interest rate credited and guaranteed charges by the Company.

Example Life Insurance Company
This illustration is not complete without all pages.
This illustration is valid for 30 days.

9:15:15 AM

March 16, 2018
Page 19 of 26

[redacted]

Ledger

Valued Client	**Face Amount:** $468,380	Indexed Universal Life
Male 30 Standard Non-Tobacco	**Death Benefit Option:** A (Level)	**Riders:** ABR, CMG, FJR, DBPR, LIBR, OPR, SAR
State: Tennessee	**Initial Premium:** $500.00 Monthly	

This illustration of [redacted] values assumes payments are made in the amounts shown and that the illustrated rates and monthly deductions will continue in the future. The interest rate used in the calculation of current values is the weighted average interest rate shown below.

			Alternative Current Illustrated Values*				Current Illustrated Values*			
Policy Year	Age	Premium Outlay	Weighted Average Interest Rate	Accumulated Value	Cash Surrender Value	Net Death Benefit	Weighted Average Interest Rate	Accumulated Value	Cash Surrender Value	Net Death Benefit
1	30	$6,000.00	3.00 %	$4,530	$0	$468,380	**6.20 %**	**$4,806**	**$0**	**$468,380**
2	31	6,000.00	3.00 %	9,156	1,685	468,380	6.20 %	9,456	1,986	468,380
3	32	6,000.00	3.00 %	13,884	6,816	468,380	6.20 %	14,569	7,501	468,380
4	33	6,000.00	3.00 %	18,722	12,080	468,380	6.20 %	19,964	13,322	468,380
5	34	6,000.00	3.00 %	23,680	17,479	468,380	6.20 %	25,666	19,465	468,380
6	35	6,000.00	3.00 %	28,839	24,516	468,380	6.20 %	31,780	27,456	468,380
7	36	6,000.00	3.00 %	34,143	30,616	468,380	6.20 %	38,262	34,735	468,380
8	37	6,000.00	3.00 %	39,586	36,888	468,380	6.20 %	45,127	42,430	468,380
9	38	6,000.00	3.00 %	45,169	43,333	468,380	6.20 %	52,396	50,560	468,380
10	39	6,000.00	3.00 %	50,884	49,948	468,380	6.20 %	60,081	59,144	468,380
		$60,000.00								
11	40	6,000.00	3.00 %	57,761	57,761	468,380	6.20 %	69,250	69,250	468,380
12	41	6,000.00	3.00 %	64,808	64,808	468,380	6.20 %	78,956	78,956	468,380
13	42	6,000.00	3.00 %	72,034	72,034	468,380	6.20 %	89,234	89,234	468,380
14	43	6,000.00	3.00 %	79,445	79,445	468,380	6.20 %	100,124	100,124	468,380
15	44	6,000.00	3.00 %	87,054	87,054	468,380	6.20 %	111,669	111,669	468,380
16	45	6,000.00	3.00 %	94,867	94,867	468,380	6.20 %	123,914	123,914	468,380
17	46	6,000.00	3.00 %	102,896	102,896	468,380	6.20 %	136,907	136,907	468,380
18	47	6,000.00	3.00 %	111,137	111,137	468,380	6.20 %	150,691	150,691	468,380
19	48	6,000.00	3.00 %	119,600	119,600	468,380	6.20 %	165,316	165,316	468,380
20	49	6,000.00	3.00 %	128,290	128,290	468,380	6.20 %	180,840	180,840	468,380
		$120,000.00								
21	50	6,000.00	3.00 %	137,179	137,179	468,380	6.20 %	197,289	197,289	468,380
22	51	6,000.00	3.00 %	146,302	146,302	468,380	6.20 %	214,753	214,753	468,380
23	52	6,000.00	3.00 %	155,663	155,663	468,380	6.20 %	233,297	233,297	468,380
24	53	6,000.00	3.00 %	165,264	165,264	468,380	6.20 %	252,992	252,992	468,380
25	54	6,000.00	3.00 %	175,098	175,098	468,380	6.20 %	273,907	273,907	468,380
26	55	6,000.00	3.00 %	185,792	185,792	468,380	6.20 %	297,163	297,163	468,380
27	56	6,000.00	3.00 %	196,809	196,809	468,380	6.20 %	321,991	321,991	470,107
28	57	6,000.00	3.00 %	208,161	208,161	468,380	6.20 %	348,480	348,480	494,842

* Benefits and values are not guaranteed. The assumptions on which they are based are subject to change by the insurer. The rates for the Percent of Premium Expense Charge, Monthly Cost of Insurance, Monthly Expense Charge, Monthly Policy Fee, Monthly Percent of Accumulated Value Charge, Rider Charge, Withdrawal Fee and Accumulated Value Enhancement, if any, are not guaranteed, will be determined by the Company and may change from time to time based on expectations of future anticipated or emerging experience. These changes may include, but are not limited to, the increase, reduction or elimination of the listed rates and amounts after a certain number of policy years. Future anticipated or emerging experience can include, but is not limited to, investment earnings, mortality, persistency, taxes and expenses which may affect these assumptions. Actual results may be more or less favorable. See page 21 for guaranteed values.

There is a charge for cost of insurance and other expenses in years when no premium is paid into the policy. Premium payments, which may be greater than the initial premium, may have to be resumed to maintain the policy in force.

2019 Series R23BS 7702-21
Version 23.5.2.A

[redacted]

This illustration is not complete without all pages.
This illustration is valid for 30 days.

December 22, 2023 9:32:29 PM

TC117753(0423)P-LS

Page 23 of 29

Example IUL Illustration Page

To do that, they use a computer program that calculates the future value of a stream of payments. The result should be at least 80% of the illustration's death benefit. If not, it means the illustration uses a rate of return or other assumptions that may be unreasonable.

If you have an accountant, he/she can do a lot of legwork for you in selecting a strong insurance company and potentially a number of choices in IULs – IF (and that's a big if) they know what to look for. I always recommend doing your own homework. Knowing what you're buying and who you're buying it from (meaning the insurance company) are the best ways to ensure you get the right plan for your particular needs.

If you need help in that regard, feel free to contact me and I will be glad to point you to unbiased, fiduciary experts who will happily work on your behalf. My contact information is on the last page of this book.

Guaranteed and Nonguaranteed Values

The guaranteed rate column (or page, depending on the illustration's format, like the example shown) in any insurance illustration assumes the worst case — that from policy inception, the carrier will credit the minimum interest and charge the maximum amount based on the standard mortality tables. For your purposes, you can assume the benefits, cash surrender value and accumulated values on this part of insurance policy illustrations will never be lower than those the insurer guarantees.

However, as I mentioned before, if the IUL were to pay the guaranteed rate for the length of time described in the illustration, that would mean the complete and utter collapse of the U.S. economy causing the stock market to go to hell in a hand basket for that entire time. Obviously, if that happened, you'd have bigger worries than what your IUL will pay you when you retire, if you lived that long. So those illustrations, while required by the various State's Department of Insurance, are basically useless for you. They do, however, offer some insight into the cost of insurance and other fees that eat away at your nest egg if the rate of return is too low.

The illustration of nonguaranteed results is not what you should expect from the actual policy performance either since they are based on averages and as I'll demonstrate later in this book, illustrations using averages can be deceptive. However, you can count on the fact that the nonguaranteed illustration is the closest that any prediction made about the future will be.

The reality is that the actual performance of the policy is subject to change at the insurer's discretion within the limits imposed by contractual provisions. The moment you buy the policy, the illustration no longer predicts future results with the exception of the worst-case scenario and the first policy year using current assumptions, both of which are guaranteed.

Some carriers provide illustrations that offer an additional "nonguaranteed" column or page. This second version reflects changes in the interest credits that are meant to be about halfway between the guaranteed and nonguaranteed assumptions. Again, don't make the mistake of thinking this midpoint is the more likely scenario for your interest credits. It is not. It's simply a random halfway point in the interest rate projections that may or may not be required by insurance regulators. Ordinarily, this intermediate rate is somewhere in the realm of 3.5%. And quite frankly, knowing that the stock market has averaged 7.45% annually from 1920 to 2023 (including reinvesting all dividends, adjusted for inflation) and has only averaged below 6% once for any 30 year period since 1921 (5.34% from 1929 – the crash year starting the depression – to 1958, which also included the three consecutive crash years just after Germany invaded Poland at the start of World War II) the idea that the stock market will average only 3 to 3.5% from now until 2053 is not a reasonable assumption.

Since no one can predict the future, both nonguaranteed illustrations — the current and the intermediate — are hypothetical representations of the company's current practices. They reflect a scenario based on rates the insurer declared to be in effect when it issued the policy and the current nonguaranteed rate is a reflection of the actual rate of return that the company had for the selected fund or funds.

The maximum illustrated rates for each strategy are determined by applying another industry regulation. This involves applying the current cap and participation rates to every hypothetical 25-year index return sequence for the past 65 years to determine an average return.

So, for example, if one company uses a 7.5% rate for their current illustration and another company uses a 7.05% rate for a similar fund, then you can rest assured that the former has a much better actual track record of gains than the latter's history.

The mortality charges do not change for either illustration.

You should look very closely at illustrations that show "vanishing" premiums. This happens when the software that produces the illustrations calculates that policy cash value and year over year earnings are projected to cover the premiums. The common presumption is that such policies are "paid up". This is not necessarily so. With the real-world rise and fall of interest rates and expenses, premiums that had vanished may, in future years, suddenly reappear. If this happens, people who haven't anticipated those premiums reappearing are in for a rude surprise. An expert agent or advisor will have third party software that can adjust the illustration to show all the premiums that are planned for, even when the cash value bumps up the death benefit.

Short version: don't accept an illustration that doesn't show exactly what your plans are for incremental increases in premiums over the years. If you're presented with one that doesn't show the full picture, find a new agent or advisor.

The Narrative Summary

Every illustration will have a section entitled the Narrative Summary. This section includes:

- ***A Policy Description; terms and features***. These descriptions give an overview of the main elements as well as any riders including your no-lapse guarantee (if applicable),

- ***The Underwriting Discussion***. This contains the policy's benefits, premiums and tax information, what happens when accelerated death benefits are accessed, descriptions of the various indexing strategies that are available and how your policy premiums are allocated amongst them, and credits and expenses to the policy if/when they occur, how interest is credited and how they determined their average illustration rates.

- ***Column Definitions and key terms***. Here the carrier defines what the terms used in the illustration mean and how they are applied. Make sure the definitions match your own understanding and how your agent or advisor defined them.
- ***A Historic Lookback***. This section shows what would have happened if you had the various strategies in place for (usually) the last 20 years. You'll notice that the average returns shown here are *not* the average returns the company uses for the illustrations. How that number is achieved should be explained in the Narrative Summary section.
- ***A Disclaimer***. The disclaimer advises readers that the illustration is not an estimate of future values and actual results could be more or less favorable. It's standard legal language for *"pay attention!"* so you know what you're getting.
- ***The Signature page***. This generally shows a summary of the illustration in 5 or 10 year increments. The applicant (you) signs a statement that he or she understands that the nonguaranteed elements are subject to change. The insurance agent (also called the producer) signs, saying he or she has explained the nonguaranteed elements are subject to change.

Illustrations are always consecutively numbered, usually in a manner that says something similar to "Page 4 of 32". Beware of any illustration an agent provides that is missing pages in the narrative summary. Just like an audit report is incomplete without all the notes related to the financial statements, so is an illustration without any part of the narrative summary.

The Ledger

Sometimes referred to as the Tabular Detail, this is the section that has the year over year projections usually shown out until age 121 or when the policy lapses, whichever comes first.

Supplemental Footnotes & Additional Information

Lastly, most illustrations have some pages of other information like statutory premiums and/or information on Modified Endowment Contracts or IRS qualifiers.

Generally, one of these pages (if there are multiple) will show the "**7-pay premium**". Remember, that's the amount that is the maximum annual premium allowed in each of the first seven years of the policy to prevent it from becoming a MEC. If your illustration has a total annual premium higher than this number, even by a single penny, your entire gains will be taxable as ordinary income. **Pay close attention to that number** and make sure that you never go over it for those first seven years.

After that you can pile money in by the bag full if you have it to invest and never have to worry about any maximum investment limitations. Now let's look at exactly why any extra money you have should go into the IUL too.

Chapter Twenty-one

DIY finance, buy a car, pay for college

Let me run something by you that you've probably heard over and over and over again, especially if you have a 401(k) plan. Never touch a penny of your retirement savings! Don't borrow from it either!

Quite frankly, good advice, ***IF*** you have your retirement money sitting in a 401(k), or an IRA or a 403(b) or even a 457(b). The tax penalties for withdrawal too early are enormous and if you borrow from your account and then lose your job (or move on in your career to a better one) you're forced to pay the entire loan balance back right away or get slammed with the same tax penalty on the unpaid balance.

Not a good result either way.

That said, saving for the future doesn't only mean saving for retirement. You have a whole life ahead of you and there are lots of things that you're going to need to finance one way or another. If you need money for a new car or a down payment on a house, or to pay for your kids' college (or just their braces), or perhaps you have a dream of a year-long purpose-driven sabbatical before you're too old to enjoy it, where are you supposed to get that money from?

Well, the savings and retirement gurus all tell you that you should be saving money that won't be used in retirement elsewhere, so you're never tempted to raid your retirement fund. You should save for a new car or a new house, or just a big vacation you're planning in the future, in some other vehicle, maybe a mutual fund or two, or even just simply a savings account. And savings for college should be done in a 529 plan, right?

First, let's look at why saving for those kinds of things is a smart idea to begin with. Let's start with saving for a new or gently used car.

Most people make car payments on car loans for almost their entire working life. However, by driving an affordable used car, paid for with cash, you could invest the money that would have otherwise gone up in smoke as the finance expense of a car payment and end up with hundreds of thousands of dollars in additional savings by the time you retire.

If becoming a homeowner is one of your long term goals and you don't have a 20% down payment, you'll waste hundreds of dollars monthly on private mortgage insurance (PMI, that ensures the bank gets paid, not you or your heirs) and could find yourself underwater if property values fall, since you'll lack some significant equity in the property.

If you had cash for the down payment, again, your savings on the PMI cost invested in your retirement plan could easily be into six digits by the time you retire.

Now how about a college fund for your kids? If you plan to have children, then the need for putting some money aside for higher learning when your kids are young is a given when you look at the skyrocketing costs of college tuitions.

Lastly, instead of going into debt for new furniture, a family trip, or even presents for holidays, save up. If you put a $3,000 vacation on a credit card at 17% interest and make minimum payments of $75 a month, it would take five years (60 months) to repay the debt and you'd pay easily $1,460 in interest. If you invested that $75 per month instead, in something that paid an average return of 6% annually for the same five years, you'd have over $5,173 to use for whatever you wanted.

So yeah, it makes great sense to save for that kind of stuff. But where?

You could find a good mutual fund. But of course, mutual funds go up and down with the market, so probably not the best place to put money for your 25th anniversary trip to Europe since Murphy's Law will be sure to sink the market the month before you go and leave you with maybe enough to scrimp by on, if not having to postpone your trip entirely. And the idea of saving for a down payment on a house or simply a good new-to-you used car in a bank savings account? You might as well save it by putting it under your mattress.

Not to mention that then you have multiple accounts you have to keep track of, multiple deposits or contributions you have to make on a regular basis, etc. All that can get pretty complicated if you're not extremely disciplined with your budgeting.

Wouldn't it be simpler if you just put money aside in one place and never had to worry about getting a decent return or losing your investment?

Now let's compare what happens if you use an IUL for saving for those kinds of things.

But wait. If your IUL is where your savings for retirement is stashed, doesn't that fly in the face of all the advice not to touch your retirement savings for those kinds of expenses?

Yep, sure does. But the thing is, if you've already planned to save for those kinds of things and that money is above and beyond what you've already earmarked as retirement savings, putting that money in an IUL, and then taking it out when you need it, not only makes sense from a financial perspective, meaning your retirement fund will benefit, not be damaged, *and* you'll actually become your own finance company!

Let's start with the idea of getting a new (or at least new-to-you) car every five to seven years.

We'll use the example of Jane, who is 24, and has been working in the business and information technology field where the median starting pay is $56,900. She lives in Long Beach, California where her take home after taxes is about 75.83% of her gross monthly paycheck of $4,827 or $3,658 per month. She just got married and her husband, who has been working in the same industry a little longer, makes about 1/3 more than she does.

Jane figures that in retirement, by age 65 she'll need an after-tax income of about $50,000 to live the way she wants to until age 100. While she really doesn't expect to live that long, she doesn't ever want to run out of money either. That is equivalent to a $65,936 income stream before taxes if she's taxed the same way she is now. Anything she gets from Social Security she'll consider as a bonus.

To achieve that she saves 12% of her current take home pay, or $450 dollars monthly, into an IUL with a starting face value (death benefit) of $323,000, and projections showing and average of 7.75% per year. She expects to increase that contribution amount to $500 per month at age 32 when she's more established in her career. And if things go the way she plans, she'll increase that contribution again at age 44, when she expects her salary (twenty years from now) to be well over $100,000, to $10,000 per year ($833.33 per month).

Age	Year	Premium Outlay	Cumulative Premium	Policy Value	Cash Surrender Value	Death Benefit
55	31	10,000	229,800	559,126	559,126	1,780,284
56	32	7,727	237,526	603,530	603,530	1,857,484
57	33	0	237,526	643,399	643,399	1,914,446
58	34	0	237,526	685,776	685,776	1,973,102
59	35	0	237,526	730,887	730,887	2,033,701
60	36	0	237,526	779,112	779,112	2,096,855
61	37	0	237,526	830,440	830,440	2,162,142
62	38	0	237,526	885,002	885,002	2,229,585
63	39	0	237,526	943,102	943,102	2,299,585
64	40	0	237,526	1,004,886	1,004,886	2,372,113
65	41	0	237,526	1,070,552	1,070,552	2,447,206
66 D	42	-49,695	187,831	1,090,445	1,090,445	2,414,485
67 D	43	-49,695	138,136	1,111,296	1,111,296	2,384,084
68 D	44	-49,695	88,441	1,133,291	1,133,291	2,356,181
69 D	45	-49,695	38,746	1,156,390	1,156,390	2,330,530

If she does that, the projections show she may even be able to stop paying into the plan at age 56, and still have a tax-free income starting at age 66 of $49,670 per month that will increase every year after the 4th year of distribution to keep pace with inflation. By age 32, Jane's car that she's had since college is still in what she thinks is good shape when she decides to get a new pre-owned car, but when she's told its trade-in value is only $3,451, she realizes that she's going to need $31,549 to buy the $35,000 car she wants. If she financed it, she finds out that even at the low interest rate of 3%, the monthly car payment would be $567 a month and so rather than pay a finance company the $2,471 in interest, she decides to pay *herself* instead.

So, at age 32, she withdraws the $31,549 from her IUL tax free (since she's already paid in $37,800 in premium by that time there is no taxable gain) and pays for the car with cash. Then she pays herself back by simply upping the amount that she pays into her IUL by the same amount that the car payment would be ($567 per month) for 60 months and as you can see below, while her cash value (her retirement fund) and death benefit take a hit initially, because she's paying that money back just like she would with a car payment, they both quickly recover and keep growing.

Age	Year	Premium Outlay	Withdrawals	Loans	Policy Value Net of Surrender Charges	Loan Balance	Loan Repayment	Cash Surrender Value	Death Benefit
30	6	5,400	0	0	25,693	0	0	25,693	354,713
31	7	5,400	0	0	32,319	0	0	32,319	361,339
32	8	-19,370	31,549	0	14,205	0	0	14,205	343,226
33	9	12,204	0	0	26,611	0	0	26,611	355,632
34	10	12,204	0	0	40,900	0	0	40,901	368,898

Remember, unlike defined contribution plans like a 401(k) or IRA, there are no limitations on how much Jane can put into her IUL on an annual basis after she's had the policy for seven years.

Now, let's say she wants to trade that car in when she turns 39, and she's making quite a bit more money than when she bought the last car, she decides she wants a car costing $50,000 now. But this time, she doesn't trade in her old car because her daughter that she had at age 25 is now just two years away from being able to drive. So, this time she withdraws $50,000 from her IUL, again tax free because having paid back the money she withdrew at age 32, and more, her cumulative premium being paid in at age 38 totaling $79,246, again there is no taxable gain.

Age	Year	Premium Outlay	Withdrawals	Loans	Policy Value Net of Surrender Charges	Loan Balance	Loan Repayment	Cash Surrender Value	Death Benefit
38	14	6,000	0	0	98,043	0	0	98,043	572,699
39	15	-33,813	50,000	0	71,074	0	0	71,074	396,905
40	16	16,212	0	0	91,455	0	0	91,455	493,328
41	17	16,212	0	0	113,194	0	0	113,194	589,709
42	18	16,212	0	0	136,388	0	0	136,388	686,142
43	19	16,212	0	0	161,112	0	0	161,112	782,546
44	20	7,200	0	0	178,781	0	0	178,781	838,246

And like last time, she ups the monthly ante to the IUL by the same amount that her car payment would have been, which quickly makes the cash value recover and keep growing. By age 44, having been in the same career for 20 years, she's now making just shy of $96,000 and so she decides to make her monthly contribution to her IUL a steady $600 a month, which equals only 10% of her *net* pay annually (well below the recommended 15% of *gross* pay) until she turns 65. How has all this borrowing and paying back affected her outcome at retirement?

Age	Year	Premium Outlay	Cumulative Premium	Policy Value	Cash Surrender Value	Death Benefit
65	41	7,200	268,681	980,928	980,928	2,242,332
66	42	0	268,681	1,044,863	1,044,863	2,313,557

If you look back at her original plan, she needed $1,070,552 at age 65, but even after borrowing out money several times, because she paid it back like she would any other loan, she's down by only $89,624 (about the same amount she would have had, had she moved her contribution up to $10,000 per year as she originally planned). Even so, she can count on a lifetime income, tax free, of more than $49,000 per year.

Age	Year	Premium Outlay	Withdrawals	Loans	Policy Value Net of Surrender Charges	Loan Balance	Loan Repayment	Cash Surrender Value	Death Benefit
100	76	-49,670	0	90,362	3,782,416	2,075,314	0	1,707,103	2,030,103
101	77	-49,670	0	92,170	3,848,235	2,167,484	0	1,680,751	2,003,751

This is where you should start to realize that you could finance almost anything you want to with your IUL as long as you pay it back just like you would any other loan. Obviously, you don't want to continually deplete your cash value, but small chunks go almost unnoticed and big chunks can still be quickly recovered if you plan your payback correctly.

How about paying for college for your kids?

Remember I mentioned that Jane had a daughter at 25? The average cost of tuition and fees for the 2017–2018 school year were $34,699 at private colleges, $9,528 for state residents at public colleges and $21,632 for out-of-state students at state schools, according to data reported to U.S. News in an annual survey. But over the past three years, the average net price increase per year was $579 at community colleges, $960 at public colleges for out-of-state residents, and $2,935 at private colleges. Of course, these things are hard to nail down but here's the ballpark cost of what Jane's daughter might be paying for a full 4-year degree by the time Jane is 43 (when her daughter turns 18):

- Two-year community colleges: $14,909
- Public colleges for residents: $19,909
- Public colleges for non-residents: $41,790
- Private non-profit colleges: $96.341

With cost increases like that 529 plans are great if you have no other alternative, but if you have an IUL, that's a much better vehicle for saving money for your kids' education. Here's why:

529 Plans vs Indexed Universal Life Insurance

	529 Plan	IUL
Distribution	Tax free gains (Conditional)	Tax free gains (Unconditional)
Flexibility	Qualified Educational Expenses: Tuition, fees, books & room; Accredited U.S. schools only	Your choice how and where you spend the funds; No restrictions
Risk	Fluctuates with the market, no locked in gains	Interest 0 to 15% with locked in gains
Financial Aid	Will reduce the financial aid: subtract up to 5.6 cents in aid for every $1 in your 529	Will not reduce financial aid at all

Knowing those figures, our hypothetical saver, decides she is going to save $80,000 for her daughter's education. However, rather than scrimp and save to increase her contributions ***before*** her daughter goes to college, Jane knows that she'll have plenty of cash value to make a tax free withdrawal of $80,000 at age 43, and all she'll have to do to still have her desired outcome number at age 65 is increase her annual savings contributions to her IUL after age 43 from her planned $10,000 to $12,000 per year, a number she knows will be easily doable if she stays on track in her career path.

Besides which, that monthly increase of $166.67 makes her total monthly savings equal to 15% of her take home pay, a number closer to what the experts say she should be saving anyway.

Let's see what that looks like in the projections.

Age	Year	Premium Outlay	Withdrawals	Loans	Policy Value Net of Surrender Charges	Loan Balance	Loan Repayment	Cash Surrender Value	Death Benefit
42	18	7,200	0	0	182,265	0	0	182,265	916,944
43	19	-72,825	80,000	0	121,000	0	0	121,000	587,718
44	20	12,000	0	0	140,587	0	0	140,587	659,164
45	21	12,000	0	0	161,492	0	0	161,492	730,819
46	22	12,000	0	0	183,790	0	0	183,790	802,685
47	23	12,000	0	0	207,527	0	0	207,527	874,675
48	24	12,000	0	0	232,792	0	0	232,792	946,890
49	25	12,000	0	0	259,706	0	0	259,706	1,019,506

You'll notice that she never pays back this withdrawal and still, her cash value has recovered by the time she's 46 and her death benefit by age 48. Let's see what this did to her bottom line at age 65.

Age	Year	Premium Outlay	Cumulative Premium	Policy Value	Cash Surrender Value	Death Benefit
63	39	12,000	284,175	889,106	889,106	2,167,925
64	40	12,000	296,175	958,967	958,967	2,263,718
65	41&	12,000	308,175	1,033,250	1,033,250	2,361,937

She's pretty much right on track. Just $37,302 below her original projection of $1,070,552. Meaning if she works just one more year (until age 66, a year shy of her full Social Security benefit retirement age) or if she pays just a small portion of that back to herself by making a slightly larger contribution in just two years between age 44 and 65, she'll be ahead of her original projections.

Starting to understand just how powerful an IUL can be as a savings vehicle?

While Jane's money came from actual cash withdrawals from her account, another option is to have the insurance company loan you money from your account.

Think of it this way. Imagine you have a $100,000 Certificate of Deposit at your current bank — say a 5-year CD paying 5% interest. You couldn't touch the money during those five years without having a substantial penalty levied against the interest credited to your account. For example, you want to buy a car for $40,000. Breaking up the CD would cost you in earned interest. So, you ask your banker if you could simply pledge the CD for a $40,000 loan. Thus, you would not interrupt the total interest being earned on the CD. The bank charges you, say, 7% interest on the car loan. You pay a net 2% above what you are earning. Not a bad deal.

Participating loans from an IUL policy work the same way. The earnings on the investment portion of the policy are not affected by either having loans or not having loans. The only cost of borrowing is the loan interest and the (temporary) reduction in cash value and death benefit. You also have to remember that policy expense charges are ongoing. Here's an important difference though. While participating loans on an IUL on the high end may cost you up to say, 6% interest (lower than the bank example), the better IUL index strategies may pay you 7%, 8%, even 10% in the long run. So, beating the loan rate is a real possibility eventually. For loans you don't pay back, it's smart to expect it to take 15 years or longer for your cumulative index credits to exceed both the policy charges and the accrued loan interest.

For a down payment on a home the formula works pretty much the same way (depending on the size of the down payment) but if we look at Jane's original projections again, by age 35 she could easily afford to loan herself the 20% down payment for a decent house.

Age	Year	Premium Outlay	Cumulative Premium	Policy Value	Cash Surrender Value	Death Benefit
35	11	6,000	61,800	72,893	68,859	468,041
36	12	6,000	67,800	83,537	80,527	517,783
37	13	6,000	73,800	94,898	92,911	567,994
38	14	6,000	79,800	107,026	106,002	618,713
39	15	6,000	85,800	119,973	119,973	669,977

Or by age 53, she could buy a $400,000 home in cash.

Age	Year	Premium Outlay	Cumulative Premium	Policy Value	Cash Surrender Value	Death Benefit
52	28	7,200	174,600	403,904	403,904	1,426,401
53	29	7,200	181,800	437,552	437,552	1,492,332

Note though in the latter case, Jane would probably have to continue working until age 70, or at least have another revenue stream to pay herself back to achieve the same retirement income she originally planned.

That latter scenario assumes Jane is a single mother with no financial contribution from a life partner, however, my point being that an IUL can be extremely useful beyond simply saving for retirement and save you truckloads of money over your lifetime in finance charges by third parties. Planned well, you can make yourself your own banker and never lose a dime.

Add to that concept that many IULs have an optional long term care rider. What that means is that you can use your IUL to set up payments for Long Term Care versus buying a separate policy for that coverage.

Long term care is the type of ongoing assistance and/or supervision that you may need if you are unable to perform normal daily activities on your own, such as bathing, dressing, eating, toileting, or getting in and out of bed or, if you are severely cognitively impaired. The need for long term care can arise from an accident or illness as well as the normal aging process.

With a Long Term Care (LTC) provision connected to an IUL, you can collect long term care benefits should you need this type of care and if you never use the long term care benefit, there is a death benefit.

The monthly benefit payments would help take care of any qualifying costs, including costs associated with long term care facility confinement, home health care services, adult day care, either at home or in an adult day care center and/or hospice care. Since any separate long term care insurance policy would require you to be in good health when you apply, having this provision built into your IUL could be a smart move.

What are the odds you'll need long term care as you grow older? Don't go by the government statistic that "70 percent of people over age 65 need some long-term care". That number was based on a government study conducted years ago, and while it may indeed be accurate, the government's definition for "long-term care" is quite encompassing and not relevant to a discussion regarding long term care insurance.

Most people purchase coverage with a 90-day elimination period — a 90-day deductible, or where you or someone else will pay for care for the first 90 days until the policy kicks in. For example, anyone spending ten days recovering in a skilled nursing facility following a hospital stay would be considered by the government as having "needed long-term care," but with most insurance policies requiring a 90-day waiting period before their benefits begin, they would not qualify for long-term care insurance benefit payments. That's why we don't use government statistics.

According to the American Association for Long-Term Care Insurance for someone with a 90-day elimination period, actuaries gauged the lifetime chance of someone buying coverage at age 60 and using policy benefits was 35%. So, 35% will use their coverage and 65% will not. As you might assume, the decline is because during those first 90 days, some people will recover and some will die.

Having that provision in place long before age 60 eliminates that 1 in 3 risk.

Chapter Twenty-two

IULs are a terrible investment

"Life insurance is a terrible investment" says the person who doesn't realize that insurance products aren't investments. Substitute "savings plan" for "investment" in that sentence and then you've got an argument with me.

Still, with all the good things that an IUL can do, you're probably saying to yourself "*There's gotta be a downside, otherwise everyone who's anyone would be recommending an IUL*".

Well naturally, there are plenty of critics if you look for them.

However, the reality is that so few advisors (including most of those you see on TV and hear on the radio) know how IULs actually work or how they can be used to your advantage in so many ways, that much of the reason they don't recommend them is either a) They're not licensed to sell them, so they either never talk about them or when they do talk about them, they make them sound like a poison pill (because every dollar you put into insurance is a dollar you can't spend with them); or b) They are licensed to sell them but they think they're too complicated for you (translation: they haven't taken the time to research them so they're too complicated for the advisor to understand and he/she doesn't want to point you to something that he/she doesn't know who to discuss); or c) They're not acting as a fiduciary.

Here's an example of text that I gleaned from a well-known advisory firm's website:

> ***If you're invested only in stocks and bonds and you're worried about a market meltdown, consider further diversifying your portfolio. Look for something that isn't correlated to the market (precious metals, for example), or talk to your adviser about safer investments (such as U.S. Treasuries) and put a portion of your savings there. That way, if the market is doing poorly, you'll have other investments that are OK.***

Their idea of "safer" investments being T-bills, which, with a little over one percent interest rates, are clearly not going to provide you with similar gains to the equity market. There's no mention of anything insurance related because they don't sell anything insurance related. They are strictly a broker/dealer with no insurance licensing, so naturally, they're only going to point you to things that they're familiar with (and licensed to sell). And, oh, by the way, that they get paid to sell.

It's pretty easy to tell if they're the kind of advisor you're looking for often by simply reading their disclaimers. Sometimes they're hard to find, often buried on separate web pages that, face it, you never look at until something goes sideways. But they are always there somewhere since they're required by regulators both on a national basis and in whatever state they do business.

On another well-known advisor's website is this disclaimer:

> *No investment strategy can guarantee a profit or protect against loss in periods of declining values. Past performance does not guarantee future results. Consult your financial professional before making any investment decision. Annuity guarantees rely on the financial strength and claims-paying ability of the issuing insurer. Any comments regarding safe and secure investments, and guaranteed income streams refer only to fixed insurance products. They do not refer, in any way, to securities or investment advisory products. Fixed insurance and annuity are not offered by [redacted] Advisors.*

Obviously, this particular firm doesn't consider an IUL an "investment strategy" and rightly so, since it's an insurance product, it's not considered an investment in the traditional (or legal) sense. And yet, while they clearly point out that they don't offer insurance or annuity products, they seem to be discounting any guarantees that insurance offerings can provide. I'll wager anyone who asks an advisor at this firm about an IUL is likely to get one of these pat responses, many of which are just parroted directly from an article that has been floating around the internet since 2012 entitled "*The Top 10 Reasons NOT to BUY Equity Indexed Universal Life*". (Note that if you Google that, you'll also find some articles from other IUL experts that refute each reason, point by point.) A good example being the following:

"Internal administration fees charged against cash value on any type of Universal Life policy that are shown on illustrations are run under current expense levels but those can change at any time at the discretion of the company. Since the insurance company uses this money to run its operations, as their internal costs go up, they may choose to substantially increase these

internal costs over time, after you have bought the policy, making the cost of insurance higher than the interest credited to your account causing the policy to eventually lapse".

As with most deceptive marketing practices, there is a kernel of truth in them that makes them believable. Yes, the insurance companies reserve the right to raise internal insurance costs, they'd be business morons if they didn't retain that right. Virtually nothing stays the same in price over multiple decades. But, in practice, these companies, many with more than 100+ years in business, realize that what that critique describes would be a huge mistake. If fact, I am not aware that any "top" company (meaning any company that myself or any well trained advisor would recommend to a client) has done that in any material way since IULs were first introduced in 1997, and I'm also not aware of any of the companies that any good advisor would put into a top ten list that has announced any plans to do so. As costs increase, they generally apply those increased administrative costs to new policies, not existing ones.

That said, no two IUL policies from different companies are identical in every way. While it's rare for expenses to increase, it's not unheard of. The expenses charged against the policy *could* increase meaning there will be less cash value in your policy because the life insurance component took some of it. From a cautionary point of view, historically, that generally happens in small companies with less financial staying power than the top dogs so your choice in that regard is important.

You have to actually read the policy you are considering and understand what is and what is not guaranteed to stay the same after the policy is issued. The key distinction here is what the industry refers to as "current company practice" versus "contractual guarantees". If you don't know the difference or don't understand any part of the language of the policy, have your agent or advisor explain it until you do understand it.

And don't press the reject button just because something can change, that alone doesn't make it bad. In fact, most policies guarantee only a handful of terms against change. You simply want to know what potentially *can* change and get some understanding as to how drastic the changes might be to make an educated decision. No nodding in agreement when they ask, "Do you understand?" if you don't.

No question is a stupid question when it comes to your financial security in the future.

Another common cautionary tale that I hear advisors tell clients interested in IULs is this:

"The point of all buying insurance is to shift the risk from the insured to the insurance company, all types of Universal Life shift the risk back from the insurance company to the insured".

This one baffles me whenever I hear it. It's baloney and I find it ironic that advisors whose mantra is "No risk, no gain", who ask to be paid in situations where you take 100% of the risk, suddenly seem to think that you, as the client, shouldn't take any. Even though with an IUL, neither the insurance company nor the insured bears *all* the risk.

The main risk that anyone takes when they buy into an IUL is that there will not be a gain *every* year. Based on past performance however, statistically, there *will* be a gain in close to 7 out of every

10 years. Since it bears repeating, in the last 50 years (1975-2024) there have only been 13 years that the S&P 500 went into negative territory, of the other 38, 37 were in positive territory (we had one 0 year in 2011), only 10 years had less than a double-digit gain. The average gain in those 37 positive years since 1970 was 15.86%.

Anyone who wants a method that is supposedly "*guaranteed*" to pay you a measly 2-3% (net) per year *every* single year – and never 0% – should buy a simple Whole Life policy.

Now don't get me wrong, aside from the incredibly slow growth factor, there's nothing wrong with owning a Whole Life policy. In fact, according to LIMRA's 2024 Life Insurance Sales Report, Whole Life remains the most popular product in the industry, having accounted for 29% of life insurance market share in 2024, followed by Indexed Universal Life at 25% (a 13% *increase* from the 2021), Term Life with 19%, Variable Universal Life at 11% (versus 33% in 2000, by the way) and finally Fixed Universal Life at 7%.

Of course, what that study doesn't show is that all 'Final Expense' (funeral/burial policies) are Whole Life policies and they're being sold by the thousands. Those policies with face values of just $25,000 or less (many in the $2,000 to $5,000 range) are ridiculously easy sales to Baby Boomers in their late sixties and seventies whose Term Life has now expired, who have saved next to nothing for retirement and they've realized that, on their death, their kids or kin may have to foot the bill for the ever growing cost of their funeral and burial.

If you're comparing an Indexed Universal Life policy to buying Term Life and investing the savings, or buying a Whole Life policy, there is no one to say which is better for you except you. Which is better should be based on your goals and your risk tolerance. It depends on what you plan to use this policy for, as well as what guarantees you're looking for.

Let's use Andy as an example and see where he would end up with his retirement nest egg using the "buy term and invest the difference" method versus a typical IUL or Whole Life policy.

Andy started saving for retirement on his 30th birthday in 2001, in the midst of a 3-year bear market because he was getting married later that year and he knew he shouldn't wait any longer.

That year was a big one for Andy. Aside from getting married, he and his new bride used up all their existing savings to put a down payment on the house of their dreams, so their retirement savings was starting from scratch.

As the sole breadwinner, naturally Andy wanted to ensure that his new bride would never have to leave their dream home should anything happen to him and his income, so Andy bought a 30 year Term Life policy with a $423,525 death benefit/face value (the exact amount of their 30 year mortgage) through his company's benefits group on the day after they bought the house. His company doesn't offer a group term life plan so Andy bought a standard individual Term Life policy from a name brand company. Now 20 years into the term of that policy, it still costs him just $38.42 per month (which is also the average monthly premium cost, for someone in better than average health aka the preferred rate, of 16 of the top Life Insurance companies for those specifications), in other words, he pays $461.12 annually.

When Andy first bought into his company's 401(k) plan in 2001, his salary was $60,000 a year. Andy decided he wanted to be able to save the recommended 15% or more of his gross salary, so he was aiming at an annual investment of $9,000 (15% of $60,000) or $750 of his pre-tax monthly salary deposited directly into his 401(k) per month. Andy's pretty sharp, so rather than trying to chase the best mutual fund, Andy and his wife decided that money should be invested 100% into an S&P ETF fund within his 401(k) so the results of his investment exactly match the results of the diversity of the entire S&P 500.

Luckily for Andy, his company matches his dollar for dollar investment up to 6% of his salary. Since Andy was putting aside far more than 6%, that match is 100% free money. A no-brainer for Andy. Since the company makes that match, Andy knew he had some wriggle room with how much he could invest monthly and still stay over that 15% target so he decided to reduce his monthly contribution by the exact amount of his life insurance and have the policy premium paid by direct deposit right from his check every month. That way he'd be sure never to miss a premium payment without even having to think about it.

So, in total, Andy started investing by having $750, less the cost of his $38.42 monthly Life insurance premium, or $711.58 monthly go into his 401(k), which rounded up to the nearest dollar is $8,539 annually. Adding the company match, the full 6% of his salary, Andy's starting annual investment was $12,139 in 2005, a full 20% of his annual gross income.

Andy works on a factory floor and likes his job so even after 20 years on the job, he plans to stick with it. Every year Andy gets a cost of living raise of 2.5% and most years, that keeps up with inflation. In keeping with his retirement savings strategy, he also increases the amount he invests every year by 2.5% as well. Since his pay goes up every year, so does the company match amount, so this year, putting all that together 20 years later in 2025, Andy's annual investment will be a total of $19,682.

Now, since we don't have a crystal ball to see the future, let's assume that the next 40 years of economic activity exactly mirrors those last 40 years, meaning we'll start to project Andy's eventual outcome by using the S&P results for 2024 and 2025 and then by using the actual results from 40 years prior (1985) as the starting point.

We know that's not what will really happen, but we can be certain there will be Bull markets and Bear markets that are similar, we just don't have any idea of the timing or the severity.

Besides comparing his results with an IUL, we'll also mirror that chart with what would happen if he invests the standard of 15% of his gross salary, meaning $9,000 a year ($750 per month) into a non-qualified (taxable) investment account and increases that amount every year by the same amount he does with his 401(k). And we'll do the same thing with a Whole Life policy to see the comparison of the other three strategies.

We'll also assume, for ease of math throughout, that Andy never experiences any long term unemployment and is a hyper-disciplined investor, continuing to contribute to his retirement savings plan, through good times and bad, every year until he retires on his 71st birthday, January 1st, 2042. Forty-one years of growth…he hopes...before he starts to take his planned distribution of $150,000 to start and increase that amount yearly to keep pace with inflation.

What do you think? Will Andy be able to hit his target with the current and future amounts he plans to invest? Or will he run out of money like most Baby Boomers will do? Let's have a look.

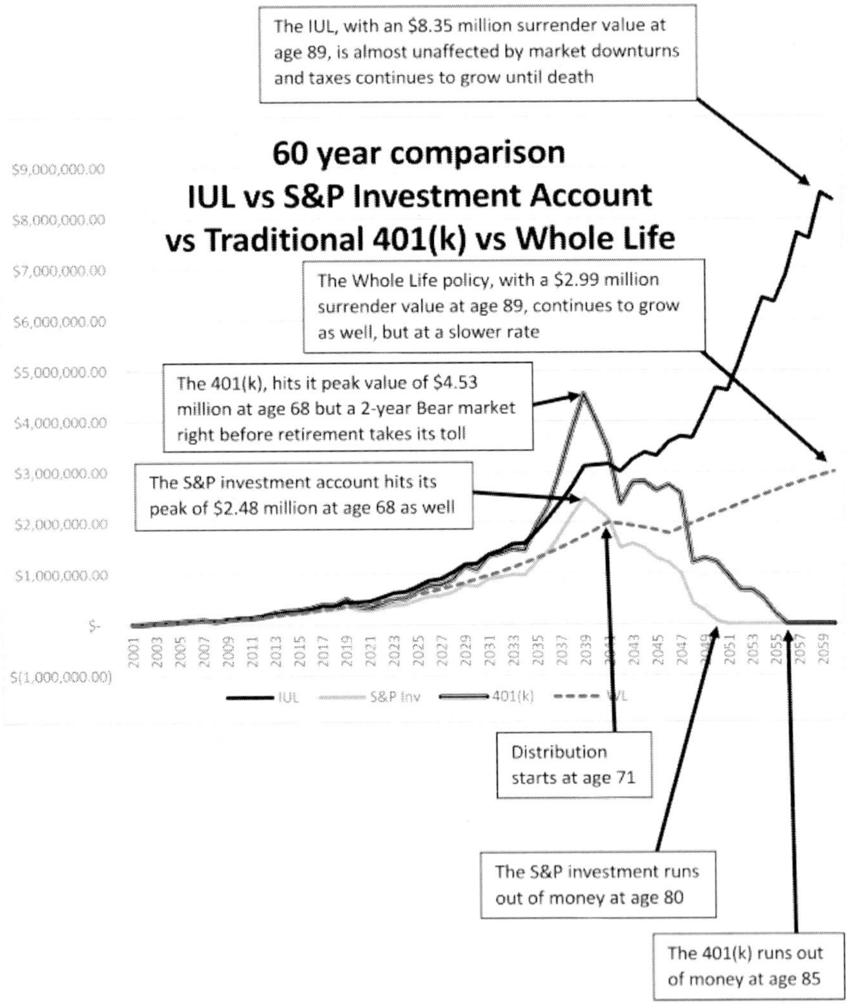

That chart shows a comparison between a properly structured Indexed Universal Life policy (tied to the S&P) with a 13.25% cap and a 0% floor, a taxable investment account invested solely in the S&P 500 index, a typical 401(k) invested in an S&P index fund and a Whole Life policy which has a guaranteed annual interest rate of 3.5% and pays an annual dividend of 2.5% (6% total being the combined average of the top 11 WL companies over the last 10 years).

You'll notice right away that for the first 19 years, the ROI for each is remarkably similar because even with the down market he started in and the financial disaster that 2008 became, Andy didn't have that much invested to make a noticeable difference compared to later on. Naturally, if we magnified this significantly the losses in 401(k) and investment account would be more obvious.

At the end of 2041, just before Andy starts taking money out for his retirement distribution, the IUL's cash surrender value of $3,156,529.13, is actually slightly less than the 401(k) value of $3,437,541.68, but remember, taxes have to be taken out of the 401(k) distributions, the IUL's distributions are tax free when structured correctly.

Also, in this chart, the years 2040 through 2042 might exactly mirror what happened in 2000, 2001 and 2002 when the S&P lost 46.55% collectively. Historically, a three in a row annual loss for the S&P is exceedingly rare, but a total loss of 46.55% in 3 years is very realistic. For Andy, this is unfortunate timing, something the financial industry refers to as '**Sequence Risk**'. Sequence risk is the danger that the timing of withdrawals from a retirement account will damage the investor's overall return. Account withdrawals taken out during a bear market are more costly than the same withdrawals in a bull market. A diversified portfolio can protect your savings against sequence risk of returns but all of Andy's investment is in equities and since he retires in 2042 and starts taking his money out during a down market, he experiences that sequential risk in a significant way unless he postpones his retirement. In this chart, the Murphy's Law-like timing is a double whammy which hastens both the 401(k) account and the S&P investment account's decline.

Meanwhile, the IUL holds its own and then starts an unending climb despite future down markets. Both the S&P investment fund and the 401(k) zero out right about the same time Andy's second (far more expensive) term policy expires, leaving him relying on Social Security (if it still exists) and without any legacy of life insurance to pass along to his family after his death.

I know what you're thinking. What if Andy's sequence of returns was different – meaning better – when he retired? Well, let's take a look and see what would happen if instead of 2040, 2041 and 2042 being negative, they were positive. Instead of negative 10.14, 13.04 and 23.37% respectively, let's substitute a positive number. Let's use 8.77 (the average return for the S&P from 1980 to 2020) making yet another record bull run of 11 years.

As you can see in the following chart, all the accounts that are tied to the S&P returns do better…temporarily…but once another market crash happens, the IUL once again gets the best of them. And while in this scenario, the 401(k) account doesn't run out of money, the difference in account value by age 89 is significant; the IUL having $9.34 million in cash value in contrast to the 401(k)'s

$2.21 million, only 23% of the IUL's cash value. And equally notable, the S&P investment account, despite a much better sequence of returns for Andy, would still run out of money by the time he reached age 85.

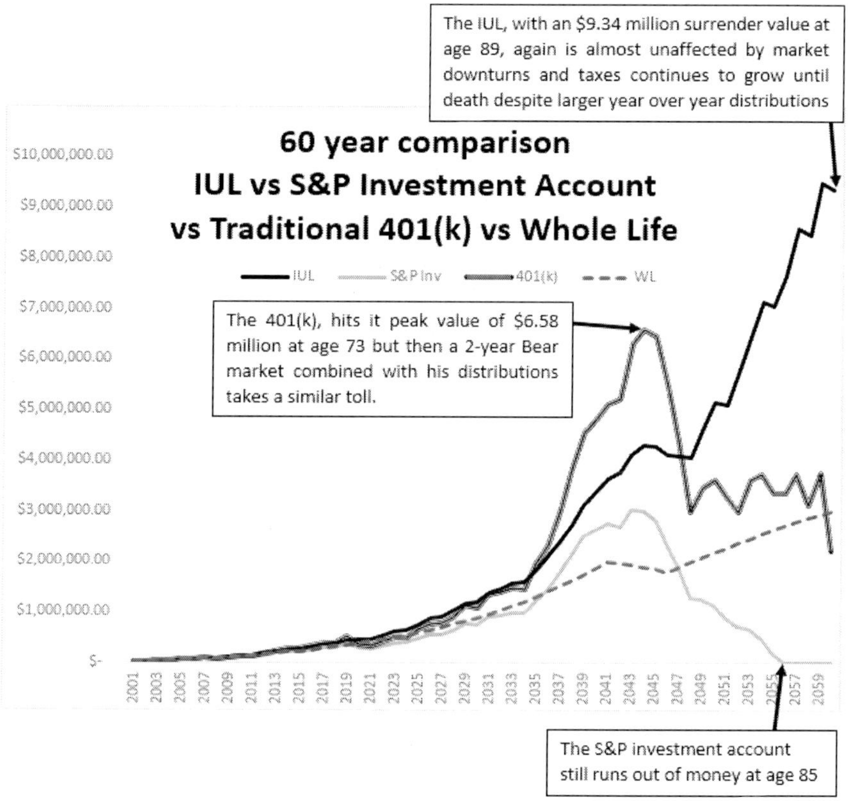

Naturally, while the 401(k) plan experiences the same gains and losses as the taxable investment account because the underlying investment is the same, it does significantly better over time because there are no income taxes being taken out every year on any investment gains.

Also, note that the 401(k) *appears* to have a better long term result than the Whole Life policy until another downturn hits late on the horizon. However, sometimes appearances can be deceiving. Remember that 401(k) plans don't *eliminate* taxes, they only delay when you are required to pay them. The tradeoff being that when he does start distributions from the 401(k), they are taxed at personal income rates, generally higher than capital gains tax rates.

Assuming, in the next 40+ years, taxes go up only slightly for Andy, meaning no crazy laws go into effect between now and then that the government uses to tap into his 401(k) savings and the highest he's ever required to pay on his income from his 401(k) is 6% higher (30% versus the 24% we used for his high end in the charts), then that money runs out a full year earlier than in the first chart.

Do you really want to ride that roller-coaster if you don't have to? If the market is even remotely similar in the future, which account would you rather have for the next 50+ years?

An added bonus that you should take note of is that with the kind of money that Andy is socking away, if that money were placed into an IUL, the face value (death benefit) of his Life Insurance policy wouldn't be a constant $423,525 for 30 years, like it would with a term life policy. Nor would he have to pay $5,801 annually *and qualify for* a <u>new</u> term policy for the same $423,525 face amount at age 60 (if he's still insurable at all by then). An IUL policy is permanent meaning he'd never have to worry about it or having to qualify ever again, and the death benefit value, by age 60 (when the Term Life policy expired) would be $1.37 million (not $423,525 like the Term Life policy) and continue to increase even after he starts taking money out, growing to an over $4.9 million death benefit by age 89.

Obviously, if he dies ahead of his time, with an IUL his family would be much better off financially than with a traditional Term Life plan.

That said, again, if you're simply looking for more guaranteed growth and predictable cash flow, then a Whole Life product may be best for you. With that type of policy, you would have a guaranteed growth rate as well as a guaranteed cost of insurance.

An IUL is typically better for long-term, after-tax retirement cash flow. With an IUL policy, insurance costs may not be guaranteed, and neither is the growth in the policy. However, while not having a guaranteed growth rate might sound like a negative situation, cash value growth through higher IUL crediting rates will almost always be *substantially* higher than a Whole Life policy (and obviously and "buy term and invest the difference" strategy, whether qualified or not).

As mentioned previously, the S&P's average investment return in the 40 years we're using is 8.77%, compared to the actual annualized return, known in the financial services industry as the **Compound Annual Growth Rate** (CAGR). The CAGR of the S&P 500 from 1871 to 2024 (153 years), including reinvestment of dividends, has been roughly 9.16%. 10.26% being the arithmetic mean, but adjusted for inflation, that's 6.91%.

While 9-ish percent might be the average, the returns in any given year are far from average. In fact, between 1926 and 2024, returns were in that "average-ish" band of 8 to 12% only eight times. The rest of the time they were either much lower or much higher. Volatility being the normal state of play in the stock market.

Nevertheless, even though the market is so unpredictable, returns *tend* to be positive in a given year, rather than negative. Meaning the apocalyptic view of the economy tanking for so many years in a row that IUL detractors (especially purveyors of Whole Life) often use as a reason not to buy one is less likely than you getting eaten by a shark, and they full well know it.

Of course, it doesn't rise every year, but over time the market has gone up on a year to year basis about 70% of the time. It's that other 30% that does the damage to retail investors and 401(k)s. And on a more micro level it's any negative month that may flip your mental switch to panic mode, causing you to cash out at or near the lowest point and missing the rebound entirely.

Imagine what's going to happen the next time some new virus gets announced. Inevitably, some people will fear the worst and panic again, selling off their portfolios trying to get ahead of any downturn. Factor in that aspect of human nature and it becomes pretty clear why most people don't get the kinds of returns they initially expect from investing in the market. The hard to swallow reality is you don't have to miss many good days to feel a negative impact. Your returns would have gone from positive to negative by missing just the 20 best days of the market over the last 20 years. Putnam Investments found comparable results by studying the data from 2003 to 2018. If you were fully invested in the S&P 500, your annualized total return would be 7.7% during that time. But if you missed only the 10 best days in the market, it dropped to a measly 2.65%.

Now take a look at those charts one more time and you'll quickly realize exactly why Pamela Yellen, author of the "Bank on

Yourself" series of books that tout Whole Life with paid-up additions to grow your wealth had said that *"IUL[s] may actually be the worst financial vehicle ever invented".* It sounds as if she hopes you'll stay uninformed and won't realize that in almost every scenario, an IUL will beat a Whole Life policy for long term growth hands down. And interestingly, since the changes to the 7702 code, Ms. Yellen has stopped heavily promoting life insurance entirely and has taken up a new banner pushing Indexed Annuities to her aging audience (IUL's cousin without any death benefit).

Any permanent life insurance should be purchased with the intent of it being a lifetime asset. From that perspective, an IUL, set up correctly, can be expected to perform better in terms of growing wealth at competitive rates, but with zero risk — and at a lower cost — than anything else available!

Speaking of permanency, you might be saying to yourself "This is a lifetime commitment. What If I lose my job?"

Good question. There is no telling what the future holds. Lots of people unexpectedly lost their jobs during the Corona virus crisis. That's why you should always have an emergency fund at the ready. However, remember that IUL policies are flexible and you aren't locked into just one payment amount. So, if you should find yourself unexpectedly unemployed, you would be able to reduce your payment down to the minimum (which is usually 20% of your normal monthly premium). Then, later on, you can catch up by putting more money back into your policy if you choose to.

Alternatively, if you have enough cash value in your policy to work with, then you can stop paying premiums altogether and just use the cash value to pay the premiums until you can resume payment. I don't recommend that, but it's an option if you've exhausted your emergency fund and find yourself in a tough spot.

Just like auto insurance, most Life insurance companies will cancel your Term policy if you miss just one month of premium. Not so with an IUL.

Another reason you'll be told to stay away from IULs is this:

"Indexed Universal Life policies don't provide the policy holder with any credit for dividends paid out by the equities making up the index. The insurance company's side fund for an IUL isn't actually invested in the index, so instead the index is used to determine the gross crediting rate for the side fund. If your money were actually invested in the stocks, the investor would get both the positive change in the net asset value [they're eternally optimistic, never mentioning what happens when the market goes down] ***as well as the dividend income. However, with IULs, any gains accrued by any dividends is left out of the equation entirely".***

This statement is actually true. However, multiple studies have back tested the S&P *with* dividends vs top selling IULs (without dividend gains) for 20-year periods going back to 1960, and the IUL always comes out ahead because the **Net Asset Value** (NAV) never goes down in an IUL (excluding internal expenses). The worst that can happen in down years in terms of investment return is a zero gain. Not to mention that the dividends you receive with any Whole life policy are those distributed only by the underwriting insurance company (not all the stocks in the S&P 500), and if you have an investment account, only those stocks that pay some small dividend, not the S&P index (ETFs pay dividends but they're taxes as ordinary income which can range from 0% to 40%) as a whole, so the total value of the dividends you might receive is vastly different from what the detractors are trying to steer you to believe.

Remember that 9.16% figure of the CAGR for the S&P 500 historically?

That includes ALL the dividends from every S&P 500 company over that timeframe. Without the dividends, the S&P's historic arithmetic average return would be just 5.97% (with a CAGR of only 4.37%).

So how does an IUL do so much better?

Simple: they don't lose money.

Again, what matters is not how much you *make*, but how much you *keep*. So, yes, it's true that with an IUL you don't get paid the dividends that you would receive if you actually owned the stock. Regardless, if the end game of how much you *net* with an IUL is more than double what you would have received if you had invested (in some form) in the actual market with dividends, which makes more sense to you? Not to mention that you'll sleep better at night knowing that with an IUL there is *zero* market risk, and not having to worry about whether or how your portfolio needs to be rebalanced to make up for a big loss.

Your profits in an IUL are locked in every year. To lock in profits from any other stock portfolio, you have to sell the stock and that money is then no longer part of your investment.

Yet another reason you'll see or hear about why not to invest in an IUL has to do with participation rates and caps. Typically, the argument against participation rates is that they are sometimes less than 100%. You'll likely be told that participation ratios are *often* less than 100%. And as mentioned above, the side fund is not invested directly in the index and many insurance companies only credit a certain percentage of the increase in the market. You'll hear something to the effect that:

"…the participation ratio is often at 80% or less meaning you are getting only 80% of the increase in the market".

Again, there is a small kernel of truth in this statement, but for the most part it is bent on scaring you. In reality, I have followed and analyzed about 100 different IUL's from 30+ companies for several years now, and for a typical annual point-to-point plan — *with a cap* — the participation rate is 100% (of the market gain up to the cap). All of the IULs I would recommend guarantee it will never be less than that. Some are more. I've seen up to 140% in several. Generally, the *only* time the participation rate is less than 100% is if there is NO cap — then it can be down to 40-60% — or more than 100% depending on the crediting time period.

From my point of view, the more complicated the IUL crediting strategy is, the less likely it is to deliver the best bang for your buck. Life insurance is a competitive marketplace and insurers are always trying to come up with some new twist that will win out over the competition. Simple and straightforward is always better.

One of the most outrageous claims that I've heard come from people pitching the Infinite Banking or Bank on Yourself Whole Life strategies, who claim that the illustrations shown by IULs are "*fictitious*" because they use averages and actual market results are never consistent. The claim is that during down years, when many

IULs have a 0% credit, there are still insurance costs and administrative fees that make the 0% years actually negative, so too many of them will deplete your cash value and cause your policy to lapse.

Again, this claim has just a hint of truth in it. In general, what you'll see in the illustrations that are presented, when you work with an insurance professional that designs IULs, are year over year projections based on the average returns that the particular fund (or funds) that you choose for your allocation have had for the last 20 years or more and then reduced even further according to highly regulated rules by the Department of Insurance in the State that you reside in. As described earlier, illustrations typically contain three sets of assumptions: the maximum they are allowed to show (which in *every* case is a highly regulated conservative estimate based on the actual historic returns of the fund used), the worst-case scenario (or, the minimum contract guarantee) and something falling in between.

They don't randomly make these things up and there are incredibly strict rules as to what they can and cannot show for the exact reason that the above claim is made – that they have to be realistic and achievable based on the actual performance history of the fund.

In fact, new rules for illustrations went into effect for Indexed Universal Life insurance products in mid-2015. The National Association of Insurance Commissioners (NAIC) adopted Actuarial Guideline 49 (commonly abbreviated as AG 49), which, for the first time, set uniform standards governing the illustrations insurers use in the sale of Indexed Universal Life insurance policies.

AG 49's first phase was meant to address what were seen by regulators as unrealistically high assumptions in illustrations of the maximum rate of return on an IUL contract. The first phase of AG 49 went into effect in September of 2015, and March of 2016 marked the implementation for the second phase.

Like fixed indexed annuities, growth in IULs is limited on the upside through features such as caps and participation rates, but there's also a buffer to the downside. Prior to the guidelines, two companies using the same index and crediting method could illustrate two different rates, according to the NAIC, and you would expect them to be remarkably similar. AG 49 is expected to keep maximum illustrated interest rates below 7% annually, but the actual allowable illustrated rate will be based on fund performance history.

The second phase of the guidelines standardized policy loan illustrations. If, for example, an investor was to borrow money from an IUL policy at an interest rate of 4% and the insurer projects a contract return of 8%, the investor may think there was a positive loan arbitrage, whereby he or she could actually make money even after taking the loan.

Regulators felt that doesn't always reflect reality though, and to some extent that's true. In poorly performing markets, if growth wasn't large enough to cover the amount owed in interest payments (i.e., several consecutive down — or flat — years), that loan (if it were big enough) could wipe out cash value and ultimately cause an investor's policy to lapse.

More recently, the NAIC has focused its attention on some new bells and whistles that some insurance companies have added to their IULs (again, in an effort to distinguish themselves against others in the industry), that "enhance" the performance of their product through the use of bonus interest crediting. Many regulators believe these types of additional crediting strategies are designed specifically to skirt the AG 49 restrictions and show higher than normally allowed illustration averages.

Lately, IUL policy options can feel a bit like shopping for a new car. Each one seems to have its own particular features, performs, and costs a little differently here and there, and has different built-in bonuses attached and nearly every carrier now employs at least one and, in many cases, more than one method to improve illustrative performance.

These add-ons, generally known as interest bonus credits frequently have different names associated with them such as "persistency bonus" or "account value enhancement". Interest bonuses vary primarily by type, amount, guarantee of the bonus, and start year but whatever they are called, they generally come in one of three forms: additional flat rate credits, multipliers, and look-back bonuses.

Flat rate credits are pretty much exactly what they sound like. A flat rate bonus pays additional interest at a fixed additional interest rate, usually beginning at a specific time (most apply after the policy has been in force for a minimum of 10 years), currently up to around 0.75%. For example, if an illustration's illustrated rate is set to 6.5% with a ½ percent interest bonus beginning in year 11, then the ledger would show values returning a 7% interest credit after the bonus activates.

Multipliers are much more complicated. They literally multiply the indexed interest returns by some factor. For example, if a policy has a 15% multiplier and the index returns a 7% interest credit, the total interest with bonus credited will be 7% times 1.15 which equals 8.05%, higher than AG 49 restrictions currently allow without them. Multipliers can take two distinct forms: as an inherent part of a specific index allocation or as a persistency bonus. If the multiplier is tied to the allocation, it most often begins when the policy does, and if it is a persistency bonus, the current trend is to begin in year 11. Normally, if the multiplier is tied to an allocation, the name of the index will have the words "multiplier account" as part of the naming convention, such as S&P 500 Multiplier Account.

Look-back bonuses provide a sort of safety net for some set number of years past. For example, one carrier will test actual cumulative index performance over the most recent eight policy years, and if the index returns have averaged less than 3% per year, the policy's account value will be adjusted to reflect a minimum of an effective 3% return for all eight years.

While that's not likely (and the insurer knows it), that certainly shoots down the criticism of extended periods of no gain years. Especially from a Whole Life perspective since 3% is right around the top of what Whole Life policies typically guarantee on an annual basis.

IUL detractors bank on the fact that you don't really understand how regulated the insurance industry is in favor of consumers. Not only will AG 49 likely be quickly enhanced to further limit the index crediting that is illustrated, but most IUL policies already have an "overloan protection" rider that (at the policyholder's discretion) essentially freezes policies where loan balances exceed a certain threshold as a percentage of cash value in the policy.

This stops the policyholder from continuing to take additional loans from the policy, but it also avoids a lapse meaning it avoids a potentially disastrous situation.

The second phase of AG 49 is viewed as a bigger deal in the application of Indexed Universal Life for use in retirement planning where investors put money into the contract and borrow it tax-free.

Don't forget that with an IUL you get to keep all your annual gains. They are locked in (less the annual insurance costs) forever. The market can never take them back from you. This is why people love IULs.

Some critics claim that because IUL illustrations use averages, they inflate the results and don't reflect real world outcomes, especially if the first one or two years of your policy experience flat (0%) growth because you bought into it during a down market.

Unsurprisingly, they are "cherry picking" what they think is a scenario that will scare you into opting for the unchangeable guaranteed interest rate of a Whole Life policy, but that's what some scheming salespeople do, right? They make a statement that they can prove in some specified scenario that they hope you'll believe is commonplace.

Well let's use some historic figures to see if that's an accurate statement. For this experiment, we'll use the actual annual returns for the timeframe that a typical person will seriously save for retirement – 30 years – the last three decades, going back to 1995.

12/29/1995	**34.11%**
12/31/1996	20.26%
12/31/1997	**31.01%**
12/31/1998	**26.67%**
12/31/1999	19.53%
12/29/2000	**-10.14%**
12/31/2001	**-13.04%**
12/31/2002	**-23.37%**
12/31/2003	**26.38%**
12/31/2004	8.99%
12/30/2005	3.00%
12/29/2006	13.62%
12/31/2007	3.53%
12/31/2008	-38.49%
12/31/2009	23.45%
12/31/2010	12.78%
12/30/2011	0.00%
12/31/2012	13.41%
12/31/2013	**29.60%**
12/31/2014	11.39%
12/31/2015	-0.73%
12/30/2016	9.54%
12/29/2017	19.42%
12/31/2018	-6.24%
12/31/2019	**28.88%**
12/31/2020	16.26%
12/31/2021	**26.89%**
12/31/2022	**-19.44%**
12/31/2023	**24.23%**
11/1/2024	**22.95%**
AVERAGE=	**10.48%**

Please note that 2024 only includes 11 months at the time of this writing. Considering the economy I'm going to assume that December of 2024 doesn't have any major change one way or the other.

How typical is this timeframe?

Well, the first five years with a total gain of 131.58% (an average of 26.32% annually) are extraordinary. However, the next three years (2000-2002) produce a triple whammy of a 46.55% loss. Then the pendulum swings back favorably with following five years producing a 55.52% gain, and so on.

Overall, for the 30 years of 1995 through 2024 the average gain was 10.48%, nearly a full point higher than where most pundits point to as the typical long term gain in the stock market. However, considering the cumulative inflation rate from 2021-2024 was 19.4%, that makes those last gains less significant.

This particular 30 year period had seven years of annual gains of more than 25% and only one year with a loss higher than 25%. It had only eight negative years, one flat year of zero gain and another eleven positive years having mostly double digit returns far higher than the 9 or 10 percent average often quoted.

Now, let's assume you invested $1000.00 per month ($12,000 annually) starting on January 1st of each year for those 30 years. You never increase that amount and never waiver regardless of the market's volatility.

If someone illustrated what your result of investing that money in the S&P during those 30 years, they might be using that 9.50 average number, and tell you that's just to simply the math.

What would those results look like?

Over $2 million dollars. Pretty darn good, right? Except that's not even close to reality. The real amount that you'd end up with *after taxes* (remember those nasty things) is just over half of that.

Using the average number throughout.

12/30/1994	10.48%	$ 13,257.60
12/29/1995	10.48%	$ 27,904.60
12/31/1996	10.48%	$ 44,086.60
12/31/1997	10.48%	$ 61,964.47
12/31/1998	10.48%	$ 81,715.95
12/31/1999	10.48%	$ 103,537.38
12/29/2000	10.48%	$ 127,645.70
12/31/2001	10.48%	$ 154,280.57
12/31/2002	10.48%	$ 183,706.77
12/31/2003	10.48%	$ 216,216.84
12/31/2004	10.48%	$ 252,133.97
12/30/2005	10.48%	$ 291,815.21
12/29/2006	10.48%	$ 335,655.04
12/31/2007	10.48%	$ 384,089.29
12/31/2008	10.48%	$ 437,599.45
12/31/2009	10.48%	$ 496,717.47
12/31/2010	10.48%	$ 562,031.06
12/30/2011	10.48%	$ 634,189.51
12/31/2012	10.48%	$ 713,910.18
12/31/2013	10.48%	$ 801,985.56
12/31/2014	10.48%	$ 899,291.25
12/31/2015	10.48%	$ 1,006,794.57
12/30/2016	10.48%	$ 1,125,564.24
12/29/2017	10.48%	$ 1,256,780.98
12/31/2018	10.48%	$ 1,401,749.22
12/31/2019	10.48%	$ 1,561,910.14
12/31/2020	10.48%	$ 1,738,855.92
12/31/2021	10.48%	$ 1,934,345.62
12/31/2022	10.48%	$ 2,150,322.65
11/30/2023	10.48%	$ 2,388,934.06

Using the real historical numbers.

12/29/1995	**34.11%**	$	16,093.20
12/31/1996	20.26%	$	33,784.88
12/31/1997	**31.01%**	$	59,982.77
12/31/1998	**26.67%**	$	91,180.58
12/31/1999	19.53%	$	123,331.75
12/29/2000	-10.14%	$	121,609.11
12/31/2001	-13.04%	$	116,186.48
12/31/2002	-23.37%	$	98,229.30
12/31/2003	**26.38%**	$	139,307.79
12/31/2004	8.99%	$	164,910.36
12/30/2005	3.00%	$	182,217.67
12/29/2006	13.62%	$	220,670.12
12/31/2007	3.53%	$	240,883.37
12/31/2008	-38.49%	$	155,548.56
12/31/2009	23.45%	$	206,838.70
12/31/2010	12.78%	$	246,806.29
12/30/2011	0.00%	$	258,806.29
12/31/2012	13.41%	$	307,121.41
12/31/2013	**29.60%**	$	413,581.35
12/31/2014	11.39%	$	474,055.06
12/31/2015	-0.73%	$	482,506.86
12/30/2016	9.54%	$	541,682.81
12/29/2017	19.42%	$	661,208.02
12/31/2018	-6.24%	$	631,199.84
12/31/2019	**28.88%**	$	828,955.95
12/31/2020	16.26%	$	977,695.39
12/31/2021	**26.89%**	$	1,255,824.48
12/31/2022	-19.44%	$	1,021,359.40
12/31/2023	**24.23%**	$	1,283,742.38
11/1/2024	**22.95%**	$	1,593,115.26

But hold on a minute. Fees. What about fees related to any form of investment account? Whether it's self-directed or not, somebody somewhere is taking a piece of your pie.

Let's use a very nominal 0.5% fee on your AUM.

		$ 12,000.00	Annually	
		Before Fees	Fees (0.5%)	Net After Fees
12/29/1995	**34.11%**	$ 16,093.20	$ 80.47	$ 16,012.73
12/31/1996	20.26%	$ 33,688.11	$ 168.44	$ 33,519.67
12/31/1997	**31.01%**	$ 59,635.32	$ 298.18	$ 59,337.15
12/31/1998	**26.67%**	$ 90,362.76	$ 451.81	$ 89,910.95
12/31/1999	19.53%	$ 121,814.16	$ 609.07	$ 121,205.09
12/29/2000	**-10.14%**	$ 119,698.09	$ 598.49	$ 119,099.60
12/31/2001	**-13.04%**	$ 114,004.21	$ 570.02	$ 113,434.19
12/31/2002	**-23.37%**	$ 96,120.22	$ 480.60	$ 95,639.62
12/31/2003	**26.38%**	$ 136,034.95	$ 680.17	$ 135,354.78
12/31/2004	8.99%	$ 160,601.97	$ 803.01	$ 159,798.96
12/30/2005	3.00%	$ 176,952.93	$ 884.76	$ 176,068.17
12/29/2006	13.62%	$ 213,683.05	$ 1,068.42	$ 212,614.64
12/31/2007	3.53%	$ 232,543.53	$ 1,162.72	$ 231,380.82
12/31/2008	**-38.49%**	$ 149,703.54	$ 748.52	$ 148,955.02
12/31/2009	23.45%	$ 198,698.97	$ 993.49	$ 197,705.48
12/31/2010	12.78%	$ 236,505.84	$ 1,182.53	$ 235,323.31
12/30/2011	0.00%	$ 247,323.31	$ 1,236.62	$ 246,086.69
12/31/2012	13.41%	$ 292,696.12	$ 1,463.48	$ 291,232.64
12/31/2013	**29.60%**	$ 392,989.50	$ 1,964.95	$ 391,024.55
12/31/2014	11.39%	$ 448,929.05	$ 2,244.65	$ 446,684.40
12/31/2015	**-0.73%**	$ 455,336.01	$ 2,276.68	$ 453,059.33
12/30/2016	9.54%	$ 509,425.99	$ 2,547.13	$ 506,878.86
12/29/2017	19.42%	$ 619,645.13	$ 3,098.23	$ 616,546.91
12/31/2018	**-6.24%**	$ 589,325.58	$ 2,946.63	$ 586,378.95
12/31/2019	**28.88%**	$ 771,190.79	$ 3,855.95	$ 767,334.84
12/31/2020	16.26%	$ 906,054.68	$ 4,530.27	$ 901,524.41
12/31/2021	**26.89%**	$ 1,159,171.12	$ 5,795.86	$ 1,153,375.27
12/31/2022	**-19.44%**	$ 938,826.32	$ 4,694.13	$ 934,132.18
12/31/2023	**24.23%**	$ 1,175,380.01	$ 5,876.90	$ 1,169,503.11
11/1/2024	**22.95%**	$ 1,452,658.08	$ 7,263.29	$ 1,445,394.79

Big difference. The result using averages would actually be $795,818.83 more than if they showed you a prediction based on a repetition of the actual market results for the last 30 years. More than three quarters of a million dollars difference! So now you understand why mutual fund providers always show averages.

We talked about fees earlier so the fact that the reduced amount after fees should be no surprise but, in this case, it is indeed a whopper of a difference from the averages. $943,539.27! And note that the typical total investment and trading expenses in a managed account are now around 1.2%, not the 0.5% we used in that example – you might pay that small a fee if you manage it yourself and only use ETFs.

You should also be aware that in this scenario, the investor is not rich and not poor (over $44,625 in personal income but less than $492,301) and over these 30 years has never sold anything for any profit (not real typical but a lot easier math) and so has never paid any taxes on this amount.

If those two things are accurate, then whenever he or she starts to take this money out, taxes between 15% (typical long term gains tax rate for that income) and 35% (at maximum personal income rates for that range of income if were all in a 401K) will apply.

The bottom line is it will be significantly less than that $1.2 million dollar number. Very likely in the realm of 25% less in spendable cash over a 20 year retirement. But let's forgo the taxes for the moment and use that $1,445,394.79 as a benchmark – which, by the way, does not include any deduction for life insurance, long term care or critical illness insurance – all of which are typically included in the premium cost of an Indexed Universal Life policy.

Interestingly, insurance laws being what they are, illustrations for any life insurance policy are not allowed to show the averages for the returns of the underlying investment (like the S&P) nor are they allowed to show historical actual numbers. Instead, they are required to show illustrations with no higher than around 7.5%. Almost a full 3 percentage points lower than the actual average of this 30 year timeframe we're using.

However, what did we find out about illustrations that show averages? They're nearly always wrong and more than likely significantly inflated, so hence the insurance law's requirement for a lower number. But does that solve the problem? Does that make it closer to reality?

Let's see.

We'll use as IUL with a 0.00% floor and a 11.50% cap (very typical numbers for today's IULs) and compare the averages to a backtest of actual results.

Using an average of 7.50 for 30 years the same we did previously, the final number would be $1,333,852.29.

That's not *too* far off the before fees and taxes historical number of $1,593,115.26. Better to underestimate it than overestimate it, right? So maybe those insurance laws restricting the numbers shown on IUL illustrations are doing their job.

Not quite. The same way that mutual fund marketers use averages to make things look rosy, insurance companies do the same thing. When you add in the cost of insurance and administration fees, etc. The real bottom line is much different than what the averages show. But how do they compare? And more importantly, how does what an IUL can produce in spendable cash

(cash value in insurance parlance) compare to what investing in the S&P will do?

Let's take a look using those historical numbers AND deducting ALL the typical fees that are embedded in any good IUL.

Policy Year			$ 12,000.00 Before Fees	Fees	Net After Fees
1	12/29/1995	11.50%	$ 13,380.00	$1,094.85	$ 12,285.15
2	12/31/1996	11.50%	$ 27,077.94	$1,110.97	$ 25,966.97
3	12/31/1997	11.50%	$ 42,333.17	$1,127.89	$ 41,205.28
4	12/31/1998	11.50%	$ 59,323.89	$1,145.70	$ 58,178.19
5	12/31/1999	11.50%	$ 78,248.68	$1,164.51	$ 77,084.17
6	12/29/2000	0.00%	$ 89,084.17	$1,184.43	$ 87,899.74
7	12/31/2001	0.00%	$ 99,899.74	$1,205.61	$ 98,694.13
8	12/31/2002	0.00%	$ 110,694.13	$1,228.21	$ 109,465.92
9	12/31/2003	11.50%	$ 135,434.50	$1,252.44	$ 134,182.06
10	12/31/2004	8.99%	$ 159,323.83	$1,278.50	$ 158,045.33
11	12/30/2005	3.00%	$ 175,146.69	$ 814.68	$ 174,332.01
12	12/29/2006	11.50%	$ 207,760.20	$ 845.27	$ 206,914.93
13	12/31/2007	3.53%	$ 226,642.62	$ 878.64	$ 225,763.98
14	12/31/2008	0.00%	$ 237,763.98	$ 915.22	$ 236,848.76
15	12/31/2009	11.50%	$ 277,466.37	$ 955.51	$ 276,510.86
16	12/31/2010	11.50%	$ 321,689.61	$1,000.08	$ 320,689.53
17	12/30/2011	0.00%	$ 332,689.53	$1,083.63	$ 331,605.90
18	12/31/2012	11.50%	$ 383,120.58	$1,158.67	$ 381,961.90
19	12/31/2013	11.50%	$ 439,267.52	$1,236.22	$ 438,031.31
20	12/31/2014	11.39%	$ 501,289.87	$1,326.27	$ 499,963.60
21	12/31/2015	0.00%	$ 511,963.60	$1,429.85	$ 510,533.75
22	12/30/2016	9.54%	$ 572,383.47	$1,547.97	$ 570,835.50
23	12/29/2017	11.50%	$ 649,861.58	$1,615.51	$ 648,246.07
24	12/31/2018	0.00%	$ 660,246.07	$1,707.35	$ 658,538.72
25	12/31/2019	11.50%	$ 747,650.67	$1,799.78	$ 745,850.89
26	12/31/2020	11.50%	$ 845,003.74	$1,892.81	$ 843,110.93
27	12/31/2021	11.50%	$ 953,448.69	$1,986.44	$ 951,462.24
28	12/31/2022	0.00%	$ 963,462.24	$2,080.70	$ 961,381.54
29	12/31/2023	11.50%	$1,085,320.42	$2,175.61	$ 1,083,144.81
30	11/1/2024	11.50%	$1,221,086.46	$2,271.17	$ 1,218,815.29

Hmmm…using the actual illustration numbers for a 30 year old, non-smoker, from a name brand company, it turns out that if the next 30 years of S&P 500 results are exactly like the last thirty, the actual results of investing in the S&P (even after fees) will be *better* than the IUL policy projection using the same backtested actual historical numbers by a whopping $226,579.50

That's right around a 15.6% difference compared to the $1,445,394.79 we calculated as the benchmarked backtested investment return in an investment account, pre-taxes.

Nearly a quarter million dollars is a lot of money. Is that enough to make you think you could still do better with some other method of investing? Well, let's not overlook a properly structured IUL's added bonus of no taxes ever having to be paid and a death benefit of over $1.2 million dollars. That's nothing to spit at.

But is this a fair comparison?

Truthfully, it's not. Using just the numbers I've shown you in those tables, it's actually still heavily biased *against* the IUL because the IUL table on the previous page includes all the expenses related to those numbers, where the returns we used for the hypothetical investment account does not.

Taxes will take a hefty bite out of any investment account outside of a Roth. In reality the real spendable cash in retirement for that example will be between $1,011.176 and $1,156,317 (and that's IF and only if the money isn't take out in a lump sum to buy an annuity, and the stock market doesn't have another lost decade), significantly less than the IUL's tax free outcome.

In addition, these tables show only 30 years of results. Your accumulation period could easily be 40 years (if you start early or retire later, or both) which would add a great deal to an IUL. Not to mention that throughout that entire time and beyond, you'd never have the stress of worrying about what the economy is doing to your portfolio. How do you put a price on that?

Remember that exercise I posed to you regarding starting with a penny and doubling it every day for 30 days? If you don't remember the result, look back on page 108 and you'll see the end result was $5,368,709.12. The thing is that after 15 days that number was only $16,384. The same compounding effect applies here. The cash value for an IUL identical to the one we used as an example after 40 years is projected at $2.7 million, more than twice what the bottom line on the table on page 324 shows, and by age 89 it's $8.4 million. Compounding gets better over time because it starts from a bigger number each period.

In order to compare apples to apples for this timespan, we should also be looking at what additional expenses would need to be taken out of those investment returns on an annual basis for the cost of life insurance that is embedded in an IUL.

Assuming this person bought a 30 year term life policy at age 30, in the same amount that we use for the IUL, the cost for that policy over those 30 years is another $13,833.68. And remember, then that policy expires at 60 leaving our investor with no life insurance at a time when they probably still have significant debt. Adding the cost of that same policy for another 25 years (to age 85) would cost an additional $139,236.48, further reducing his or her next egg with lost opportunity expense by reducing compounding impact.

But even that lost opportunity cost doesn't take into account the behavioral science aspect that after two years of consecutive losses, like in 2000 and 2001, the typical investor (like you) is not likely to continue 'throwing good money after bad' and would likely opt to stop putting in the $12K until the market recovered – missing out on most or all of the big gain when it does.

Assuming those costs even *without* the in and out market behavior, the spendable cash total of the investment account in the example shown, after taxes and all expenses, if the next 30 years exactly imitated the last two decades of market results, would certainly not be that $1,445,394.79 we originally used as a benchmark.

How much less? There are tons of variables to consider for that number but figure around 35 to 40 percent less. Pretty significant difference.

Even Dave Ramsey (who has some *seriously* misguided perceptions about IULs) will tell you that since no one can predict the future, the only way to reasonably judge a particular investment is to look back at its history. Meaning the market is likely to do over a long period of time, what the market has done over a long period of time, plus or minus any "*Wow, that was great*" and any "*Wow, that was terrible*" events. The critical issue being that no one can accurately predict when either of those will or won't happen. It would be nice to be party to the former, and IULs (up to their cap) will do that while 100% protecting you against the loss of gain and/or principal related to the latter.

Nay-sayers will refute that example by finding examples of IULs whose illustrations predict some "blue sky", higher than actual results over the same time period that seem totally unrealistic – and maybe are. But even without some of the new add-ons that some insurers are using, not every IUL performs the same over time, but there's more than enough historic data to look at to find those that *do* consistently perform well. Think about that for a second. Why would you consider those IULs that critics point to when there are better performing plain, vanilla versions that they will never talk about?

What the detractors fail to point out to you is that there is no 4 or 5 year "recovery" period with IULs (even when the market doesn't cooperate early on) so, because you never lose money, when the market recovers, the asset growth is exponentially faster.

Of course, there are internal expenses that impact your IUL during flat years, like the cost of insurance usually being the largest, but your incoming premium will always cover that early on and in later years it might come from your cash value. If the IUL is designed right, those kinds of expenses will be almost imperceivable in contrast to the growth over time.

In contrast, the people that hawk the Bank on Yourself and Infinite Banking strategies using paid up Whole Life as the foundation of the program, being that Whole Life policies used to be able to guarantee 2-4% interest annually, and have no market correlation, naturally those strategies have to compete against the conservative 6-8% annual crediting generally shown in IUL illustrations. While it may be true that some IULs with lower caps may not outperform the S&P over time (Not all IULs are alike and the low cap ones I'm describing now shouldn't even be on your list to consider, but they do exist), in general, they will still out perform *any* Whole Life policy whose low interest never changes, even with the gain from dividends. Remember, most of the companies that offer IULs also sell Whole Life insurance and every IUL has an option to put some of your premium into their guaranteed fixed rate fund which normally matches the guaranteed interest rate of Whole Life policies they offer. They're certainly not going to ruin their business by purposefully offering some product that doesn't do what they claim it will.

For several years Whole Life insurance companies self-reported on themselves in something called the Blease report. Part of that report compared the distributions from various policies given a constant premium ($10,000) paid for 25 years and documented what each policy was illustrated to earn at the point of sale, and then what it *actually* earned 20 years later. Roger Blease died in 2013 and no one took over doing these, but in the last report the result for the 12 top performing companies, the projected (illustrated) **IRR** (Internal Rate of Return is a term used in accounting to define the metric that estimates the profitability of potential investments) was 6.72%, whereas the *actual* IRR 20 years later was only 3.81% — that is 43% less than projected. It's no wonder that salespeople pitching Whole Life strategies want to downplay the much higher (actual) returns of IULs by saying the illustrations don't match reality, when in truth, many IULs have outperformed even their highest illustrated projections.

Another point that salespeople who try to sway you to a Whole Life policy will talk about is consistency. They tout that the interest crediting for Whole Life never changes versus the ups and down of the market. They also make it seem like dividend payments never change, and often imply that when they do change, they go up. That's a load of hooey too.

The chart below is based on historical dividend data provided by topwholelife.com, a Whole Life insurance aggregator, about the six largest Whole Life insurance companies.

Historical Whole Life Insurance Company Dividend Rate Changes by Year						
Year	MassMutual	New York Life	Northwestern	Penn Mutual	Ohio National	Guardian
2024	Increased	Increased	Increased	Maintained	Maintained	Increased
2023	Maintained	Maintained	Maintained	Maintained	Maintained	Increased
2022	Maintained	Maintained	Maintained	Maintained	Decreased	Maintained
2021	Decreased	Decreased	Maintained	Decreased	Decreased	Maintained
2020	Decreased	Increased	Maintained	Maintained	Decreased	Maintained
2019	Maintained	Decreased	Increased	Decreased	Maintained	Maintained
2018	Decreased	Decreased	Decreased	Maintained	Decreased	Maintained
2017	Decreased	Increased	Decreased	Maintained	Decreased	Decreased
2016	Maintained	Maintained	Decreased	Maintained	Maintained	Maintained
2015	Maintained	Increased	Maintained	Maintained	Maintained	Decreased
2014	Increased	Increased	Maintained	Maintained	Maintained	Decreased
2013	Maintained	Increased	Decreased	Maintained	Decreased	Maintained
2012	Increased	Decreased	Decreased	Maintained	Maintained	Maintained
2011	Decreased	Maintained	Decreased	Maintained	Decreased	Decreased
2010	Decreased	Decreased	Decreased	Maintained	Maintained	Decreased
2009	Decreased	Decreased	Decreased	Maintained	Decreased	Increased
2008	Increased	Maintained	Maintained	Increased	Maintained	Increased
2007	Increased	Maintained	Maintained	Maintained	Maintained	Increased
2006	Increased	Maintained	Maintained	Increased	Decreased	Decreased
2005	Decreased	Maintained	Decreased	Maintained	Decreased	Increased
2004	Decreased	Maintained	Decreased	Decreased	Decreased	Decreased
2003	Decreased	Decreased	Decreased	Decreased	Maintained	Decreased
2002	Decreased	Decreased	Decreased	Maintained	Decreased	Decreased
2001	Maintained	Maintained	Maintained	Maintained	Maintained	Maintained
2000	Maintained	Maintained	Maintained	Maintained	N/A	Decreased
1999	Maintained	Maintained	Maintained	Decreased	N/A	Maintained
1998	Maintained	Maintained	Increased	Maintained	N/A	Increased
1997	Maintained	Maintained	Maintained	Decreased	N/A	Increased
1996	Decreased	Decreased	Maintained	Maintained	N/A	Decreased
1995	Decreased	Decreased	Maintained	Decreased	N/A	Decreased

As you can see, in the last 30 years, the decreases in dividend rates *far* outweigh the increases. Consistent is not a word I'd use to describe dividends unless you meant only in terms of how often they're paid.

And those decreases are really no surprise since Whole Life dividend rates often correlate with the bond market (because the allocation of assets are similar) and since the bond market reacts very closely with interest rates, so go the Whole Life dividends.

But what about those darn cap limits?

The short answer is caps change annually based on interest rate environments and market volatility, affecting policy performance.

The insurance company uses caps as the basis of how they fund the IUL. The company takes a portion of your premium and they buy options on the index that the funds in your policy are allocated to. How much they can buy depends on the portfolio performance rate of the insurance company's general investment fund (which consists primarily of high quality, fixed income instruments such as bonds and mortgages), which determines how much they have to spend. However, IULs differ from most general account products in two ways: 1) the way that it credits interest to policyholders, and 2) the participation limits that it sets on a policyholder's upside potential.

Life insurance companies do not invest their money (a sizable chunk of which is *your* premiums paid into any policy) using the same stock options that retail investors use because, by law, they are not allowed too. Solvency laws ensure that insurance companies' assets in reserve are far more than what their risk exposure is. They are mandated by strict regulations to maintain the actual cash assets in highly regulated, prudent, and relatively secure assets. With an IUL, you get to base your gains in a life insurance policy (risk free) on market gains – they cannot!

All that said, there are occasionally moving parts – primarily the cap. Rising interest rates typically lead to increasing caps, but this relationship is lagging; sustained increases in rates (generally for a year or more) are needed for caps to reflect those changes. Higher market volatility can lead to lower caps, as it becomes more expensive for insurance companies to hedge against risks. Conversely, in periods of low market volatility, caps may increase, illustrating the dual nature of how market conditions affect policy caps.

Typical cap rates for an Indexed Universal Life policies range between 8% and 12% per year. According to Wink Intel (Wink is an insurance marketing and consulting company that provides competitive intelligence to life insurance and annuity companies), the range of average caps on IUL contracts at this writing is between 10 and 12 percent.

Ordinarily, any of these rates are guaranteed for one year at a time, and historically, depending on the insurer, they can and do change from time to time. The only reason a company would need to lower these is if the interest they have earned is less, so they can only buy less options than the year before. Most companies will happily provide a cap history if you ask for one – and you will likely see it hasn't changed much in recent years. Also, caps are near the lowest they have ever been since they started around 20 years ago and yet many are still 14% or more.

However, the cap rate also depends on internal several factors as well, including:

- The specific IUL product you choose, and the terms and conditions of your coverage.
- The index or group of indexes your policy is connected to.

And to a lesser degree:

- How well you keep up with your premium payments
- And any adjustments you make to your policy, such as loans, withdrawals, or changes to your account value

If the underwriters haven't already dropped them to the guaranteed minimums during the recent low interest rate environment, then chances are they are unlikely to ever do so. Also, this works both ways. Caps and participation rates have gone up in the past and probably will again.

And naturally, you should consider that until recently, interest rates were at the lowest point since the mid 1950's, that's more than 60 years ago. The odds of interest rates going further down at the writing of this book, to a point that insurance companies would be forced to reduce their caps, is slim to none. The odds of interest rates going up in the future, however, are pretty high, meaning insurance companies are more likely to raise caps in the future than to lower them from where they are today.

Is that a too optimistic point of view? Hardly. Google historic interest rates and you'll quickly get the picture of what the future may look like.

The participation rate usually only changes if it is for an IUL with no cap, or if it is one (with a lower cap) for more than 100%.

It is very difficult for many insurance agents – let alone you, the consumer – to analyze (or even know what to analyze) to compare IUL's and have a sense of how they can be expected to really perform. What you should never do is compare IUL's using the illustration rates because almost all have different caps, costs, features, etc. The new AG 49 Illustration Rate rules are some help in this regard by making them all adhere to the same formula of how things are shown, but as mentioned before, some companies are using creative bonus features to basically circumvent those restrictions.

It'll probably come as no surprise to you to learn that the main force behind the lobby for AG-49 came from carriers that don't offer any Indexed Universal Life insurance. There is little doubt that they saw that companies that offered IULs were gaining market share at their expense, mainly stealing clients from their go-to product line, Whole Life Insurance. So, if you read or hear the argument about agents or companies cherry picking historic averages to make returns look rosy, consider the source, it's simply not accurate in today's marketplace.

I've also seen videos on YouTube from people who clearly have never actually read an IUL illustration ranting about how this "expert" or that "authority" said that the actual rates of return in IULs are dismal. It's pretty obvious they don't know that, by law, each IUL illustration <u>must</u> contain a page that shows at least the last 20 years (many show 25 now) of historic annual rate of return results in every fund that they offer. You can be the judge on that.

Even so, how well an IUL may perform is also determined by how it is designed. Remember, <u>no</u> illustration can accurately predict the future. If caps on a recently purchased policy are declining while interest rates have increased, this may be a potential cause for concern and should prompt a policy review. Caps should behave according to market trends, and any policy exhibiting abnormal performance may require examination to assess its health and long term suitability

Before I get off this subject, I'll point out that I already know you're going to go online and search for every video and article there is about why IULs may be a bad choice, if for no other reason than simply to see if I've given a good argument against ALL of them. In that vein, I'll relate a story that Kevin Nuber, Vice President of LifePro Financial Services tells in a video refuting those ten reasons not to invest in an IUL I mentioned earlier.

Kevin talks about a time when he was having serious chest pains. And just like you or I would do, he went online and listed his symptoms to get an idea of what his problem might be *before* he went to see his doctor. Common sense practice, right?

Well, what Kevin read online convinced him that he had somehow contracted a ***terminal*** disease! All the symptoms were the same, the progression was the same…it had to be that…after all, these were expert medical opinions he was reading.

So, Kevin went to the doctor, told him everything he'd learned on the internet and what his symptoms were, and the doctor's reaction wasn't at all what Kevin had expected. Instead of showing grave concern, he smiled, poured something into a glass, told Kevin to drink it and left the room. A few minutes later, the doctor returned and asked Kevin how he felt. Kevin responded that his chest pain was gone and he hadn't felt that good in a long time! The doctor's reply was "Kevin, you have heartburn".

I'm relating this story for the same reason that Kevin did. The internet is great place to access a lot of information about any subject. The problem is that there's no filter for you to know which information is good and which information is bad, or at the very least, misleading. And generally, for the latter, with the hidden purpose to dissuade you from further investigation and/or guide you away from the competition.

Without some objective expert guidance, you may end up with what you think is a terminal disease of your finances. In fact, that's part of the reason I included this whole chapter. Buying into an IUL should be a fully educated decision and to do that, you need to know what the facts *really* are and weigh them against what's in your best interest.

For the same reason you wouldn't go to an Optician for eye surgery, to put together a well-designed IUL you must work with a financial advisor who is also licensed to sell insurance and/or insurance professional who knows and understands how to do this, what companies offer the best IUL for your needs, and how the features and benefits compare to the other companies in the market. Few have that advanced training, but I'll happily help you find one if you have trouble on your own or simply want a second opinion on who you're planning to use.

The final caveat isn't really a red flag as much as it is a limitation.

Not everyone will qualify for an IUL. Like any other life insurance plan, you have to meet a minimum health standard before you can buy one. However, even if you, personally, don't qualify (for whatever reason) you could own (pay into and control) an IUL that insures a family member, and generally use the plan for the same long term results. It's all perfectly legal and above board and any competent agent or advisor can explain how that is done.

The good news on that front is that qualifications for an IUL aren't any more stringent than any other life insurance plan, and in some cases not qualifying for one company doesn't mean you won't qualify with another. If you have minor health problems, your agent or advisor can find the best company that you *will* qualify for.

Chapter Twenty-three

More examples

Just so you can see what's possible (and realistic) let's see what happens when, Jim, a 25-year-old saves just $100 a week ($400 a month) to age 65 and puts that money in an IUL with 12.25% cap, coverage of $220,000, that maximizes the cash value by minimizing his death benefit and an average illustration credit of 7.06%.

Age	Year	Premium Outlay	Cumulative Premium	Policy Value	Cash Surrender Value	Death Benefit
26	1	4,800	4,800	3,736	638	223,736
27	2	4,800	9,000	7,722	4,801	227,722
28	3	4,800	14,400	11,979	9,233	231,979
29	4	4,800	19,200	16,627	14,030	236,527
30	5	4,800	24,000	21,394	19,073	241,394
41	16	4,800	76,800	114,684	114,684	334,684
42	17	4,800	81,600	127,921	127,921	347,921
43	18	4,800	86,400	142,162	142,162	362,162
44	19	4,800	91,200	157,487	157,487	377,467
45	20	4,800	96,000	173,970	173,970	393,970
61	36	4,800	172,800	693,459	693,459	913,459
62	37	4,800	177,600	750,572	750,572	970,572
63	38	4,800	182,400	811,959	811,959	1,031,959
64	39	4,800	187,200	877,933	877,933	1,097,933
65	40	4,800	192,200	948,845	948,845	1,168,845

By age 65, with no increase in contributions, he has almost $950,000 in cash value and a $1.1+ million plus death benefit.

Even with a mediocre IUL company, that would allow Jim to take a $55,000 tax free annual distribution starting at age 66.

Age	Year	Annual Cash Flow	Annual Outlay	Policy Value	Cash Surrender Value	Death Benefit
96	71	55,000	-55,000	1,777,935	1,777,935	1,997,935
97	72	55,000	-55,000	1,814,164	1,814,164	2,034,164
98	73	55,000	-55,000	1,850,160	1,850,160	2,070,160
99	74	55,000	-55,000	1,885,696	1,885,696	2,105,696
100	75	55,000	-55,000	1,920,513	1,920,513	2,140,513

And by age 96 he still has a death benefit of more than $400K (after subtracting the loan balance) and by that time he's taken out more than $1.3 million *more* than he paid in premium. Not bad, eh?

Well, let's look at what would happen if his contributions kept pace with his increasing salary.

Age	Year	Premium Outlay	Cumulative Premium	Policy Value	Cash Surrender Value	Death Benefit
61	36	12,000	288,000	1,305,546	1,305,546	1,697,209
62	37	12,000	300,000	1,413,619	1,413,619	1,809,432
63	38	12,000	312,000	1,529,901	1,529,901	1,927,676
64	39	12,000	324,000	1,655,011	1,655,011	2,052,214
65	40	12,000	336,000	1,789,629	1,789,629	2,183,347

By simply increasing his contributions $50 per week ($200 per month) every five years, Jim could increase his retirement savings at age 65 by more than $840,000, which would allow for a substantially higher starting income after retirement. Of course, that assumes that Jim's ending salary is just over $120,000 at age 65 (40 years from now) and he saves 15% of his after-tax income. Imagine what these numbers would look like if Jim's starting salary is in the low six figures!

But let's say you're not 25 years old when you start. Okay, let's say Anne is a 30-year-old IT administrator and she's making just over $100,000 in annual salary, but even though her take home pay is only about 1/3 of that she knows that she needs to catch up, so she starts an IUL with a face value of $500,000 and paying about $833.33 per month ($10,000 annually) for the first five years.

Age	Year	Premium Outlay	Cumulative Premium	Policy Value	Cash Surrender Value	Death Benefit
31	1	10,000	10,000	7,426	0	507,426
32	2	10,000	20,000	15,629	5,039	515,629
33	3	10,000	30,000	24,496	13,906	524,496
34	4	10,000	40,000	34,136	23,546	534,136
35	5	10,000	50,000	44,690	34,100	544,690
39	9	12,500	100,000	107,596	97,006	607,596
40	10	12,500	112,500	126,650	117,860	626,649
43	13	14,000	154,500	197,040	193,546	849,249
44	14	14,000	168,500	223,678	221,878	932,238
59	29	16,000	396,500	933,867	933,867	2,360,796
60	30	16,000	412,500	1,010,489	1,010,489	2,472,949
64	34	18,000	484,500	1,378,926	1,378,926	2,972,577
65	35	18,000	502,500	1,486,062	1,486,062	3,106,523

As her salary grows, so do her contributions so that by age 60, she already has more than $1 million in cash value, and by age 65 she's got over $1.4 million. At that point, if she chose to, she could easily withdraw $1.25 million and buy herself a Qualified Longevity Annuity Contract (QLAC) that would guarantee her a lifetime income, but she'd have to pay taxes on her gain over the $502,500 that she paid in premium.

So, Anne decides she's going to work a few more years, but not add anything else to her IUL after age 66.

Then at age 70 she wants to have a tax-free income from her IUL of $80,000 per year. Here's how that looks.

Age	Year	Premium Outlay	Withdrawals	Loans	Policy Value Net of Surrender Charges	Loan Balance	Loan Repayment	Cash Surrender Value	Death Benefit
66	36	10,007	0	0	1,592,095	0	0	1,592,095	3,228,626
67	37	0	0	0	1,694,846	0	0	1,694,846	3,335,373
68	38	0	0	0	1,803,653	0	0	1,803,653	3,445,771
69	39	0	0	0	1,918,835	0	0	1,918,835	3,559,995
70	40	0	0	0	2,040,694	0	0	2,040,694	3,678,311
71	41	-80,025	80,000	0	2,089,178	0	0	2,089,178	3,660,303
72	42	-80,025	80,000	0	2,140,059	0	0	2,140,059	3,646,618
73	43	-80,025	80,000	0	2,193,271	0	0	2,193,271	3,637,146
74	44	-80,025	80,000	0	2,248,886	0	0	2,248,886	3,631,995
75	45	-80,025	80,000	0	2,306,988	0	0	2,306,988	3,631,198
76	46	-80,025	80,000	0	2,367,663	0	0	2,367,663	3,634,646
77	47	-80,025	32,507	48,442	2,478,683	48,442	0	2,430,241	3,665,171
78	48	-80,000	0	82,569	2,625,452	131,011	0	2,494,441	3,710,499
79	49	-80,000	0	84,220	2,775,453	215,232	0	2,560,221	3,753,415
80	50	-80,000	0	85,905	2,928,646	301,136	0	2,627,510	3,794,254
96	66	-80,000	0	117,929	5,549,260	1,934,361	0	3,614,899	4,158,505
97	67	-80,000	0	120,287	5,713,729	2,054,648	0	3,659,081	4,159,081
98	68	-80,000	0	122,693	5,885,068	2,177,341	0	3,707,727	4,207,727
99	69	-80,000	0	125,147	6,046,789	2,302,488	0	3,744,301	4,244,301
100	70	-80,000	0	127,650	6,196,374	2,430,138	0	3,766,236	4,266,236

For the first few years she takes tax free withdrawals totaling just under the amount she paid in premium (so no tax on any gain) and from then on, she loans herself the money (all tax free). And by age 100, she still has some $3.76 million in cash value yet to be dispersed, and if she died that year her, her heirs would still receive her death benefit (less the loan balance) of over $1.8 million dollars, even though (at that age) she would have already taken out $2.4 million over those 30 years which is $1.8 million more than more than she paid into her IUL in premium.

Or let's look at Ginny, who is 37 and just heard about IULs. Ginny is already a super saver. She has a decent savings in a 401(k) but she knows she can't take that money out without being heavily penalized in taxes. And the same goes for her Roth IRA. So, Ginny takes the $10,000 she had been saving in a side account because she couldn't hyper fund her defined contribution plans and plunks down that lump sum to jump start her IUL. Here's what Ginny's plan looks like.

Age	Year	Premium Outlay	Cumulative Premium	Policy Value	Cash Surrender Value	Death Benefit
38	1	15,935	15,935	12,182	497	512,182
39	2	12,000	27,935	21,593	9,908	521,593
40	3	12,000	39,935	31,849	20,164	531,849
41	4	12,000	51,935	43,025	31,340	543,025
42	5	12,000	63,935	55,272	43,587	555,272
43	6	12,000	75,935	68,586	56,901	568,586
44	7	12,000	87,935	83,110	71,425	583,110
45	8	12,000	99,935	98,849	87,164	598,849
46	9	12,000	111,935	115,948	104,263	615,948
47	10	12,000	123,935	134,450	124,752	634,450
48	11	12,000	135,935	154,502	146,673	654,502
49	12	12,000	147,935	175,903	170,060	675,903
50	13	12,000	159,935	198,737	194,881	698,737

With a starting face value of $500,000, to keep her IUL from becoming a Modified Endowment Contract, Ginny only pays in $494.58 per month her first year, so her total contribution in year one is $15,935, just seventeen cents less than the maximum 7 pay test amount (shown in every illustration) that keeps the policy from becoming a taxable MEC. From that point on, she pays in $1,000 per month until age 55 and then $1,200 per month until age 70.

At 71 she plans to take out $75,000 per year in tax free income. She has a family history that portends a lower life expectancy than most and unless some medical miracles happen between now and then, Ginny doesn't expect to live past 95, and she doesn't need to leave any to her heirs because at that point, they're already set, so her income plan looks like this.

Age	Year	Premium Outlay	Withdrawals	Loans	Policy Value Net of Surrender Charges	Loan Balance	Loan Repayment	Cash Surrender Value	Death Benefit
68	31	14,400	0	0	1,022,342	0	0	1,022,342	1,953,124
69	32	14,400	0	0	1,101,548	0	0	1,101,548	2,043,690
70	33	14,400	0	0	1,185,430	0	0	1,185,430	2,136,714
71	34	-75,025	75,000	0	1,185,311	0	0	1,185,311	2,076,700
72	35	-75,025	75,000	0	1,184,597	0	0	1,184,597	2,018,529
73	36	-75,025	75,000	0	1,183,367	0	0	1,183,367	1,962,400
74	37	-75,025	75,000	0	1,181,654	0	0	1,181,654	1,908,394
75	38	-75,025	75,000	0	1,179,252	0	0	1,179,252	1,856,142
76	39	-75,025	60,935	14,346	1,190,394	14,346	0	1,176,048	1,813,053
77	40	-75,000	0	76,787	1,262,452	91,133	0	1,171,319	1,800,297
93	56	-75,000	0	105,412	2,127,736	1,551,012	0	576,724	1,076,724
94	57	-75,000	0	107,520	2,117,250	1,658,532	0	458,718	958,718
95	58	-75,000	0	109,671	2,090,174	1,768,202	0	321,972	821,972
96	59	-75,000	0	111,864	2,044,881	1,880,067	0	164,814	664,814
97	60	-75,000	0	75,000	1,955,067	1,955,067	0	0	0

Her $75,000 income, that she increases every year after age 75 to keep up with inflation, will last her until she's 97 (if she lives that long).

But what if you're in your forties when you get this book? Is there no hope for you? Of course there is. You've still got 20 – 30 years to save depending on when you plan to retire. Here's a good example of a 40-year-old, Mark, who starts out at a $500,000 face value IUL and paying in $10,000 annually, again with the idea that he will increase his contributions by a couple thousand dollars per year every 5 years or so, up to a maximum of $18,000 when he turns 61 and plans to continue working until age 70. He already has some real estate investments that pay him some passive income and he expects to increase those holdings to make up a sizable portion of his retirement income. His goal with an IUL is to have at least $1 million by age 72 to use for a lifetime income annuity that will pay him about half of his ending salary.

You'll notice in the following table that he is able to do just that.

Age	Year	Premium Outlay	Cumulative Premium	Policy Value	Cash Surrender Value	Death Benefit
41	1	10,000	10,000	6,258	0	506,258
42	2	10,000	20,000	13,286	1,021	513,286
43	3	10,000	30,000	20,922	8,657	520,922
44	4	10,000	40,000	29,389	17,124	529,389
45	5	10,000	50,000	38,716	26,451	538,716
46	6	12,500	62,500	51,381	39,116	551,381
47	7	12,500	75,000	65,261	52,996	565,261
48	8	12,500	87,500	80,369	68,104	580,369
49	9	12,500	100,000	96,791	84,526	596,791
50	10	12,500	112,500	114,689	104,509	614,689
51	11	14,000	126,500	135,546	127,329	635,546
52	12	14,000	140,500	157,795	151,663	657,795
53	13	14,000	154,500	181,530	177,482	681,530
54	14	14,000	168,500	206,842	204,757	706,842
66	26	18,000	372,500	718,675	718,675	1,457,407
67	27	18,000	390,500	781,522	781,522	1,537,997
68	28	18,000	408,500	848,254	848,254	1,620,538
69	29	18,000	426,500	919,168	919,168	1,705,322
70	30	18,000	444,500	994,179	994,179	1,791,987
71	31	0	444,500	1,056,390	1,056,390	1,850,828
72 D	32	-1,000,025	-555,525	118,677	118,677	618,677
73	33	0	-555,525	121,373	121,373	621,373
74	34	0	-555,525	123,568	123,568	623,568
75	35	0	-555,525	125,189	125,189	625,189

The point of these examples is simply to show what IULs are capable of. And while the last three examples are all from the same company whose IUL has a 15% cap and uses a 7.75% illustration average, the COI from the IUL that we used for Jim has lower overall expenses, meaning even though the cap and historic averages are higher, the actual outcomes in terms of long term savings for might be significantly better over time for Anne, Ginny and Mark if they used the same IUL as Jim. Not to mention that all these examples use the simple average for the projections and we know from comparison that the actual market results over the same time period might be superior as well.

Little differences can mean a lot over time.

Chapter Twenty-four

End game

So now that you've got the lowdown on how IULs work and how they'll benefit you, you probably want to know how to plant your Money Tree as soon as possible.

First, let's review what you learned:

An Indexed Universal Life policy is a type of insurance that allows the policy holder the opportunity to increase the funds in the policy's cash value component based on the return on an underlying market index. Some of the most common indexes that are used within IUL policy include the Dow Jones Industrial Average (DJIA), EURO STOXX 50, Russell 2000, NASDAQ 100 Stock Price Index (NASDAQ 100), Standard & Poor's 400 (S&P MidCap 400), and Standard & Poor's 500 (S&P 500).

An IUL policy's cash value 'account' can never lose money due to a downturn in the market. IULs guarantee a minimum annual account value, locking in gains from each year. Which means that when you own an IUL insurance policy, whenever the underlying index's return is positive, you will have an increase in your policy's cash value – typically up to a set maximum called a "cap". However, if the underlying index performs negatively in a given year, the return that is credited to your cash value is usually 0% (or in some IULs up to 2%). This means that, while there may not be any increase during that period, there is also no loss. These policies will also allow you to allocate some (or all) of the money in the cash value component to a fixed account.

Here are eight reasons why you should want to use an IUL as a means to save for your future:

1. **The safety of zero chance of negative returns.**

   People who got burned by cliff dropping values of their investments in the stock, bond, and real estate markets since the turn of the century understand the value of an absolute guarantee that their annual returns will never be negative. That guarantee is exactly what Indexed Universal Life policies provide. If the index used by the policy declines over the time period measured, you are completely protected from that risk. There is never a decline in the contract's value due to declining values in the index, regardless of which one is selected.

2. **The insurance company absorbs the investment risk.**

   The insurance underwriting company provides interest credits to the index universal life product by investing in bonds and index options. What if any one (or more) of the bonds default? What if the counterparty to the index options defaults, like Lehman Brothers did to many insurers? The answer in both cases is that the insurer bears this risk and protects its contract holders (you) from it.

3. **The possibility of higher positive returns.**
   Safe alternatives without investment risk right now are suffering from incredibly low yields. Many are still at historical lows, and that makes them unattractive to many savers. With an IUL, if the index performs well over the point to point time period, the policy can result in an interest credit that often beats the pants off other safe methods of saving. Some IUL products even include interest crediting formulas that compare multiple indices and more heavily weight the better performing indices.
4. **The ability to create a tax-free cash flow in retirement.**
   Most other vehicles that are used to save for retirement create taxation. For example, IRAs and 401(k)s delay but do not eliminate taxes. In fact, in reality they allow you to save a small amount of taxes on your income now in only to have to pay a much larger amount in taxes later. Properly structured Indexed Universal Life policies, on the other hand, can create a totally tax-free cash flow in retirement. Through the use of contract loans after the paid in basis is met, your cash flow can be free of federal, state, and local income taxes, as well as free of the alternative minimum tax. And, it will also create a tax-free death benefit. This tax-free feature allows an IUL to be far more attractive than other alternatives, even if those alternatives create a higher pre-tax return.

5. **The death benefit provides pre-funding of your retirement plan for your family if you die.**
For any married couple, the ability to save for retirement usually depends upon the ability of one (or both) of the spouses to continue working and earning an income. As a result, the death of a working spouse can devastate the best-laid plans to fund retirement. The Life and Health Insurance Foundation for Education reports that a 35 year old man has more than a one in six chance of dying before retirement, and a man at age 45 has more than a one in seven chance of dying before age 65. IULs eliminate this risk by providing a life insurance death benefit. In addition, many insurance carriers now offer IULs with a Long Term Care rider and a waiver of premium in the event of disability. According to the Social Security Administration's Disability and Death Probability Tables for Insured Workers Born in 1997, more than one in four of today's 20-year-olds can expect to be out of work for at least a year because of a disabling condition before they reach the normal retirement age, some will never recover enough to go back into the workforce.
6. **Guaranteed return of premium.**
With most Indexed Universal Life products, your agent can use the carrier's illustration software to design a scenario where you can be assured of being able, at some point in time, to cancel the contract and receive back at least what you paid in over time. While most carriers do not provide a guaranteed return of premium beyond the free look period, it's not unusual for your agent or advisor to be able to create

a scenario where the guaranteed cash value equals the premiums paid after a period of time, for example, 10 years. This provides additional assurance to you that the IUL you're considering is safe.

7. **Insurance for a lifetime without paying for a lifetime.** One of the maybe unexpected bonuses for someone who uses an Indexed Universal Life policy to save for their golden years is that once you stop paying in premiums and start taking out a cash flow, the insurance coverage does not end. In fact, in a properly structured IUL, you can often continue to be insured for the rest of your life without ever having to pay an additional dime to the insurance company.
8. **No chance of government interference** We also know that compared to 401(k) and IRA plans, IULs have several advantages, like the fact that there are few restrictions on the amount that may be contributed annually to an IUL. Once you pass year seven, there are no limitations. However, our trusted government representatives have been known to change the rules and regulations where finances are concerned when times get tough. But since insurance products aren't regulated by the IRS, the likelihood of any government-imposed changes on Indexed Universal Life policies are next to zero.

All those things are great, but they don't help you if you don't take advantage of them. For most folks, retirement saving is something that you learn on the job – literally – often without a lot of help from anyone who's really knowledgeable. Most of us don't even think about how we might save for retirement before we have a decent paying job and someone from our HR group started handing us forms and talking about setting up our 401(k) or IRA.

It doesn't matter if you are someone who seeks out advice from the legitimate pros or simply someone who likes to do your own research and makes decisions that way, everyone struggles initially with trying to grasp the importance of just getting started.

Almost all of us procrastinate. The thing is, time is on your side only if you use it. Like everything else around you, common wisdom about your retirement, meaning doing what everyone else is doing because you don't know any better is no longer an option for you.

Consider yourself 'enlightened'.

However, below are a few common retirement savings mistakes that are all too common:

- ***Waiting to start saving for retirement until after you pay off debts or after you buy a house.***

If you're just starting out and you make enough to pay your bills and spend a couple bucks here and there, you're probably more focused on stuff that you think deserves your immediate attention, like repaying student loans or credit card debt. We already discussed why paying off student debt too early doesn't make sense from a growth standpoint, and even with some debt, you're far better off in the long run if you start saving as soon as you start working because, as you've see in the examples in this book, the sooner you start socking money away in the right place, the more time your money has to grow and compound on that growth.

Not to mention that I've seen far too many young couples use every dime of liquid capital they have available to put down on a house. Doing so leaves little room for "what if's" and may result in lost opportunity cost. Better to rent a little longer and save up more than be "house rich and cash poor". The reality is you'll probably end up with a nicer house to begin with.

- ***Not understanding that diversification doesn't mean "pick one from each column"***

It's highly likely that any retirement savings plan you're exposed to will offer multiple investment strategies, however, you probably won't achieve the right level of risk and diversification by simply dividing up your contributions across the board. Rather, match your goals with the strategy that's going to help you achieve them best, and knowing that all IULs rebalance their funds to help you make the most of the market should give you great peace of mind.

- ***Only focusing on past performance history***

It's tough to ignore past performance when you're trying to gauge where to invest money that you know you'll need down the road. However, there's a good reason why investment advertisements always include something to the effect of "Past performance is not a guarantee of future results". In reality, even with an IUL, past performance is completely unconnected to future results, but history sometimes repeats itself and the diversified portfolios of IULs never chase yesterday's high performers because we know that slow and steady wins the race every time.

- ***Not maximizing your savings rate***

Anyone who has an employer sponsored 401(k) plan has probably had some HR sponsored meeting where they talked about how much you *should* be saving. And again, if you have an employer who matches any percentage of your income, do enroll in that plan and invest up to that match rate. That's a 100% immediate gain. Use it to your advantage. However, regarding a savings rate, most employers set what's called 'default savings rate' – that's usually the percentage of your salary that they will match when you save toward retirement, typically between 3 and 6 percent. You should think of this as only a starting point. Generally speaking, it will have *zero* correlation to the amount you *should* be saving in order to meet your planned financial goals. Hopefully, you've already mapped that out, or if you haven't done that yet, get busy. Start increasing the amount you save by 1 to 3 percent every quarter until you find that you're one step past your comfort zone, then take a single step back. Or sit down with a financial planner and have them help you develop a personalized savings plan using an IUL.

- ***Panic selling when the market goes south***

We know now that human nature habitually reacts stronger to losses in the market than to gains that are slow and steady, which commonly leads most people whose savings are exposed to the market to "buy high and sell low" rather than the opposite. You already know that the bigger problem with trying to time the market is that you must somehow masterfully time it not just once, but twice – first when you sell (to dodge big losses), and then a second time when you buy back in (to capture the rebounding gains).

And you know that when you have money safely tucked away in an IUL, you can shrug off the news of market crashes knowing that you haven't lost a dime, and when the market recovers your savings will be growing at an even faster rate, not hoping just to get back where you started.

Learning how to save was a matter of trial and error for me and most of my friends and coworkers because we weren't exposed to the level of information that you have (maybe in your hand, in form of a cell phone) until we were much closer to retirement age. There was no Siri or Alexa that we could randomly ask questions that crossed our minds and get immediate answers or point us to where to find them. We often had to pay for the information we needed and many times it was just plain wrong. This book is written so you won't make those same mistakes.

That said, like anything else, with IULs, one size does *not* fit all.

An IUL policy is best suited for someone who plans to make contribution increments in a steady stream but may need the occasional flexibility that most any other type of investment that is exposed to the market can offer, but with zero risk of loss; someone who knows that they will eventually have a need for life insurance protection or the ability to create a legacy to be passed onto heirs tax free and wants the potential of significantly tax advantaged cash flow in retirement.

Certain aspects of where you are in life and your mindset about saving in general can greatly affect whether an IUL policy is the best choice for you. If you can answer "yes" to the following, then the Millennial Money Tree strategy is the right choice for your savings for the future:

- ✓ Can you commit to a long-term savings strategy (however big or small)?
- ✓ Are you (or perhaps the person you may be buying a policy for) still 20 or more years from retirement?

- ✓ Are guarantees against loss of your savings investments important to you?
- ✓ Are you concerned about the potential negative impact of taxes on your retirement income, both now and in the future?

As I've mentioned before, Indexed Universal Life insurance policies should only be purchased by someone who understands the pros and cons of an IUL policy. And, no, that does not mean that you just went on YouTube and searched for "Pros and Cons of an IUL policy". While that's a good start, consider the sources. Too many of those are primarily promotional messages meant to point you in one direction or another. What I mean is that you read this book – thoroughly – so go back and re-read parts that you just skimmed or skipped altogether.

More important than that, I highly recommend finding an unbiased and reputable financial advisor or an insurance specialist as part of your decision making process. The former will help you narrow down the choices of providers that will meet your needs, but he or she may not be licensed with the insurance company you ultimately want to use. That may require contacting the company to find a licensed insurance agent near you that can take your application (based on your consultation with your financial advisor). Or I can recommend several I know.

Now I know many of you are tempted to skip the financial advisor cost (usually you can find a good fee-based advisor — remember to ask if they act as a fiduciary — that won't charge you for an initial consultation), but I'll warn you against trying to wingit on your own. Remember, you're making what should be a lifelong decision.

That said, doing some research to narrow down the best IULs to consider is fairly easy. There are several companies that consistently appear in any list of the top providers of IULs and they are there not just because they have great marketing and aggressive salespeople. Some of the highest ranking in terms of sales and value (in no particular order of recommendation) include:

- AIG
- American National
- AXA Equitable
- John Hancock
- Lincoln National
- Minnesota Life
- Mutual of Omaha
- National Life Group
- North American Company
- Pacific Life
- Penn Mutual
- Prudential
- Symetra
- Transamerica

Some you may have heard of, others you may never have heard of. But these are all A+ rated insurance companies, so from a financial strength perspective, they all pass with flying colors.

However, all IUL policies do come with their own set of variables that some would look at as risks. We've already covered many of those in the previous chapter but there are some other things that you'll want to check on with any IUL. Make sure you fully understand the cap, (the rate of growth that your policy may be limited to receiving in any given crediting period) and the amount of "growth" that is credited or given to the policy, based on the underlying market index performance.

The best IUL companies will demonstrate a history of maintaining both attractive IUL Caps and Crediting rates, and a highly trained IUL professional can help you find the best IUL product for your specific needs.

Also, make sure you understand what happens if interest rates go up once you have loans borrowed against the policy. This is why it's smart to choose a policy with a limit or guarantee on the interest rate you are charged on an IUL loan. Be sure to ask your IUL expert about what companies offer this provision in your market.

Since IUL's are written to be annually renewable, this means that insurance costs will increase as you age. To combat the COI eating away at your policy value, it would be beneficial to start with a company with a low fee structure and always structure the policy in a way that minimizes the death benefit and maximizes the funding for the cash value side of the policy. This can have an impact on your future insurance costs. There are a few scenarios where you wouldn't want to do that, but they are rare.

Each IUL policy will have costs, of course, as does any financial instrument. And those costs can vary by your age, gender, health, and type of benefits you are looking to secure, etc. Note that IUL fees are determined by the product that you select, not the person helping you secure the solution. So instead of only trying to find the answer to the question of how much IUL fees are, you should also be asking the question, "What are my needs and goals and will an IUL provide me an opportunity of achieving these needs and goals better than some alternative solution?"

When you're considering Indexed Universal Life insurance as that solution, then any risks may be heavily outweighed by the obvious benefits, such as cash value, and no loss guarantees, for example. However, the biggest risk with Indexed Universal Life insurance may not be the product itself. The biggest risk with IUL may be working with a professional who doesn't fully understand the product or someone who may not be the most reputable salesperson. The value of working with a well-regarded IUL expert cannot be overstated.

There are probably several insurance marketing organizations across the US that have contracted with all the top companies, but every advisor will have their "favorite" IUL for one reason or another. Listen to why they think their recommendation is the best choice and if it doesn't fit your goals, don't be swayed. I always, always, always recommend getting a second opinion from another unbiased (fiduciary) professional if you're being pitched by someone who is simply an insurance agent.

If you want to do your own research (which I always recommend), a useful resource that I've found is a blog article on an objective insurance and estate focused website entitled "Top 10 Best Indexed Universal Life (IUL) Insurance Companies". It's updated multiple times a year and on there you can click on any of the specific IUL insurers listed or go to their life insurance company reviews page for more on the top IUL companies. Here's the link:

(https://www.insuranceandestates.com/indexed-universal-life-iul-insurance)

Note that I am certainly not casting any dispersions on insurance salespeople, but in the overall population of insurance professionals that I've experienced, only a small minority in the industry are what I would consider as having 'expert level' knowledge when it comes to comparing IULs. Ideally, you want to work with an agent who specializes in IULs and will be able to help you determine which are the best Indexed Universal Life insurance companies for your needs.

On the other hand, if you already have a financial advisor that you trust, you might ask them why they hadn't mentioned an IUL before.

As I mentioned before, when you look at companies like banks, brokerages, mutual fund companies, etc., what incentive do their representatives have to teach you about these policies? Usually, a dollar that is put into an insurance policy ends up being a dollar out of the large investment firm's pocket.

In addition, regulators have put tight restrictions on the manner in which these products can be marketed and promoted, therefore it is unlikely you would see these types of products advertised on TV or promoted the way auto insurance is, for example. That also means that if you're not a licensed insurance agent, it's literally illegal to pitch them to anybody, so your financial advisor may say that they are just adhering to the law by not recommending them to you, but that's hugely misleading. They could *always* bring in someone who IS licensed to speak to you about them if they are truly working in your best interest.

Lastly, again, these policies are also relatively new. Remember that IULs were first introduced in 1997 it's only taken from then until now to go from close to $500,000 in initial year sales to over $3.4 Billion in annual sales as of this writing in 2024. Quickly becoming the dominant choice of life insurance policy owned by consumers with multiple record gains in market share, leaving Term Life in the dust and only 4% behind the leading insurance product, Whole Life.

Is there any reason a good financial advisor wouldn't have already mentioned an IUL as a viable method for you to save for retirement without any risk of loss of principal. If they don't have a good answer for that question – find a new advisor. Finding the right advisor is half the battle, then your job is to be the person who defines the end game. Your advisor's job is to determine the best vehicle to use to get there.

Chapter Twenty-five

Some parting thoughts

A lot of what I'm about to tell you in this chapter may sound like I have a negative outlook on life. I can assure you that is the farthest from the truth. However, I am pragmatic. Shit happens. I can pretty much guarantee that your life isn't going to be smooth sailing for the next 30-40 years, so sooner or later you're going to suffer a setback or get knocked down unexpectedly. The old maxim of "It's not what happens to you, but how you react to it that matters" are wise words. Take them to heart so that no matter how often you get knocked down, you'll always get back up again.

With that in mind, I, too often, come across both Millennials and GenZ folks that have the mindset that they can achieve *anything* they want simply with a strong enough passion for what they do, a good work ethic and some discipline. For some, that is absolutely true. However, for the hoi polloi, not so much.

I sincerely admire the optimism and enthusiasm, but there is no guaranteed formula for living out your dreams either before or after retirement. Certain steps, strategies and disciplines can improve your odds tenfold, but achieving *any* goals you want in life requires effort, planning and, frankly, some luck.

I, myself, often use the quote, attributed to the Roman philosopher Seneca, that "*Luck is what happens when preparation meets opportunity*". Unfortunately, "opportunity" sometimes evades even the most well prepared. So, for many, giving up on something they thought they wanted to do is merely a steppingstone to success in another field.

That said, buying a lottery ticket isn't going to help your chances of success either. Especially considering that if you drive just ten miles to purchase your lottery ticket, it's between three and twenty times more likely that you'll be killed in an auto accident along the way to buy the ticket than to win the jackpot.

Here's the thing. You've been taught practically since you could add two and two that the "safe and practical" path for you would be to go to school and get a good job, live on less than you make, and invest your money so you can quit your job at 65-ish years old and live out your dreams in retirement. Right?

If that was such a "safe" path, why is the average Baby Boomer retiring with less than $28,000 saved?

Avarice? Lack of forethought? Maybe. But recently I had a craving for a Big Mac and rather than go through the drive-through, I went inside. The woman who took my order had to be in her late seventies, *at least*. I thought to myself, here she is, instead of living out her dreams in her "Golden Years", she's working under the "Golden Arches".

Who knows why? Maybe her husband died without any life insurance, and she didn't have the means to make ends meet on her own. Maybe she just ran out of money in retirement and doesn't have the skills to work for any more than minimum wage. So much for "traveling the world" when you have to clock in at McDonalds every day just to be able to pay your bills.

Do you want to live like that?

I'll wager the answer is no.

Just as sad are those who *were* prepared and had their retirement dreams crushed in the stock market crash in 2008. The list is long of people who diligently contributed savings to their retirement funds month after month, year after year, only to have their entire lifetime savings wiped out by the failing of Lehman Brothers. For them, in what seemed like the blink of an eye — their entire life savings vanished. Others consider themselves lucky because they only lost 50% of their savings, even though it took them almost a decade to recover.

The COVID-19 pandemic, considered a Black Swan event, led to significant losses in retirement savings for many individuals. Nearly three in ten Americans decreased or stopped their retirement savings altogether due to the economic fallout of COVID-19. Furthermore, the stock market's fall has wiped out nearly $3 trillion in U.S. retirement accounts. The pandemic's unprecedented impact resulted in widespread financial repercussions, affecting retirement savings on a large scale. Could that happen again? Of course.

During the 1920s, the U.S. stock market quadrupled. If you didn't have a strategy that got you out before the historic crash of 1929, it would have taken you 26 years to recover. If you invested $100 in the S&P 500 at the beginning of 2009, you would have about $689.83 at the end of 2023, assuming you reinvested all dividends. That's more than quadrupled, that's just shy of five times. Has your money multiplied by nearly 5X since then?

If not, why not? Do you even have an exit strategy? If so, are you sure it will work?

When the correction finally comes, and we all know it will eventually, how long do you think it will take you to recover?

These are critical life-changing questions you need to be asking yourself before it's too late. More importantly, why would you want to take that kind of risk if you could get the same or better rewards with zero risk of loss?

The lesson is this: the traditional methods we've all been taught, in many ways, are smoke and mirrors. An illusion.

There is no such thing as "job security". While they're coming back into fashion, you're still unlikely to be offered any form of "pension" that you can actually rely on through your Golden Years. Pensions can go broke too if they're badly managed. And you already know that relying on a 401(k) with no alternative for when the market dives is just dumb. If the control is out of your hands, then make sure you have solidly backed guarantees in place. Take the factor of "luck" out of any equation wherever and whenever possible.

Well known life coach Tony Robbins has often been quoted as saying "*If you want to be successful, find someone who has achieved the results you want and copy what they do, and you'll achieve the same results".*

And while that's great advice for anyone, the "copy what they do, and you'll achieve the same results" part is not true in many cases. If the industry you're in is a very duplicatable business, like the insurance industry for example, then finding a highly successful mentor (better yet, mentors, plural) is a great way to learn the right steps, the right way, so you avoid trial and error on your own, the outcome is very likely to be success.

However, 99.9% of all advice from successful people, in any industry, that you'll read or hear (especially on the internet) is tainted by something called "**survivorship bias**". Rather than paraphrase it, I'm simply going to quote the "In highly competitive careers" section from the Survivorship Bias article on Wikipedia because that says it much better than I would:

> *"Whether it be movie stars, or athletes, or musicians, or CEOs of multi-billion-dollar corporations who dropped out of school, popular media often tells the story of the determined individual who pursues their dreams and beats the odds. There is much less focus on the many people that may be similarly skilled and determined but fail to ever find success because of factors beyond their control or other (seemingly) random events. This creates a false public perception that anyone can achieve great things if they have the ability and make the effort. The overwhelming majority of failures are not visible to the public eye, and only those who survive the selective pressures of their competitive environment are seen regularly".*

Survivorship bias is just one of a multitude of cognitive biases that need to be understood and catalogued in your brain if you ever hope to view the world without any false predisposition.

Just as importantly, be aware that general purpose advice is vastly different from high-performer advice. Getting from 'just okay' to 'stupendous' takes a particular set of steps with methods or skill sets, which are likely quite different from those that take you from 'just starting out' to 'mediocre' and from 'mediocre' to 'pretty good', etc. Make sure that the advice you're following reflects your stage of proficiency – especially with regards to your finances. Regardless of what anyone tells you, there is no get-rich-quick secret that only a special few know. The under-educated are the least likely to recognize opportunity even when it falls in their lap. Never stop learning and eventually you'll find your path and know an opportunity when you see it.

For most people, playing the market is like playing poker, meaning every time someone gains money, someone else loses it, only you're playing against the best poker players in the world, and just like in Las Vegas, the "house" always has the advantage. And yes, I realize that when the stock market is doing really well, it can be like a Siren's song to some, but what you don't risk, you can't lose.

Money can be fuel to move forward, or it can be an anchor to keep you from moving forward. You've probably heard the saying "golden handcuffs" before. If you haven't, it's often used as a descriptor by someone who likely dislikes their job and would much prefer to do something else but the money they make is so good (or they're so far in debt they can't do without it even for a short time) that they feel like they're confined to it. People who think that way simply don't know a way to get out of the box they're in. Having read this book, you already do. Here's how I know that.

Have you ever wondered how certain professionals, lawyers for example, can command so much money for the time they spend with you? It's not just their credentials, there are lots of talented, well-schooled attorneys that don't make $850 an hour and never will. However, some lawyers make that and more because the free market has determined that their time (not just their talent) is worth that much because others (their clients) are more than willing to pay it. Their time is limited, so if you want some of it, you're going to pay a high price for it. It's their value in the marketplace that determines that cost, the more perceived value they have (whether it's real or not) the more they can charge…and get.

Your time is limited too. But trading time for money caps your income no matter what kind of job you're in or service you offer because there is a limit to how many hours you work in a day. So, if you want to increase your income, you can either increase your perceived value in your marketplace, or you can learn how to separate your income from hours worked so that you can make money in your sleep. Passive versus active income. Like in Chapter 18, finding ways to increase your income, whether it's a side gig or your full time venture that can be scaled to increase your income without increasing the number of hours you work will get you to financial freedom faster than you can imagine.

Finally, fear of missing out (FOMO) is an entirely internal emotional state.

A 2023 study done by Qualtrics on behalf of Credit Karma among 1,005 adults ages 18 and older, showed that nearly 40% of Millennials and GenZ went into debt just to keep up with their peers. What's scarier is that they were too often afraid to admit it to anyone else.

The study found that they often feel peer pressure to spend money they don't have on things like travel, sporting events, concerts and music festivals, weddings, or simply social activities such as dinner and drinks with friends at places too pricey for their budget. When a friend suggested doing something they can't afford, 27% felt uncomfortable saying "no" for fear of missing out on "quality time" with their friends or being part of a once-in-a-lifetime experience.

Millennials are worse off however, with 15% admitting they've taken on $500 or more in debt as a result of spending time with their spendthrift friends, compared to just 2% of GenZ respondents in the same boat.

If that sounds like you (regardless of your age), you're not alone. Out of the 39% who've gone into debt to keep up with their friends, nearly three-quarters (73%) have kept it a secret.

Why?

In the Credit Karma/Qualtrics study, 36% said they spent money they didn't have because they were afraid they wouldn't be included in a future activity if they didn't; 27% said they didn't want to feel like an "outsider;" 26% thought they would lose friends and 23% said they didn't want to be judged.

Here's some tough love. Nobody's life is going to change if you skip going to that concert you can't afford, except maybe your own – possibly for the better.

Not spending money you don't have doesn't equal being a "Debbie Downer". There's no reason to be ashamed of being temporarily unable to afford a night out or some pricey vacation because you have that money earmarked for the future, or simply because it's way out of your budget right now. Chances are, by being honest with your friends, you might learn they feel the same way.

If you're afraid you'll kill the mood when your friend invites you to do something you can't afford, suggest something less expensive (better yet, free) you could do instead.

There are dozens of cheap or free activities you could suggest as an alternative. You could even plan a money-free travel adventure where the only cost is the gas to get there.

And this FOMO spending often extends beyond social activities. Especially when some well-moneyed friend you admire tells you of their latest investment success and urges you to make the same investment.

Most certainly, while not putting your money at risk in the market means you're not going to catch the next Google or Amazon rising star in the stock market, it also means you won't lose a dime. When your zero-risk Money Tree savings strategy is in place and working for you, you're already way ahead of the game long-term. Focus on what you can control, automate as much as you can, and let your good habits compound on themselves. Over time, you'll be shocked at how great the outcome will be and it'll be your turn to brag a little.

So now, having been presented with all this information, one of three things will happen next. The first possibility is that you will choose to do nothing. If that's what happens after you put this book down, I've failed in my mission miserably and you will likely become part of the ninety-plus percent who wait until it's too late to take action that will really make a difference in your and your future generations' lives. I sincerely hope that's not what you do.

The second involves you maybe shifting your spending and investing in several small areas and hopefully creating (or adhering to) a budget plan, but not taking action on the Money Tree Strategy of using an IUL – for whatever reason. If that's the case, I'd love to hear your reasons because, again, from my point of view, I've failed you.

The third option involves you hitting a reset button and taking immediate action. People who choose this path take advantage of every strategy described in this book that is available to them and destroy every other potential obstacle to their wealth-building for the future.

The fact is that anyone can build enough savings to retire without having to reduce their standard of living if they plan far enough in advance, even without a high income, or a side-gig, as long as you pay yourself first, live within your means, have a high enough savings rate, use the right vehicle, make your savings and investments automatic and you don't lose money in the process. Put those pre-determined amounts aside before you ever see them, and don't touch a penny more than what your strategy allows until you retire, and I can guarantee your Money Tree will bear fruit for you and generations to come.

Now you know it can be done. You now have the knowledge to change not just your own life, but to change the lives of generations of your family that come after you. That's powerful stuff. But knowledge, by itself, is not power – it's only *potential* power. Execution of that knowledge is the power. Knowing doesn't move anything. Doing moves you forward.

Get busy.

Resources

The Millennial Money Tree Blog – Want even more info?
https://millennialmoneytree.blog

Test Drive an IUL with an IUL Calculator
https://www.iulresource.com/Calculators/Test-Drive-IUL

National Financial Educators Council Financial Capability Quiz
https://www.financialeducatorscouncil.org/national-financial-capability-test/

FINRA National Financial Capability Study Financial Literacy Quiz
https://www.finra.org/financial_literacy_quiz

Investor.gov Compound Interest Calculator
https://www.investor.gov/financial-tools-calculators/calculators/compound-interest-calculator

National Life Save Now vs Save Later Calculator
https://www.nationallife.com/Financial-Calculators-Save-Now-vs-Save-Later

Life Insurance Statistics
https://www.policygenius.com/life-insurance/life-insurance-statistics/

Feedback on this book is always welcomed. I can't guarantee I'll respond to every email but I'll try darn hard. Contact me at:

john.logan@moneytree.ventures

Made in United States
North Haven, CT
10 November 2026

22106125R00211